FIGHT
LIKE A
GIRL

FIGHT LIKE A GIRL

This edition published in 2017 by Summersdale Publishers Ltd

First published by Zest Books Ltd in 2016

Illustrations by Summer Pierre and Marianne Thompson

An Hachette UK Company
www.hachette.co.uk

Summersdale Publishers Ltd
Part of Octopus Publishing Group Limited
Carmelite House
50 Victoria Embankment
LONDON
EC4Y 0DZ
UK

www.summersdale.com

Printed and bound in the Czech Republic

ISBN: 978-1-78685-204-5

Substantial discounts on bulk quantities of Summersdale books are available to corporations, professional associations and other organisations. For details contact general enquiries: telephone: +44 (0) 1243 771107 or email: enquiries@summersdale.com.

LAURA BARCELLA

FIGHT
LIKE A
GIRL

50 FEMINISTS
WHO CHANGED THE WORLD

summersdale

CONTENTS

INTRODUCTION

I've been a feminist since forever – or at least since before I fully understood what the word meant. It all started around sixth grade. I don't remember which one of us got the abortion-rights bug first, but a few girlfriends and I started fervently attending pro-choice rallies in our home town of Washington, DC.

We'd wear purple and wave handmade signs and shriek along with the surging crush of mostly older, mostly female masses demanding things like 'abortion on demand without apology'. At twelve, I didn't quite grasp all the specifics (or even the basics, having yet to experience so much as a proper kiss). But I knew enough to believe, soul deep, in women's freedom to choose what happens to our bodies, regardless of what kinds of accidents or outside forces intervene.

I don't remember all the details of the rallies themselves (hey, it was a super-long time ago), but I vividly recall how they made me feel. Namely, I felt addicted – swept up in the blustery power of so many impassioned women smushed elbow to elbow on the National Mall. I loved the life-affirming awesomeness of hearing tens of thousands of people recite powerful rallying cries in unison. I was blown away by how huge it felt, how real and tangible and… important.

The foundation of my passion for feminism started then, and over the years it's only grown. In high school, my best friend and I launched our own fanzine, and in college I grew smitten with the riot grrrl scene, turning to music and the world of zines to help me process both my own life and the bigger world around me. I launched a new zine in college, and started working as my college newspaper's women's issues editor.

After college, I continued dabbling in feminist journalism and indie media. I was obsessed with using my voice as a writer to help spread the word about all the kick-ass women out there who do, say, and make cool things – things that don't always get noticed just because they happen to have been created by someone other than a white dude.

I've dreamed of writing a book about some of the world's ballsiest lady-heroes for years. And 2016 just happens to feel like the right moment to do it. Why? Well, for starters, there's a surplus of fierce women – of all ages, races, faiths, and cultures – doing fierce things.

Plus, as you might have noticed, feminism has been having a bit of a media moment lately. It's a unique time to be a feminist – hell, it's a unique time to be a woman – because the cohesively defined women's rights movement of the seventies isn't really around anymore. Today's feminism is broader in the scope of issues it addresses, and it can sometimes feel a bit splintered and amorphous. Plus, there are more people rightfully confronting the question of who feminism is – and should be – for. Professor Kimberlé Crenshaw coined the term 'intersectionality' back in 1989, writing, 'Cultural patterns of oppression are not only interrelated, but are bound together and influenced by the intersectional systems of society. Examples of this include race, gender, class, ability, and ethnicity.' Feminism is not and should not be one-size-fits-all – there are women of every religion, race, size, ethnicity, background and sexual orientation aligning themselves with feminism these days, and that's exactly the way it should be. To help effect change for every woman, feminism needs to be as broad and inclusive as possible – it needs to reach far beyond the concerns of white, middle-class, cisgendered, able-bodied women.

Every movement is flawed, and we have a long way yet to go. But it's heartened me to see more and more powerful women publicly aligning themselves with women's rights in recent years, or even just talking about it in the first place. Feminism doesn't mean subscribing to a certain magazine or marching on the Mall three times a year. It doesn't mean listening to one particular kind of music, or dating one particular kind of person, or reading one particular kind of book, or forcing yourself not to hate-watch *The Bachelorette*. Your feminism can be self-defined.

Mine can, too. And I would have devoured a book like this when I was a teenager. The problem was that I couldn't find one. That's why I wanted to write this book as a sort of 'feminist heroes' primer.

The women I selected for inclusion are from a range of eras, from today through the early days of the suffragist movement. There are popular names you'll instantly recognise (hi, Beyoncé!), and lesser-known ones with colourful histories. Those lesser-known figures made powerful social and political strides that benefited women, but they weren't always widely embraced by the mainstream.

I didn't want this book to exist solely as a refresher course on a bunch of stuff you already know about people you're already familiar with (for that reason, some big-name mainstays weren't included, like Gloria Steinem). I wanted this book to be broad, showcasing the valuable work of the underdogs alongside the power icons. And I won't lie – sometimes personal taste came into play. For instance, Madonna and Kathleen Hanna are in here because they've both had a huge role in shaping my own personal feminism.

Not all of the women in this book actively self-identify as feminists (Yayoi Kusama, for example), and not all were specifically linked to the women's movement, per se (see folks like Jane Goodall and Rosa Parks). I chose to include them anyway because even though some of these women might think twice about donning a 'This is what a feminist looks like' T-shirt, every woman here is a trailblazer and world shaker in her own right, and to me, that's what mattered.

Now go forth and get your feminist on!

Laura Barcella, 2016

1.
MARY WOLLSTONECRAFT
(1759–97)

'I do not wish [women] to have power over men, but over themselves.'

Claim to Fame	Country of Origin
Writer, philosopher	England

HER LEGACY

Mary Wollstonecraft was a philosopher, a theorist, and a liberal feminist author (some have even called her 'the first feminist') whose pot-stirring writing caused a major ruckus in the eighteenth century. She wrote a number of books that suggested that women should be autonomous creatures of their own making.

Wollstonecraft felt it was wrong that women were generally treated as little more than pretty, servile playthings for their husbands. She believed that expecting women to stay home and be, essentially, 'convenient domestic slaves' wasted their talents and led them to become mothers and wives by mandate rather than by choice (at a real cost to their happiness as well). Confining women to such rigid roles was destructive to society, she argued; providing more education to them would only make women – and, by extension, everyone else! – stronger and happier, both at home and out in the world.

HER LIFE STORY

Wollstonecraft grew up in London with an alcoholic, abusive father, who beat both her and her mother. The nightmare at home only fuelled her desire to escape her family and forge her own way in the world. Though she didn't have a formal education, the resourceful Wollstonecraft began supporting herself by age nineteen as a teacher, governess, and 'lady's companion'. She went on to found a school with her sister, Eliza, and her best friend, Fanny, though it eventually went bankrupt.

After living in Ireland for three years before moving back to London, Wollstonecraft began working as a translator for Joseph Johnson, who published radical books. She contributed to his publication, *Analytical Review*, and then published *A Vindication of the Rights of Woman* four years later (after first putting out a political pamphlet called *A Vindication of the Rights of Men*, a response to Edmund Burke's *Reflections on the Revolution in France*).

At this time, Wollstonecraft noticed that boys were gaining access to a national education system. Why shouldn't girls have the same high-quality education opportunities as well? Recognising this hypocrisy, Wollstonecraft publicly argued that exempting women from full civic status held back society as a whole. She also argued for women's right to support themselves via the same career paths as men (law, medicine, etc.), and that women should have representation in Parliament. In a time when women had significantly fewer rights than they do now, Wollstonecraft's ideas about gender equality were nothing less than revolutionary.

In December of 1792, Wollstonecraft went to France and took up with the blooming intellectual and philosophical circles there. One of those was the enlightenment school of thought, which centred on reason, science, and individualism rather than old-school customs, tradition, and blind faith. She was also a member of the Rational Dissenters, a religious group that did not believe in sin or damnation.

Critics attacked Wollstonecraft for her unconventional lifestyle and her progressive beliefs, misinterpreting them as a hatred of men. Some of those critics even felt the need to offer their nasty opinions years after Wollstonecraft's death, including authors Ferdinand, Farnham, and Lundberg, who lamented in the 1949 book *Modern Woman: The*

Lost Sex: 'Mary Wollstonecraft was an extreme neurotic of a compulsive type…' Luckily, history was on Wollstonecraft's side in the end.

HER COOL CREDENTIALS

★ Wollstonecraft was an early proponent of free thought when it comes to religion. She believed women should live independently and form their own opinions that aren't based on blind faith in a divine deity.

★ She's the mother of Mary Wollstonecraft Shelley, the pioneering author who wrote *Frankenstein*.

★ When she decided to pursue a career as an author, she dreamed big. She didn't want her books to fizzle out of the public consciousness. Instead, she intended to become 'the first of a new genus', as she expressed in a 1787 letter to her sister.

QUOTABLES

'Make women rational creatures, and free citizens, and they will quickly become good wives; that is, if men do not neglect the duties of husbands and fathers.'

'Taught from infancy that beauty is woman's sceptre, the mind shapes itself to the body, and roaming round its gilt cage, only seeks to adorn its prison.'

'Independence I have long considered as the grand blessing of life, the basis of every virtue...'

2.
SOJOURNER TRUTH

NÉE ISABELLA BAUMFREE (1797–1883)

'And ain't I a woman?'

Claim to Fame	Country of Origin
Abolitionist, women's rights activist	USA

HER LEGACY

Sojourner Truth was a former slave who accomplished extraordinary things in her lifetime. First, and arguably most important, she escaped slavery – a major coup in and of itself. But she didn't get free only to sink into a life of isolated silence. She used all the horrors she'd witnessed as motivation and dedicated the rest of her life to ending slavery as an institution. She became a prominent abolitionist and women's rights activist who played a big role in launching the suffrage movement that eventually gave women the right to vote.

Truth was famous for her impassioned mix of religion and activism when she worked on behalf of freed slaves during the Reconstruction era (a time after the Civil War when the United States tried to atone for the political, social, and economic blights of slavery). She also spoke out about the importance of working toward a just society for all people, not just the lucky few who happened to be born white and male. Truth's 'Ain't I a Woman?' speech, which she presented at a women's convention in Ohio in 1851, is considered one of the most important feminist speeches of all time, and it's been referenced in countless other works by feminists.

HER LIFE STORY

Truth was born into slavery in the late 1700s in Ulster County, New York. Her original name was Isabella Baumfree, but she changed it in 1843 to Sojourner, which means 'wanderer'. Growing up, she only spoke Dutch, and she never learned to read or write (which was common among slaves).

She was bought and sold as a slave four times, and was 'owned' by various families, some of whom were violent. In 1827, New York law finally emancipated slaves, but by then Truth had already escaped to freedom with her baby daughter after her owner reneged on a promise to free her. Soon after she'd made a run for it, Truth learned that her five-year-old son, Peter, had been illegally sold to someone in Alabama. She brought the matter to court and eventually won – she was thrilled when Peter was returned to her. It was one of the first cases in which a black woman successfully battled a white man in an American court.

Truth became a travelling preacher in 1843; by then she had embraced Methodism after having an intense spiritual experience in the woods one day. She travelled around the country advocating for abolition, human rights, women's rights, prison reform, temperance, and a ban on capital punishment.

During her travels, she met and sometimes befriended important figures in the abolitionist and suffrage movements, including William Lloyd Garrison, Amy Post, Frederick Douglass, Harriet Beecher Stowe, Lucretia Mott, and Susan B. Anthony. Truth was among a handful of escaped slaves, including Harriet Tubman and Frederick Douglass, to become big abolitionist leaders, and in 1850 she published a celebrated memoir, *The Narrative of Sojourner Truth*, which helped spread her convictions to a wider audience. That year, she also spoke at the first National Women's Rights Convention in Massachusetts.

Some of Truth's opinions were considered 'out there', even among the more radical circles she was part of. She advocated for political equality for every woman of every race, and scolded abolitionists who didn't work to gain civil rights for black women as well as men. She was worried that the movement would leave women in the cold, without fundamental rights of their own (like, duh, the right to vote).

During the Civil War, Truth helped recruit black soldiers for the Union Army. She had a chance to meet with more than one US president: in 1864 she met Abraham Lincoln at the White House, and later she convened with President Ulysses S. Grant to try to help ex-slaves secure land grants from the government. (Sadly her attempts didn't work, though she pushed for that cause for seven years.)

Truth died in 1883 at her home in Michigan, where she was commemorated in a Michigan Legal Milestone raised by the State Bar of Michigan. Though she died impoverished, she had a full life of rule-breaking and change-making, a legacy that still inspires people today.

HER COOL CREDENTIALS

★ Truth wasn't afraid of a challenge. At a meeting in 1852, Frederick Douglass suggested that black people must use force to win their freedom. Truth, a proponent of nonviolence as a key component of her Christian faith, pushed back against Douglass's assertions, exclaiming, 'Is God gone?'

★ She was ballsy when she had to be. In 1858, during a speech, someone interrupted her to rudely yell out their belief that she was actually a man. To prove a point — and showcase her womanhood without shame — Truth opened her top and revealed her breasts. (She was almost six feet tall and had a deep voice that led some impressively obnoxious people to question her gender.)

★ Harriet Beecher Stowe once attested to Truth's potent charisma, saying that she had never 'been conversant with anyone who had more of that silent and subtle power which we call personal presence than this woman.'

QUOTABLES

'If women want rights more than they got, why don't they just take them, and not be talking about it.'

'I am glad to see that men are getting their rights, but I want women to get theirs, and while the water is stirring I will step into the pool.'

'And ain't I a woman? Look at me! Look at my arm! I have ploughed and planted, and gathered into barns, and no man could head me! And ain't I a woman? I could work as much and eat as much as a man – when I could get it – and bear the lash as well! And ain't I a woman? I have borne thirteen children, and seen most all sold off to slavery, and when I cried out with my mother's grief, none but Jesus heard me! And ain't I a woman?'

3.
EMMELINE PANKHURST
NÉE EMMELINE GOULDEN (1858–1928)

'We have to free half of the human race, the women,
so they can help to free the other half.'

Claim to Fame	Country of Origin
Women's rights activist, suffragette	England

HER LEGACY

Dubbed 'the mother of British suffrage', Emmeline Pankhurst was an exceptionally powerful women's rights figure who left behind an unmatchable legacy in UK history. Pankhurst was a women's rights activist who fought bravely – and sometimes bitterly – for British women to obtain the right to vote.

The tactics she used were not always totally peaceful. In fact, she sometimes used violent approaches, like arson, to fight for what she believed in, and Pankhurst and some of her daughters – who fought alongside her – found themselves in prison multiple times.

In a tragic twist, she died a mere two weeks before English women were finally granted full voting rights.

HER LIFE STORY

Pankhurst was born in Manchester, England, in 1858, and was the eldest daughter in a bustling house of ten children. Agitation ran in her blood; both of Pankhurst's parents were anti-slavery and women's suffrage activists who introduced her, at a young age, to the importance of freedom and equal rights for all. In fact, Pankhurst's mother took Emmeline to her first suffrage meeting when she was just fourteen years old, after much begging on the teenager's part. After that event, Pankhurst considered herself a dedicated suffragist.

Pankhurst grew up in a warm, comfortable home. But, as she wrote in her autobiography, *My Own Story*, she began to notice – and resent – subtle differences in the ways she and her brothers were treated. Specifically, she was bothered by the way her parents seemed to devote more attention to her brothers' education than they gave to hers or her sisters'. She believed the boys' school choices were given more weight simply because, well, they were male. (Girls, back then, weren't expected to do much beyond marrying and raising babies, so their education wasn't a big priority.) This unnerved her, *especially* because her parents were women's rights activists! (It just goes to show that everyone has a blind spot, even those who are committed to the cause.)

After going to school in Paris for a few years, she returned home to Manchester and married a barrister, Richard Pankhurst, in 1879. Pankhurst shared his new wife's radical leanings, and was an avid suffragist working to advance various bills that benefited women. They had five children (one of whom died of diphtheria as a boy), and eventually moved to London, where Pankhurst kept busy with a life of activism. In 1889, she founded the Women's Franchise League, which campaigned to permit both married and single women to vote in their towns' elections.

After her husband died in 1898, Pankhurst descended into depression and grief, but her commitment to her ideals never waned. In 1903, she launched a new organisation called the Women's Social and Political Union, which was exclusively dedicated to voting rights ('deeds, not words'). The WSPU began gaining more attention for its militancy, especially after one of Pankhurst's daughters, Christabel, was arrested during a protest. Believing that more direct, even abrasive forms of action might be more effective than quieter protests, some of her group members began using aggressive tactics like smashing windows and attacking police officers during their demonstrations.

When Pankhurst and her affiliates inevitably got arrested and imprisoned, they'd launch hunger strikes, a tactic first employed by British suffragette Marion Wallace Dunlop. They weren't striking to protest their imprisonment, but because the government refused to label their crimes 'political acts' (political prisoners got better treatment and more respect). Instead of releasing the suffragettes, some prisons started force-feeding them, an act akin to torture.

When World War One began, Pankhurst stepped back from all that direct action and urged women to help support the war effort. The government released all the imprisoned WSPU protesters, and in 1918 the government gave women a limited right to vote, in part because of how helpful they had been during wartime. Another bill passed that year allowing women to be elected to Parliament.

Pankhurst passed away in London at age sixty-nine, just weeks before Parliament finally gave complete voting rights to women.

HER COOL CREDENTIALS

★ The *New York Herald Tribune* posthumously dubbed Emmeline Pankhurst 'the most remarkable political and social agitator of the twentieth century and the supreme protagonist of the campaign for the electoral enfranchisement of women.'

★ In 1930, Pankhurst was immortalised with a beautiful statue of her likeness in London's Victoria Tower Gardens. The plaque reads, 'This statue of Emmeline Pankhurst was erected as a tribute to her courageous leadership of the movement for the enfranchisement of women.' Ironically, Prime Minister Stanley Baldwin – who had opposed voting rights for women – unveiled the statue.

★ Megastar Meryl Streep played Pankhurst in the wildly successful 2015 film *Suffragette*.

QUOTABLES

'Trust in God. She will provide.'

'Men make the moral code and they expect women to accept it.'

'You have to make more noise than anybody else, you have to make yourself more obtrusive than anybody else, you have to fill all the papers more than anybody else, in fact you have to be there all the time and see that they do not snow you under.'

4.
MARIE CURIE

NÉE MARIA SALOMEA SKŁODOWSKA (1867–1934)

'I was taught that the way of progress was neither swift nor easy.'

Claim to Fame	Country of Origin
Physicist	Poland

HER LEGACY

Marie Curie is one of the most famous scientists in history, and one of the most celebrated scientists of her time. Though she's known primarily for discovering the elements radium and polonium, Curie made other major scientific advancements, including reaching the conclusion that radioactivity is an intrinsic atomic property of matter. She faced down many obstacles – both internal and external – throughout her career, including chronic depression and intense sexism, but she eventually became the first woman to win a Nobel Prize.

HER LIFE STORY

Curie grew up in Warsaw, Poland, during a time when Poland was not an independent country but was split up among Austria, Prussia, and czarist Russia. She and her family lived in the part of Poland that was run by the Russian czar, who did not believe women should be allowed to go to college. Her parents were teachers, so education and learning were prioritised in her family. Her mum and dad were also

Polish nationalists who supported uprisings aimed at making Poland independent from Russia.

When Curie was ten, her mum died. Curie remembered her passing as 'the first great sorrow' of her life, which 'threw [her] into a profound depression'. Curie did extremely well in school, but at one point she had to leave due to a 'nervous disorder' (later believed to be the depression she reportedly continued to struggle with throughout her life). She planned to continue her studies to get an advanced degree, but the medical school at the local University of Warsaw did not yet admit any women. In 1891, however, the University of Paris (a.k.a. the Sorbonne) granted Curie admission on a scholarship. 'So it was in November, 1891,' she later said, 'at the age of twenty-four that I was able to realise the dream that had been constantly in my mind for several years.'

Though she'd feared she was unprepared for the rigours of the programme, Curie finished first in her master's degree physics course in 1893 and second in maths a year later. Before completing her maths degree, she was commissioned to do a study on the magnetic aspects of different steels. While searching for a lab to do this work, she met Pierre Curie, a scientist and lab chief who was also researching magnetics. They began working together, then fell in love and married in 1895. By the time of their marriage, she already had two master's degrees!

Having successfully published some of her research, Curie decided to pursue a doctorate, a feat no other woman in the sciences had accomplished at the time. Her doctoral thesis focused on uranium rays, and in the course of her work Curie formed a hypothesis that would revolutionise the science world: that the emission of rays by uranium compounds could be an atomic property of the element uranium – which means it could be something built into the core structure of its atoms. At the time, no one understood the complicated internal composition of atoms, so her theories were pretty revolutionary. Curie also went on to discover the natural elements polonium and radium, and essentially coined the concept of radioactivity, which became its own new scientific field.

Curie's career, though great, was marred by sexism. In 1911 she received the Nobel Prize in Chemistry for her earlier work with polonium and radium, but the fantastic news was offset by scandal. A weekly newspaper published letters believed to prove that Marie

Curie and the married physicist Paul Langevin were having an affair. When a Nobel committee member asked her not to attend the award ceremony because of this, Curie pushed back and told him that 'there is no connection between my scientific work and the facts of private life'. Earlier in the year she had also endured a major disappointment when she was denied election to the French Academy of Sciences by a margin of two votes, reportedly because she was Polish and (of course) female. Academy member Émile Hilaire Amagat told her, 'Women cannot be part of the Institute of France.' She never put herself in the running as a candidate again.

Curie died of a rare blood disease in her late sixties. Her death was reportedly caused by exposure to excessive radiation; at the time no one knew that radioactive elements could be deadly.

HER COOL CREDENTIALS

★ As mentioned, Curie was the first woman to win a Nobel Prize (in physics, along with her husband Pierre). She was also one of the few Nobel laureates (and the only woman!) to win the prize twice – she won again in 1911 for chemistry.

★ Curie's wedding ceremony with Pierre was not religious. They didn't exchange rings, and she wore a navy outfit instead of a white dress. These were all pretty notable feminist actions, especially back then.

★ She is the first and only woman to be entombed in France's national mausoleum, the Pantheon, based solely on her incredible achievements.

★ Her long-time friend Albert Einstein named Curie as one of two scientists he respected most. He said, 'Not only did she do outstanding work in her lifetime and not only did she help humanity greatly by her work, but she invested all of her work with the highest moral quality. All of this she accomplished with great strength, objectivity, and judgement. It is very rare to find all of these qualities in one individual.'

QUOTABLES

'Be less curious about people and more curious about ideas.'

'I have frequently been questioned, especially by women, of how I could reconcile family life with a scientific career. Well, it has not been easy.'

'Life is not easy for any of us. But what of that? We must have perseverance and above all confidence in ourselves. We must believe that we are gifted for something and that this thing must be attained.'

5.
VIRGINIA WOOLF

NÉE ADELINE VIRGINIA STEPHEN (1882–1941)

*'As a woman, I have no country. As a woman
my country is the whole world.'*

Claim to Fame	Country of Origin
Author	England

HER LEGACY

Virginia Woolf is one of the pre-eminent feminist and modernist writers of the twentieth century. Despite this, much of her work wasn't widely acclaimed until years after her death, which is surprising given how impactful her work has been. For example, many of her books were later made into popular films (see 1997's *Mrs Dalloway*) and Woolf herself is a character in Michael Cunningham's Pulitzer Prize-winning novel *The Hours* (which was also turned into an Oscar-winning movie!).

Growing up, Woolf prioritised books and writing over, well, almost anything else, which predisposed her to a lifelong obsession with literature. (She once said, 'I am ashamed, or perhaps proud, to say how much of my time is spent in thinking, thinking, thinking about literature.') Part of the reason she was so invested in her work was because it helped her stay afloat from her continuous dips into mental illness. Woolf suffered a number of breakdowns in her life, and her debilitating struggle with manic depression ultimately led to her suicide.

In her too-short stint on earth, Woolf was a fierce advocate for the rights of women. In fact, her work largely centred on the inner workings of women's minds and lives. Though she wasn't necessarily a 'marching in the streets' type of activist, the vast number of essays, novels, and letters she wrote reveal a quiet commitment to capturing the thoughts, pains, feelings, and losses of modern women's everyday lives. Her groundbreaking extended essay *A Room of One's Own*, first published in 1929, is nothing short of a feminist classic. It uses a fictional narrator to advance the idea that women need both financial security and private spaces of their own – both literal and figurative – to be happy and successful.

HER LIFE STORY

Virginia Woolf was born into a large, upper-class Victorian family. Though aspects of her childhood seemed idyllic – she was born into an elite, book-loving family – there were dark aspects that haunted both her life and work. Woolf's mother, Julia Jackson Stephen, was her life's great love, and the Mrs Ramsay character in Woolf's heralded novel *To the Lighthouse* was written for her mum. Woolf's father, philosopher and

author Leslie Stephen, was a prominent literary figure in his own right, and served as the first editor of the *Dictionary of National Biography*.

Virginia Woolf's beloved mother was a beautiful, well-connected woman who abandoned any religious beliefs she had when her first husband, Herbert Duckworth, died suddenly while picking a fig for her, of all things. After that, Jackson reached out to neighbour Leslie Stephen after reading some of his essays about agnosticism. When Stephen's own wife passed away, he and Jackson fell in love and joined families. Julia already had three children of her own from her first marriage, and Stephen had one. They subsequently had four more children of their own, and their large eight-person family was complete. Woolf was exceptionally close to her three full siblings, but reportedly had some issues with the others. For instance, after her two half-brothers, George and Gerald Duckworth, died in 1939, Woolf confessed in an essay that they had molested both her and her sister Vanessa.

When her mother died of rheumatic fever at age forty-nine, Woolf – then thirteen – was devastated. (She called it 'the greatest disaster that could happen'.) One of her half-sisters, Stella Duckworth, also died, and later her father, and Woolf began experiencing the mental breakdowns that would persist throughout her life.

After the death of their father, Woolf's sister Vanessa took on a more maternal role, and together they moved to the Bloomsbury section of London. Soon the young women began hosting parties and events with intellectuals, artists, and writers like Clive Bell (who married Vanessa but later fell in love with Woolf). As a clique, they became known as the creative, controversial, and sexually free Bloomsbury Group.

Woolf married writer Leonard Woolf in 1912. Throughout all this, she was refining her voice as a writer on her own terms, and her first novel, *The Voyage Out,* was published in 1915. Woolf was still grappling with mental illness during this time, however, and attempted suicide in 1913. By 1917 she was more stable, and she and her husband founded Hogarth Press together. (It still exists as an imprint of Crown today!)

Over the rest of her life, Woolf released a steady stream of profound, often highly complex literary works, including *Orlando, Mrs Dalloway,* and *To the Lighthouse.* She also got involved in an array of romantic entanglements with both men and women. Many of these relationships also played out in her books.

But by the time World War Two was beginning, Woolf again found herself in a pit of despair and self-doubt. In 1941, she loaded her pockets down with stones and drowned herself in a river outside her house.

HER COOL CREDENTIALS

★ When Woolf was growing up, famous writers like Henry James and James Russell Lowe would stop by her family's London house just to hang out.

★ Woolf was ahead of her time in believing that gender and sexuality were fluid (she famously touched on some of these ideas in *Orlando*). She believed that gender was largely a result of socialisation.

★ *The Guardian* published some of the very first articles Woolf ever wrote.

QUOTABLES

'Take no advice, to follow your own instincts, to use your own reason, to come to your own conclusions.'

'A woman must have money and a room of her own if she is to write fiction.'

'As long as she thinks of a man, nobody objects to a woman thinking.'

6.
AMY JACQUES GARVEY

NÉE AMY EUPHEMIA JACQUES (1895–1973)

'No line of endeavour remains closed for long to the modern woman.'

Claim to Fame	Country of Origin
Writer, activist	Jamaica

HER LEGACY

Amy Jacques Garvey was a radical leader in the community feminism and pan-African movements of the 1920s, committed to fighting racism and negative stereotypes about black people. Pan-Africanists generally believe that people of African descent should live together in one separate, united nation on their own because they were so commonly mistreated and marginalised by the non-black masses.

Though Jacques is most famous for her ties to Marcus Garvey (she was his second wife; he was a black nationalist who became an icon in the civil rights movement), she deserves major props in her own right for the great strides she made for her community. Jacques served as the secretary and office manager of the Universal Negro Improvement Association and African Communities League and kept it running while her husband was imprisoned. She courageously vocalised bold ideas about race and nationhood that would benefit women of colour for years to come.

HER LIFE STORY

Jacques was born in Jamaica, where she grew up in an upper-class household. She immersed herself in books at a young age and went to very good schools, and with her dad's encouragement and help, she became interested in international issues, politics, and current affairs.

When she moved to Harlem in 1917, she got involved in the Universal Negro Improvement Association after hearing Marcus Garvey speak about racial inequity. The UNIA became one of her passions – maybe her biggest one – for years to come. The group's mission was to empower black people all over the world, with a focus on creating professional and educational opportunities for all people of African descent. Founded in 1914, the organisation was a bit slow to take off, but by 1918 it had various branches and was gaining more supporters all the time.

Then in 1923, Marcus Garvey went to prison on charges of mail fraud. Jacques took up the mantle and served as her husband's personal representative, travelling all over the country to give speeches at local UNIA divisions and conferring with public officials to continue spreading the group's message. From 1924 to 1927, Jacques worked as the associate editor of the UNIA's newspaper (the biggest black-owned newspaper in the world then), *The Negro World*. She even launched a new section dubbed 'Our Women and What They Think', which centred on feminism, black nationalism, and profiles of famous black women.

Her work as a journalist was notable because she wrote about black women as political beings in their own right, a concept that wasn't exactly popular at the time. She believed black men needed to stand up for their female counterparts, not repress women's choices and voices. Though she agreed with certain ideas that other feminists would go on to disdain – like the notion that men should be breadwinners – her contributions to the public discourse on these matters are seen as a key step in the advancement of black feminism, and she was an avid proponent of women taking strides to better themselves intellectually, politically, and personally.

When Marcus Garvey was released from prison and then deported, Jacques followed him back to their homeland of Jamaica. After he passed away in 1940, Jacques kept ploughing forward in the fight for African independence and women's rights. In 1944 she wrote 'A Memorandum Correlative of Africa, West Indies and the Americas', which she used to push UN reps to launch an African Freedom Charter. She later published her own book, *Garvey and Garveyism*, and went on to publish two essay collections, *Black Power in America* and *The Impact of Garvey in Africa and Jamaica*.

She died in Kingston, Jamaica, in 1973, but her adamant mission to further the strength and power of black women has secured her place in the history books.

HER COOL CREDENTIALS

★ Jacques experienced 'a political rebirth' after her husband's death. She began expanding her horizons to include helping exploited workers and other important concerns.

★ After her husband died, Jacques became a contributing editor to a black nationalist journal, *The African*.

★ In the late forties, she formed the African Study Circle of the World in Jamaica to study African history.

QUOTABLES

'The women of the East, both yellow and black, are slowly but surely imitating the women of the Western world, and as the white women are bolstering up a decaying white civilisation, even so women of the darker races are sallying forth to help their men establish a civilisation according to their own standards, and to strive for world leadership.'

'The doll-baby type of woman is a thing of the past, and the wide-awake woman is forging ahead prepared for all emergencies, and ready to answer any call, even if it be to face the cannons on the battlefield.'

'Negroes everywhere must be independent, God being our guide. Mr. Black man, watch your step! Ethiopia's queens will reign again, and her Amazons protect her shores and people.'

7.
FRIDA KAHLO

NÉE MAGDALENA CARMEN FRIEDA KAHLO Y CALDERÓN (1907–54)

'Feet, what do I need you for when I have wings to fly?'

Claim to Fame	Country of Origin
Painter	Mexico

HER LEGACY

Frida Kahlo is the most legendary and, arguably, revolutionary female painter in history. Though some people question whether she would be considered a feminist by today's standards, she was ahead of her time in nearly every way when it comes to flouting traditional ideas about womanhood. She succeeded in a time when women were routinely held down, both personally and professionally, and transcended other norms of that time, too – her art explored taboo topics like miscarriage, gender inequity, abortion, death, and sex. She also rebelled against traditional ideals of female beauty, not only refusing to remove her unibrow and moustache, but making them darker with a black pencil.

HER LIFE STORY

Kahlo was born in Coyoacán, Mexico, in 1907, to a Mexican mum and German-Jewish immigrant dad. From a young age, Kahlo suffered from physical ailments and ill health, both of which later became prevalent themes throughout her artwork. When she was just six years old, Kahlo contracted polio, causing her right leg to become visibly shrivelled (much to the delight of her cruel classmates). This made Kahlo delve deep into her own imagination for comfort.

While studying to be a doctor at the exclusive Escuela Nacional Preparatoria (she was one of only a handful of girls admitted), Kahlo began dabbling in leftist politics and joined a student socialist group. Then, at age eighteen, she was in a terrifying bus accident in which she was impaled by a handrail. She had to endure thirty-two surgeries, and doctors weren't sure if she'd ever walk again (she did); the accident also made her infertile, leading to several miscarriages. It was while she was bedridden that her father, Guillermo Kahlo – also an artist – suggested she try painting.

During her long recovery, Kahlo created colourful paintings, mostly self-portraits, in a style that would become her trademark. She once explained, 'I paint myself because I am so often alone, because I am the subject I know best.' Her work during that time was very emotion-driven, and some of it was difficult to look at. Much of it centred on her recovery – images of her alone in a series of hospital beds – but also on childbirth and fertility.

A few years after she started painting, she married the famed Mexican muralist Diego Rivera, who would become one of her life's most intense, ongoing sources of both pain and inspiration. Their relationship was passionate and stormy; though there are many accounts of his frequent infidelities, Kahlo had her own fair share of extramarital dalliances with both men and women. Rivera once wrote of his wife, 'I recommend her to you, not as a husband but as an enthusiastic admirer of her work, acid and tender, hard as steel and delicate and fine as a butterfly's wing, lovable as a beautiful smile, and as profound and cruel as the bitterness of life.'

FRIDA SELLS

Frida Kahlo isn't just an artist – she's practically a mythic figure. Even sixty-two years after her death, her dramatic life and work still fascinate and titillate admirers all over the world. An art dealer once told *Vanity Fair* magazine that 'Frida has been carved up into little pieces. Everyone pulls out that one piece that means something special to them.' It's true – and savvy companies have jumped on the painter's power to pull in dollars. Here are just a few of the ways we're keeping Frida alive:

★ She appeared in Volvo ads. Because, y'know – a Swedish car company and a Mexican communist artist have soooo much to do with each other.

★ She appeared on a US postage stamp. Back in 2001, the United States Postal Service turned one of Kahlo's 1933 self-portraits into a commemorative stamp. Mexico also released its own version. Hey, I'd buy 'em.

★ Her life was made into an opera. When composer Robert Xavier Rodriguez got the chance to turn the turbulent life of Kahlo into an opera back in 1991, he had to say yes. The two-act finished product, *Frida*, was originally commissioned by the American Music Theater Festival, and it got glowing reviews.

★ Her life was also the subject of the 2002 movie, *Frida*, which starred Salma Hayek.

★ Her house was turned into a museum. Kahlo's cobalt-blue home in Mexico City, known as the Blue House, is now a popular museum and tourist attraction. And for good reason: it's the home Kahlo grew up in. She also lived there with Diego Rivera, and eventually died there. Both her artworks and her personal effects can be found inside, and hundreds of people line up to take a peek every day.

Diego and Kahlo shared a passion for politics, and both belonged to the Mexican communist movement. Her beliefs were also strongly informed by Marxist theory (Marxism is a social theory constructed by philosopher Karl Marx about how class struggle dominates society), and in her youth read and discussed the writings of Nietzsche, Hegel, and Kant. She fought for a variety of social issues, oftentimes featuring them in her work; the personal really was political when it came to Kahlo. Among other things in her art, she insistently questioned the power dynamics between first- and third-world countries, and also the role of women in a patriarchal society.

From 1926 until her death by a pulmonary embolism in 1954, Kahlo created almost 200 paintings, drawings and sketches, fifty-five of which are self-portraits. She's a legend: a fiery, supremely resilient risk-taker who bucked the trends of the time to be wholly, unapologetically herself. Her artistic epilogue continues to serve as a huge inspiration to women everywhere.

HER COOL CREDENTIALS

★ Though Kahlo was born on 6 July 1907, she listed 7 July 1910 as her birth date because it marked the beginning of the Mexican revolution. She wanted her personal story to align with the start of modern Mexico.

★ All over the world people loved Kahlo, and she had many noteworthy friends and lovers. For example, she was praised and befriended by the French surrealist André Breton, and wined and dined with Pablo Picasso in Paris.

QUOTABLES

'I was born a bitch. I was born a painter.'

'I must fight with all my strength so that the little positive things that my health allows me to do might be pointed toward helping the revolution. The only real reason for living.'

'My painting carries with it the message of pain… Painting completed my life… I believe that work is the best thing.'

'I already know everything, without reading or writing. Not very long ago, maybe only a few days back, I was a girl going her way through a world of precise and tangible colours and forms.'

8.
SIMONE DE BEAUVOIR

NÉE SIMONE ERNESTINE LUCIE MARIE BERTRAND DE BEAUVOIR (1908–86)

'I am too intelligent, too demanding, and too resourceful for anyone to be able to take charge of me entirely. No one knows me or loves me completely. I have only myself.'

Claim to Fame	Country of Origin
Author, philosopher	France

HER LEGACY

Some consider Simone de Beauvoir the 'grandmother' of the second wave of feminism, and her monumental 1949 book *The Second Sex* has been dubbed 'the feminist bible'. In an introduction to the book, Judith Thurman wrote that no woman writer before de Beauvoir had opened up in quite such a brazen way about 'the intimate secrets of her sex'. De Beauvoir was a wildly controversial figure who wrote about wildly controversial subjects, and people today still debate her feminist cred. (In my eyes, anyone who makes such a powerful, long-lasting impact on cultural attitudes about women is someone worth knowing about.)

A prolific author of novels, biographies, and poems, de Beauvoir didn't necessarily consider herself like a philosopher (which she was) or even feminist. But she's widely thought of as one of the most influential intellectuals of the twentieth century – and certainly one of the most celebrated thinkers in France – whose ideas were way ahead of their time. For instance, she was outspoken in her criticism of gender essentialism (the idea that men and women are different because of certain innate traits), arguing in *The Second Sex* that 'one is not born, but rather becomes, a woman'. She later explained: 'There is no biological or psychological destiny that defines a woman as such… Baby girls are manufactured to become women.'

HER LIFE STORY

De Beauvoir was born in Paris in 1908 to a family descended from aristocracy. Her father was an atheist and her mother a devout Catholic, and de Beauvoir, who had learned to read at the age of three, at one point wanted to be a nun. Her parents eventually hit major financial troubles, sending the family to live in squalid apartments with a 'no waste' policy. This helped fuel de Beauvoir's lifelong disdain for materialism.

At fourteen, de Beauvoir turned to atheism, a belief system that stayed with her forever and also prompted her interest in philosophy.

She took classes at the Sorbonne in Paris; she was the ninth woman to receive a degree from the esteemed university. When she was twenty-one she became the youngest philosophy teacher in France.

As a young woman, de Beauvoir fell in love with Jean-Paul Sartre, the famous existentialist philosopher who would become her fifty-year-long partner, both intellectually and romantically. The couple never lived together, had kids, or married. He proposed, but she turned him down because she disapproved of marriage as an institution. Instead, they signed a pact of 'transparency', allowing them both to take lovers (de Beauvoir was bisexual, so many of her dalliances were with women).

She gained some success after writing the novel *She Came to Stay* and publishing essays about existentialist ethics, but it wasn't until the publication of her 700-page masterwork, *The Second Sex*, that de Beauvoir rocketed to fame. The book was revolutionary in its ideas about female oppression, specifically that throughout history men had relegated women to the status of 'the Other', a separate, inferior, and profoundly misunderstood second class. The book was both passionately celebrated and attacked for its assertions that women's subpar treatment in the world was a result of messed-up social attitudes and mores, not innate female characteristics.

De Beauvoir was a very prolific writer and remained active in both feminism and existentialism throughout the 1970s. Though she was famous for the rest of her life, people often demeaned her intellectual contributions, claiming she leeched off Sartre's theories. Plenty of major feminists recognised her significance, though. Gloria Steinem once said that 'if any single human being can be credited with inspiring the current international women's movement, it's Simone de Beauvoir.'

HER COOL CREDENTIALS

★ In 1971, when abortion was still illegal in France, de Beauvoir signed the Manifesto of the 343. This was a groundbreaking list of famous women who claimed to have had abortions. The political power of being open about having an abortion became more common – though still not accepted – many years later, of course, but de Beauvoir was among the first to do it.

★ When de Beauvoir died of pneumonia in 1986 at the age of seventy-eight, a newspaper headline blared, 'Women, you owe her everything!'

★ She hung out with a range of awesome luminaries, from Che Guevara and Albert Camus to Kate Millett.

QUOTABLES

'Self-knowledge is no guarantee of happiness, but it is on the side of happiness and can supply the courage to fight for it.'

'She [woman] is the inessential in front of the essential. He is the Subject, he is the absolute. She is the Other.'

'For me, my books were a real fulfilment, and as such they freed me from the necessity to affirm myself in any other way.'

'I am an intellectual, I take words and the truth to be of value.'

9.
PAULI MURRAY

NÉE ANNA PAULINE MURRAY (1910–85)

'I am determined that my country shall take her place among nations as a moral leader of mankind. No law which imprisons my body or custom which wounds my spirit can stop me.'

Claim to Fame	Country of Origin
Activist, lawyer	USA

HER LEGACY

Pauli Murray was an African American activist, lawyer, writer, and priest who was once dubbed a 'one-woman civil rights movement'. She's not remembered as one of the glamorously bold-faced names of that era though, which is a travesty because her feminist legacy is towering – indeed, she's considered an unsung pioneer of her time.

She was instrumental in bridging the chasm between civil rights and women's rights, making sure people worked to include black women in both movements. As she wrote in her book *Words of Fire*, 'By asserting a leadership role in the growing feminist movement, the black woman can help to keep it allied to the objectives of black liberation while simultaneously advancing the interests of all women.'

Murray fought for a wide swath of intersecting human rights. Though she didn't publicly identify as a lesbian throughout most of her life, friends and colleagues knew about her long romantic relationships with women, and she was passionate about fighting for LGBT causes. She may have actually been transgender, though that term had not yet been invented at the time. She reportedly identified as a heterosexual man and once said she was 'convinced that she was really a man, forced… to occupy a woman's body'. Murray was a co-founder of the National Organization for Women (NOW) and of the hugely important civil rights organisation Congress of Racial Equality (CORE), one of the 'Big Four' civil rights groups of that time.

HER LIFE STORY

After spending her early life in Baltimore, Maryland, Murray moved to Durham, North Carolina, to live with her grandparents (her parents died separately when she was young). Durham was a segregated city that Murray was itching to escape, so she hightailed it out of there after graduating from high school with distinction.

After getting her degree in English from New York's Hunter College, in 1938 Murray applied to graduate school at the then-all-white University of North Carolina. She was denied entry because of her race, even though her white great-great-grandfather had been a trustee of the university. Though she was turned away, her bold move gained national publicity, thanks to support from the National Association for the Advancement of Colored People.

After graduating from Howard Law School at the top of her class and then getting a master of laws degree at the University of California's Boalt Hall, Murray became the first African American female deputy attorney general of California. She eventually moved back to New York, where she was hired as the only black attorney at the law firm Paul, Weiss, Rifkind, Wharton, and Garrison, and was just one of only three women lawyers there. Murray's dedication to activism was the most enduring thread throughout her life. She was arrested and imprisoned for refusing to sit at the back of a bus in 1940, fifteen years before Rosa Parks did the same. (She even coined the term 'Jane Crow' as a way to describe a life lived under both racist and sexist policies of the time.) She also organised desegregation protests and sit-ins in Washington, DC, and was an advocate of using nonviolent resistance techniques popularised by Mahatma Gandhi.

Though she shared Martin Luther King Jr's vision of a fair, equitable society for all Americans, Murray didn't think King or anyone else was above criticism. She was one of several black women activists who were vocal in their anger about the lack of female leaders included in the planning of the historic 1963 March on Washington, a rally on the political and social struggles of African Americans. Never one to sit idly by and watch injustice happen, Murray said women's lack of inclusion in preparation for the March was 'bitterly humiliating', and she called out the men involved, saying in one speech, 'There is much jockeying for position as ambitious men push and elbow their way to leadership roles. Not a single woman was invited to make one of the major speeches or to be part of the delegation of leaders who went to the White House. This omission was deliberate.'

In 1961 President Kennedy put Murray on the President's Commission on the Status of Women Committee on Civil and Political Rights. In 1965, she published an article with fellow NOW founder Mary Eastwood, 'Jane Crow and the Law: Sex Discrimination and Title VII'. The authors noted that 'the most serious discrimination against both women and Negroes today' took place in the workplace, and wrote that employment discrimination based on sex and gender was as detrimental as the kind based on race. When the landmark Civil Rights Act of 1964 was signed into law by President Lyndon Johnson, it prohibited employment discrimination based on race, colour, religion, and national origin – but it didn't include sex. Murray and other activists lobbied to have sex discrimination included in Title VII of that bill, and their efforts paid off.

Her groundbreaking accomplishments didn't end there. Murray wrote many articles and books, including, in the early fifties, a powerful biography of her family's journey from slavery to emancipation, *Proud Shoes*. And at age sixty-six, Murray became the very first African American woman to be ordained as an episcopal priest!

HER COOL CREDENTIALS

★ Murray was a lifelong friend of Eleanor Roosevelt's and also maintained a long correspondence with Langston Hughes.

★ In 1947 Murray was named Woman of the Year by *Mademoiselle* magazine. She was the first African American to earn a doctor of science of law degree from Yale Law School.

★ Thurgood Marshall, head of the legal department at the National Association for the Advancement of Colored People, described Murray's book, *States' Laws on Race and Color*, as the bible for civil rights lawyers.

QUOTABLES

'One person plus one typewriter constitutes a movement.'

'As an American I inherit the magnificent tradition of an endless march toward freedom and toward the dignity of all mankind.'

'I speak for my race and my people – the human race and just people.'

[Letter to President Franklin Roosevelt, 1938:] 'Negroes are the most oppressed and most neglected section of your population. Twelve million of your citizens have to endure insults, injustices, and such degradation of the spirit that you would believe impossible.'

10.
ROSA PARKS

NÉE ROSA LOUISE McCAULEY (1913–2005)

*'I would like to be remembered as a person who wanted to be free…
so other people would be also free.'*

Claim to Fame	Country of Origin
Activist	USA

HER LEGACY

Rosa Parks, a.k.a. 'the first lady of civil rights', is a legend known all over the world for that one super-famous instance in 1955 when she refused to give up her seat to a white passenger on a bus in Montgomery, Alabama. Not that this simple move wasn't awesome; it did help spark a huge boycott. Though the former seamstress is often described as a quiet, humble woman – a sort of accidental activist whose interests were generally more traditional and domestic – that isn't the reality. Parks has a much richer legacy of activism and audacity than people give her credit for. (As one writer noted in a *Ms.* magazine blog post, 'Rosa Parks did more than sit on a bus!!!') For example, Parks created a group, the Alabama Committee for Equal Justice, expressly to investigate the brutal gang rape of a black Alabama woman named Recy Taylor, and in the thirties she attended secret meetings to help defend the Scottsboro boys.

HER LIFE STORY

Parks was born in Tuskegee, Alabama, during a time that was rife with a horrific amount of violence, injustice, and inequality for African Americans. As a child she was told to sleep with her clothes on in case she had to run from the Ku Klux Klan in the middle of the night. She later said of that time, 'Back then, we didn't have any civil rights. It was just a matter of survival, of existing from one day to the next. I remember going to sleep as a girl hearing the Klan ride at night and hearing a lynching and being afraid the house would burn down.'

With her grandparents being former slaves and firm advocates for racial equality, her family's experiences with racism set the stage for Parks's future activism. She dropped out of high school in her junior year to take care of her ailing mother and grandmother, and then went to work as a seamstress in Montgomery. (She got her high school

diploma later, in 1934.) After marrying a man named Raymond Parks, who was involved with the National Association for the Advancement of Colored People, she became the first woman to join the NAACP in Montgomery, where she served as the chapter's youth leader. She also worked as the secretary to the organisation's president.

In the 1930s, Parks participated in secret meetings to help fight the death sentences imposed on the Scottsboro boys, nine African American boys who had been wrongfully convicted of raping two white women. And in 1943, twelve full years before her famous showdown on the bus, Parks refused to give up her seat on another bus and was then thrown off for it. That same year, she tried to register to vote but was denied. She eventually earned a voting certificate in 1945, after trying to register three times.

On 1 December 1955, Parks was riding home from work on a Montgomery bus when the bus driver asked her to move to the 'coloured' section so a white boarder could take her seat. 'When he saw me still sitting, he asked if I was going to stand up, and I said, "No, I'm not,"' she remembered. 'And he said, "Well, if you don't stand up, I'm going to have to call the police and have you arrested." I said, "You may do that."' When the policemen came and asked her why she didn't stand, she calmly explained, 'I didn't think I should have to stand up.'

Parks's action prompted the Montgomery Bus Boycott, in which African Americans protested the segregated seating by refusing to ride local buses. It also launched a nationwide movement to end segregation in public areas in general. She was put in prison and found guilty of disorderly conduct, but she appealed her conviction, thereby formally challenging the legality of segregation altogether. The bus boycott lasted 381 days, until the US Supreme Court finally changed its tune and ruled that the segregation law was unconstitutional, and the buses were integrated.

Parks continued her commitment to activism, routinely challenging racism, violence, and oppression on both large and intimate scales. For example, an essay she reportedly wrote in the 1950s, but which only emerged in 2011, described a time when she was almost raped by a white man she dubbed Mr Charlie. She wrote, 'I would never yield to this white man's bestiality. I was ready to die, but give my consent, never… If he wanted to… rape a dead body, he was welcome, but he would have to kill me first.'

Parks received many accolades during her lifetime, including the Spingarn Medal, the NAACP's highest award for outstanding achievement by an African American person, and the prestigious Martin Luther King Jr Award, for her quiet but powerful leadership in the community. She was also given the Congressional Gold Medal, the highest civilian award from the US legislative branch, for the everlasting impact she has made on society.

Rosa Parks will be forever remembered not just for refusing to give up her bus seat to a white guy, but also for spending so many years of her life boldly leading the fight against racist hate and oppression. In 2010 *Time* magazine named her one of the twenty-five most influential women of the twentieth century.

HER COOL CREDENTIALS

★ In 1996 President Bill Clinton awarded Parks the Presidential Medal of Freedom. Along with the Congressional Gold Medal, this medal is considered the highest honour given to a US civilian. At the ceremony, Parks was called 'the first lady of civil rights' and 'the mother of the freedom movement'.

★ During her life, Parks wrote four books: *Rosa Parks: My Story*; *Quiet Strength: The Faith, the Hope, and the Heart of a Woman Who Changed a Nation*; *Dear Mrs. Parks: A Dialogue With Today's Youth*; and *I Am Rosa Parks*.

★ In 1998 the Rosa Parks Museum and Library opened at the site of her arrest in Montgomery to commemorate her activism and her spirit.

QUOTABLES

'Each person must live their life as a model for others.'

'Knowing what must be done does away with fear.'

'I would like to be remembered as a person who wanted
to be free... so other people would be also free.'

'I had given up my seat before, but this day, I was especially tired. Tired
from my work as a seamstress, and tired from the ache in my heart.'

'Stand for something or you will fall for anything. Today's
mighty oak is yesterday's nut that held its ground.'

11.
FLORYNCE KENNEDY

NÉE FLORYNCE RAE KENNEDY (1916–2000)

'You've got to rattle your cage door. You've got to let them know that you're in there, and that you want out. Make noise. Cause trouble. You may not win right away, but you'll sure have a lot more fun.'

Claim to Fame	Country of Origin
Attorney, activist	USA

HER LEGACY

Florynce Kennedy was an African American feminist rabble-rouser and a high-profile civil rights attorney known for her ballsy, take-no-prisoners stance in the courtroom – not to mention her trademark cowboy boots, pink sunglasses, and penchant for holding nothing back when it came to speaking her mind. (*People* magazine once called her 'the rudest mouth on the [feminist] battleground.') Though she hasn't gotten much in the way of history-book recognition, Kennedy was one of the most prominent black feminists of the sixties and seventies.

Kennedy helped repeal New York's restrictive abortion laws; launched a new political party, the Feminist Party; and was committed to fighting for civil rights, the Black Power Movement, and consumer advocacy (way before Ralph Nader made it his big platform). Gloria Steinem wrote about the powerhouse in *Ms.* magazine, 'Just as there was only one Eleanor or Winston… there was only one Flo.'

HER LIFE STORY

Born in Kansas City, Missouri, in 1916, Kennedy looked to her dad, Wiley Kennedy, as an example of strength and determination. Wiley owned his own taxi company and bought a home in a largely white neighbourhood. The Ku Klux Klan once came calling and demanded that the family leave town. As Kennedy recalled in her autobiography, '[Daddy] brought his gun... out with him and said, "Now the first foot that hits that step belongs to the man I shoot. And then after that you can decide who is going to shoot me." They went away and they never came back.'

She credited her parents with helping to instil self-esteem, confidence, and an anti-authoritarian streak in their girls, noting, 'My parents gave us a fantastic sense of security and worth. By the time the bigots got around to telling us that we were nobody, we already knew we were somebody.'

Kennedy knew she wanted to be an attorney way back before she even started high school, and she fought her way to admission at the prestigious Columbia Law School. When she first applied to Columbia, she was turned away, supposedly because the school's quota of female students had already been met, though it was more likely because she was black. But Kennedy refused to take no for an answer: she was brilliant and she deserved to be there. She threatened to file a discrimination lawsuit, and the university promptly admitted her. She was the only black person in her class.

After graduation, in 1954, she launched her own law practice and was one of the few black women to practise law in New York City. The legal maven went on to represent influential African American musicians, like Billie Holiday and Charlie Parker, as well as female members of the Black Liberation Front and the Black Panthers.

Growing fed up with the law as a tool for change, Kennedy turned to her true passion: political activism (though she continued taking legal cases for causes she believed in). She sued the Roman Catholic Church in 1968 for interfering with abortion laws, and she led campaigns against big-time political honchos like Richard Nixon, George Wallace, and New York City Mayor Edward I Koch. In 1966 she founded an organisation, Media Workshop, to fight racism in advertising.

Getting swept up in the budding feminist movement, Kennedy was one of the original members of the National Women's Political Caucus. She helped found the National Organization for Women (NOW), though she eventually walked away because she didn't believe the group was radical enough. 'When I saw how retarded NOW was, I thought, "My God, who needs this?"' she once said. The political party she launched, the Feminist Party, nominated famed African American politician Shirley Chisholm for president. Kennedy was also a co-founder of the National Black Feminist Organization.

In 1968 Kennedy protested against the Miss America Pageant and later co-authored (with feminist lawyer Diane Schulder) a groundbreaking book about abortion, *Abortion Rap*, which collected the stories of women who had had underground or illegal abortions. In the seventies she began lecturing with folks like Gloria Steinem. Steinem recalled in *The New York Times* that she would often speak first during their appearances together. This wasn't because Steinem thought she deserved top billing, but because speaking 'after Flo I would have been an anticlimax'.

HER COOL CREDENTIALS

★ Kennedy was an activist her whole life. She first dipped her toe in the water of social justice when she was young, organising a boycott of Coca-Cola after a local bottling plant refused to hire African American truck drivers. In 1978 she started her own New York City cable-access programme, *The Flo Kennedy Show*, and she participated in activist movements even into her eighties.

★ Speaking of TV, she also moonlighted as a film actor! Kennedy appeared in *The Landlord* (1970), *Black Roots* (1970), *Who Says I Can't Ride a Rainbow!* (1971), and the feminist classic *Born in Flames* (1983).

★ She was nothing if not creative. Throughout her career, she created hilarious new words like jockocracy (hyper-masculine, sports-obsessed American culture) and Pentagonorrhea, which likened the toxic, imperialistic U.S. government to a social/sexual disease.

QUOTABLES

'If men could get pregnant, abortion would be a sacrament.'

'I never stopped to wonder why I'm not like other people. The mystery to me is why more people aren't like me.'

'Being a mother is a noble status, right? So why does it change when you put "unwed" or "welfare" in front of it?'

'There are very few jobs that actually require a penis or vagina. All other jobs should be open to everybody.'

12.
MAYA ANGELOU

NÉE MARGUERITE ANNIE JOHNSON (1928–2014)

'I'm a feminist. I've been a female for a long time now. It'd be stupid not to be on my own side.'

Claim to Fame	Country of Origin
Writer	USA

HER LEGACY

Writing about racism, poverty, power, sexism, single motherhood, sexuality, and so much more with command, poise, and bucketloads of heart, Maya Angelou recorded history – both her own and the outside world's – through her years of dedication to advocacy and the arts. Though she's best known for her work as a writer, she was a radical activist first, working for civil rights and social justice causes as she helped document the racial and political upheaval happening at the time, especially in the Jim Crow South.

And she wasn't just an activist and writer. Though she first achieved fame for her 1969 autobiography, *I Know Why the Caged Bird Sings* (the very first non-fiction bestseller by an African American woman), she was also quite successful as a poet, singer, director, playwright, screenwriter, and more. As journalist John Nichols noted, she 'danced with Alvin Ailey, cut a fine calypso album, sang at Harlem's Apollo Theatre, performed in the touring company of *Porgy and Bess*, appeared in the television mini-series *Roots*, wrote songs with Roberta Flack'. It's hard to imagine anyone personifying the notion of 'grabbing life by the balls' better than Angelou.

HER LIFE STORY

Angelou grew up in Stamps, Arkansas, mainly with her grandmother, her brother, Bailey, and her uncle, Willie (her parents split when she was young). Though her grandmother was loving, Angelou experienced terrible violence at age seven, when her mother's boyfriend raped Angelou and then her uncles killed her attacker. Traumatised, Angelou went mute for five years. 'Just my breath, carrying my words out, might poison people and they'd curl up and die,' she wrote. But when she was in eighth grade, Angelou thankfully found her voice again after reciting a poem for a family friend.

When she was a teenager, she won a scholarship to study dance and drama at the California Labor School in San Francisco. At age fourteen, she left school and became San Francisco's first female African American cable car conductor. Angelou later finished high school and took odd jobs as a cook and waitress, but her heart was always in the arts and entertainment. Throughout the fifties and sixties, she worked as an actor and singer in a number of productions across the country.

In 1969 her first memoir, *I Know Why the Caged Bird Sings*, was published to great fanfare. It was nominated for a National Book Award and maintained a coveted place on *The New York Times*' paperback bestseller list for two years. The book focused on her childhood in Arkansas and the racism and strife she eventually managed to overcome. It made Angelou a star, but it was not without critics. Some close-minded people thought *Caged Bird* was too in-your-face in its coverage of issues like racism, teen pregnancy, and the church – it has been widely banned from school classrooms for those reasons. One Virginia organisation, Parents Against Bad Books, was formed with the sole mission of preventing young people from reading Angelou's book!

The controversy disturbed her – 'I feel sorry for the young person who never gets to read it,' she once said – but it didn't stop her. Angelou published many more memoirs and branched out into poetry (which earned her a Pulitzer Prize nomination) and other forms of writing. When she began working in film as an actor, screenwriter, and director, she broke new ground in Hollywood for African American women.

Angelou became close with Martin Luther King Jr after he heard about her activist work. In 1959 King made her the northern coordinator for the Southern Christian Leadership Conference, an important African American civil rights organisation. She later worked with revolutionary Black Power activist Malcolm X and helped him build the Organization of African American Unity. Angelou wrote of Malcolm X, 'Up close he was a great red arch through which one could pass to eternity… I had never been so affected by a human presence.' She also helped found the Cultural Association for Women of African Heritage.

Angelou drew tons of other esteemed cultural figures into her personal orbit – she was good buddies with writer James Baldwin (he was the one who first encouraged her to write an autobiography), and she was tight with the beloved jazz crooner Billie Holiday for a while. She later famously became close with Oprah Winfrey, who would throw lavish birthday celebrations for her dear friend. In 1974 President Gerald Ford appointed Angelou to the Bicentennial Commission; later, President Jimmy Carter put her on the Commission for International Woman of the Year.

Angelou had a knack for boosting people's spirits, especially those of the oppressed and downtrodden, and many of her words have been immortalised on posters, cards, magnets, you name it. Later in life, she kept singing and working in film. She won three Grammys for her spoken word releases, and before she died in May 2014 she was working on an album called *Caged Bird Songs*, which was released posthumously.

As a truth- and justice-obsessed writer, activist, and entertainer extraordinaire, Angelou helped illuminate her own path out of the darkness. She inspired generations of girls to follow in her journey to transcend a painful past and make something beautiful of one's life – which she did, to the utmost.

HER COOL CREDENTIALS

★ In 1993 President Bill Clinton invited Angelou to his inauguration. She wrote a poem for the event – which she was asked to read aloud – called 'On the Pulse of Morning'.

★ Angelou wrote, produced, directed, and starred in countless productions for stage, film, and television.

★ In 2010 President Barack Obama awarded her the Presidential Medal of Freedom, which is considered one of America's highest civilian honours. He also said Angelou's work had 'spoken to millions, including my mother, which is why my sister is named Maya'.

★ Angelou earned a Tony Award nomination for her acting in the play *Look Away* (1973) and an Emmy nomination for her work on the television mini-series *Roots* (1977).

QUOTABLES

'There is no greater agony than bearing an untold story inside you.'

'If I am not good to myself, how can I expect anyone else to be good to me?'

'I love to see a young girl go out and grab the world by the lapels. Life's a bitch. You've got to go out and kick ass.'

'You alone are enough. You have nothing to prove to anybody.'

13.
YAYOI KUSAMA

(1929–)

'I am just another dot in the world.'

Claim to Fame	Country of Origin
Artist, writer	Japan

HER LEGACY

Yayoi Kusama is a trailblazing Japanese avant-garde artist who has worked in many different mediums: painting, sculpture, collage, installation, writing, and fashion, just to name several. She is now in her late eighties, and many folks think of her as Japan's greatest living artist. Though Kusama doesn't consciously associate herself with feminism, viewers have long noted strong feminist themes in her work, which explores cultural identity, sex, gender, and race. One professor wrote that Kusama, like Yoko Ono, seems 'obsessed by the refashioning of the Japanese female body', noting that both women's art 'displaces any easy or overdetermined notions of the objectified Japanese female "Other"… that is often… received as exotic, inscrutable, small, cute…' Her work is considered a precursor to the minimalist and pop art movements, and she's influenced lots of megastars, such as Andy Warhol.

Many young women look up to Kusama as an icon – not just for her artistic prowess, but because she has been very open about her struggles with mental illness, which has helped other people with similar challenges to feel less alone. She incorporates her illness into her art, making something truly beautiful out of it. Kusama has said her work originates from 'hallucinations only I can see', and she translates those 'obsessional images' into her sculptures and paintings. She remembered first experiencing hallucinations as a child: 'One day, I suddenly looked up to find that each and every violet had its own individual, human-like facial expression, and to my astonishment they were all talking to me.'

HER LIFE STORY

Kusama was born in Matsumoto City, Japan, into a wealthy, conservative family. Her childhood was far from idyllic. Her father was a womaniser who wasn't home much. Her mother was physically abusive and tried to prohibit Kusama from painting, even going as far as destroying the canvases she was working on. Having such a violent,

difficult mum bred a firm thread of anti-authoritarianism in Kusama that would persist her whole life.

She went off to study art in Kyoto as a means to escape her turbulent home life. There she mastered Nihonga painting, an intricate Japanese style developed during the Meiji period (1868–1912). In 1958 she moved to New York City, and within eighteen months she accomplished something unthinkable in the art world in that short time: she landed a solo show. Most of the exhibit comprised five huge canvases covered in infinity nets. The work was compared to that of superstar painter Jackson Pollock.

Kusama also drew attention for her sexually charged performance pieces supporting civil rights and free love. In one, she painted polka dots all over naked men and women (including herself). Speaking of dots, they are a running theme throughout her work; their repetition, she said, helps soothe her anxieties. She said, 'Since my childhood, I have always made works with polka dots. Earth, moon, sun and human beings all represent dots; a single particle among billions.'

After conquering New York City in the sixties, Kusama moved back to Japan in 1973. There she began writing surrealistic novels, poetry, and short stories, including the novel *The Hustler's Grotto of Christopher Street* (1983), which won the Tenth Literary Award for New Writers. Still suffering from obsessive-compulsive disorder, Kusama checked herself into a psychiatric hospital, where she resides today. Though some have claimed she's 'faking' her illness to get attention, Kusama denied this offensive idea, saying, 'My artwork is an expression of my life, particularly of my mental disease.' She does all her artwork at her studio near the mental hospital and created a large sculpture that resides on the hospital grounds. She described the sculpture as 'a store-bought rowboat completely covered with stuffed canvas protuberances'.

Despite not identifying herself as a feminist, Kusama has had a profound influence on women artists across the world. Yoko Ono reportedly called her an influence, and Kathleen Hanna's punk-electro band Le Tigre mentioned Kusama, along with dozens of other important women artists, in its song 'Hot Topic'.

HER COOL CREDENTIALS

★ Kusama collaborated with legendary Louis Vuitton creative director Marc Jacobs on the fashion collection LOUIS VUITTON × YAYOI KUSAMA.

★ She was good friends with legendary artist Georgia O'Keeffe. After finding a book by O'Keeffe in a bookstore in her hometown, Kusama sent the artist some of her watercolours and O'Keeffe wrote back. O'Keeffe eventually even went to visit Kusama when she lived in New York.

★ In 2006 Kusama became the first Japanese woman to receive the Praemium Imperiale, one of Japan's most prestigious prizes for internationally recognised artists.

QUOTABLES

'I devote my energy to both telling my personal life story and seeking self-obliteration. However, I will not destroy myself through art.'

'I have painted since I was around ten and I still work every day.'

'Growing up, I was constantly told to behave appropriately as a girl. When I wanted to get a driver's licence, my mother said that I could get a chauffeured car if I married well. When I said I wanted to be a painter, she told me to be an art collector instead. But I was not discouraged because I knew I was talented.'

14.
FAITH RINGGOLD

NÉE FAITH WILLI JONES (1930–)

*'I just decided when someone says you
can't do something, do more of it.'*

Claim to Fame	Country of Origin
Artist, writer	USA

HER LEGACY

Faith Ringgold is an important African American artist and writer who has been working to promote feminist and anti-racist causes since she first started out in the early sixties. Though she has worked in a huge variety of mediums, Ringgold is best known for her colourful story quilts. With her quilts, she politicised what was often thought of as a 'women-only' art form, bringing new meaning to the classic feminist catchphrase, 'The personal is political.' She has described her work as 'an expression of the African American female experience'.

Ringgold's intricate, painted quilts tell stories through panelled images seamlessly woven with elaborate accompanying text. Many works focus on the horrors African Americans have been forced to endure through the years. 'The reason why I began making quilts is because I wrote my autobiography in 1980 and couldn't get it published... my story didn't appear to be appropriate for African American women... and that really made me so angry,' Ringgold explained.

To date, Ringgold has made more than ninety-five quilts, with each section of each quilt equalling one page of a book. She said that the works she created in the sixties kept her out of the traditional art world because they depicted 'the struggle for independence and freedom that black people were pursuing during the civil rights era' – a subject that made some people uncomfortable (as all great art is wont to do!).

FAITH RINGGOLD'S CORNUCOPIA OF CHILDREN'S BOOKS

In addition to being a celebrated artist, Faith Ringgold has written beautiful books for kids. Many of the colourful tomes feature her iconic story quilts, translated onto the page. The books may be for kids, but the themes and storylines are universal, and the art is gorgeous, making them worth checking out no matter what your age.

TAR BEACH

Ringgold's 1988 story quilt of the same name was the direct inspiration for this book, which won more than ten awards. It tells the story of Cassie Louise Lightfoot, an eight-year-old growing up in Depression-era Harlem (just like the author herself!) who vividly fantasises about flying over New York City, high above the 'tar beach' of her apartment building rooftop where she hangs out and eats with her family, and making right all the many wrongs in her 1939 world.

MY DREAM OF MARTIN LUTHER KING

Ringgold used a dream she had about Martin Luther King Jr as a springboard into a creative retelling of the life of the civil rights hero. It's an important feat, and one she pulls off effortlessly. Her language is infused with poetic drama as she recounts King's early days, his home life, and his activism, as well as the racism and segregation that were par for the course during his time. The art is amazing.

IF A BUS COULD TALK: THE STORY OF ROSA PARKS
In this vivid picture-book biography, Ringgold tells Rosa Parks's life story through a talking bus, which shares Parks's tale with little protagonist Marcie. It all begins when Marcie finds herself on a weird, driverless bus one day instead of her usual school bus. The talking bus tells Marcie all about Rosa Parks's childhood and activism, as well as her refusal to give up her seat to a white dude, a singular act that spawned sweeping change. At the end of the crazy ride, Marcie meets Rosa Parks herself when she strides onto the bus.

HER LIFE STORY

Ringgold was born and raised in Harlem during the Great Depression. She picked up a love of fabric and textiles from her mother, Willi Posey, who was a fashion designer and seamstress. Sick often with asthma as a child, Ringgold was forced to stay home with her mum, which is how she learned to sew and be creative with fabrics. Her mum also took her to lots of museums and cultural events, which helped expand Ringgold's worldview.

After graduating with a master's degree in art from City College of New York, Ringgold began teaching college in 1970 in New York City. Her work in the sixties was primarily made up of paintings about racism, injustice, and civil rights. In the early seventies, she abandoned traditional painting and began embracing different mediums like dolls and sculpture. She began creating her famous story quilts with the help of her mum. When Posey died in 1981, Ringgold committed to making a quilt every year in her honour.

Some of Ringgold's quilts are graphic in their depictions of African Americans' history of systemic oppression at the hands of white people. For example, one creation, 'Flag Story Quilt', tells of a paraplegic, armless African American war vet who gets wrongly accused of rape and murder. But not all her quilts relate the same type of painful story. Another, 'Picnic on the Grass... Alone', from her 1997 series *The American Collection*, seems to offer messages of both hope and loneliness – a reflection on female solitude. As journalist William Zimmer wrote, it features a young woman named Mariena, 'a successful artist with wealth, fame and beauty, finding herself picnicking alone. She is wistful, perhaps, but she might just be smiling, enjoying the solitude.'

A dedicated activist since the 1970s, Ringgold is quite the feminist badass. In 1970 she formed an ad hoc group with Poppy Johnson and Lucy Lippard to protest how few women artists were selected for the prestigious annual exhibits at the Whitney Museum of American Art in New York City. Their goal, Ringgold said, was for that year's exhibit to feature at least 50 per cent women artists. In response, they left raw eggs at the museum, then added sanitary napkins to the gross-out mix. 'Unsuspecting male curatorial staff would pick up the eggs and experience the shock of having raw egg slide down the pants of their fine tailor-made suits,' she recalled in her memoir.

Ringgold's artworks can be found in the permanent collections of many prominent museums, including the Metropolitan Museum of Art, the Museum of Modern Art, and the Guggenheim Museum. She has also written a number of popular books for children.

HER COOL CREDENTIALS

★ Ringgold was a founding member of the 'Where We At' Black Women Artists, a New York-based women's art collective connected to the Black Arts Movement (an artistic arm of the Black Power Movement).

★ Ringgold has won more than seventy-five prestigious awards, including twenty-two honorary doctorate of fine arts degrees.

★ Her first book, *Tar Beach*, won more than thirty awards, including the Ezra Jack Keats New Writer Award and the Coretta Scott King Award for Illustration.

QUOTABLES

'There are very many artists who just want to paint colours. That's fine. I couldn't do that. I have something else I want to make my story about.'

'I became a feminist because I wanted to help my daughters, other women and myself aspire to something more than a place behind a good man.'

'I always knew I wanted to be somebody. I think that's where it begins. People decide, "I want to be somebody. I want to make a contribution. I want to leave my mark here." Then different factors contribute to how you will do that.'

'I don't think America's the centre of the world anymore. I think African women will lead the way [in]… women's liberation.'

15.
YOKO ONO
(1933–)

'If you allow them, women bring out their true self, which is strong and talented and powerful. But the world didn't want to know about that. The world wanted to keep women down.'

Claim to Fame	Country of Origin
Artist, musician	Japan

HER LEGACY

Yoko Ono (her first name translates to 'Ocean Child' in Japanese) may be best known for her high-profile 1969 marriage to beloved Beatle John Lennon. But the eighty-something's massive feminist legacy shouldn't be underestimated – Ono is a multifaceted, envelope-pushing, avant-garde artist and musician who has become infinitely more than simply the shadow of her former husband. In feminist anthems like 'Sisters, O Sisters', she wailed against the patriarchy and urged her fellow women to 'shout from our hearts'. Ono has said that for her, 'art is a means of survival', and she's used her art as a tool to address gender discrimination, as well as to tackle themes of peace, social justice, and anti-consumerism.

Despite all this good stuff, Ono was a constant target of derision in the primarily white-male music scene of the sixties and seventies. As an outspoken Japanese woman who stood firmly by Lennon's side instead of wilting into the background, she was bashed, trashed, and dragged through the mud by fans, critics – well, almost everyone. But Ono only used that misogynistic hate as fuel to make her art and activism stronger.

HER LIFE STORY

Ono's childhood was largely spent on the move: her family relocated from Tokyo to the States and back again, several times over. After dropping out of Sarah Lawrence College, she moved to the legendary arts hub of New York City's Greenwich Village, where she immersed herself in art and poetry. She began creating controversial artworks that invited viewers to participate in the work. Many viewers simply didn't 'get' her avant-garde sensibilities – at one point, Ono adopted the housefly as an alter ego – but that didn't bother her.

One of Ono's most popular works was a conceptual art piece she first performed in 1964 called 'Cut Piece'. Viewers were invited to chop off bits of her clothes until Ono was left wearing absolutely nothing. The piece could be seen as a statement on the ownership of women's

bodies, on the artistic relationship between viewer and creator, or on shedding American materialism. As for much of Ono's work, the larger meaning was ultimately determined by each individual who experienced it.

John Lennon was a fan of Ono's work. The duo married in 1969 and began collaborating extensively, as well as becoming active in the anti-Vietnam War effort sweeping the country. They famously staged 'bed-ins' for peace – their honeymoon was a weeklong bed-in! – in which they holed up in a hotel room, stayed in bed, let their hair grow, and invited press into the room to talk about world peace for twelve hours a day. Together they launched a mini art movement, Bagism, which involved wearing a bag over one's body as a statement against 'isms' and stereotyping people based on race, gender, and appearances.

Ono challenged ideas of what a female musician was supposed to be, do, and look like, which she got routinely insulted for. She never let her attackers silence her, though. In her awesome 1974 song 'Yes, I'm a Witch', she talked back to the critics who had torn her down, singing, 'I'm a witch, I'm a bitch, I don't care what you say. My voice is real, my voice speaks truth, I don't fit in your ways.'

Ever since Lennon was gunned down outside the couple's apartment building in 1980, Ono has worked even more tirelessly to promote peace, tolerance, anti-racism, and women's rights. In 2002 she launched the LennonOno Grant for Peace, a $50,000 award given to two people every two years. (Fun fact: Lady Gaga won it in 2012.) Ono and her son, Sean Lennon, founded the group Artists Against Fracking (the controversial practice of drilling and injecting fluid into the ground to release natural gas from rocks).

Her work has kept Ono passionately busy and fulfilled. As she said in 2013, at age eighty: 'I have had an incredible life. I don't mean that in a fairy-tale way, but an incredible and busy working life.'

HER COOL CREDENTIALS

★ Her 1980 album *Double Fantasy* – which she performed on with John Lennon and released three weeks before his death – reached number one in the *US Billboard* chart.

★ After the devastating World Trade Center attacks on 11 September 2001, Ono placed a full-page, unsigned ad in *The New York Times*. All it said was, 'Imagine all the people living life in peace.' Ono's rep explained that she left the ad anonymous because 'she felt it would be more effective if her name wasn't on it'.

★ In 1951 Ono became the first female student admitted to study philosophy at Gakushuin University in Tokyo.

★ In 2009 she judged the world's first Twitter haiku competition in London. Ono has a massive social media presence, with nearly five million followers on Twitter and 197,000 on Instagram.

QUOTABLES

'The male society is letting the men think of the women as something pretty and soft and that kind of thing… So I just wanted to show what we were. Women are the ones who actually created the human race.'

'The whole world is starting to realise that it was the most unwise thing for our society to have ignored women power, to run the society with male priorities.'

'It's a waste to not say anything with art.'

16.
AUDRE LORDE

NÉE AUDRE GERALDINE LORDE (1934–92)

'I am deliberate and afraid of nothing.'

Claim to Fame	Country of Origin
Poet	USA

HER LEGACY

Audre Lorde called herself a 'black lesbian feminist poet warrior mother', a smorgasbord of intermingling, often marginalised identities. One of the greatest things about Lorde was how she overtly celebrated all those parts of herself, even in the face of blatant social injustice. A self-proclaimed 'outsider' – in fact, her best-known book is titled *Sister Outsider* – Lorde was proud of who she was and didn't try to shrink down to make anyone else feel comfortable. She was determined to define herself on her own terms, far from the rigid constraints placed upon women of colour. Lorde often wrote about female sexuality, a taboo topic that was considered even more out of bounds from a black lesbian. Today she is remembered as one of the twentieth century's most influential African American female writers and educators – someone who didn't just accept differences among people, but encouraged them.

Lorde received broad critical praise for tackling powerful subjects with grace and sensitivity in her writing, but – like many other feminist fighters who dared speak up against oppression, abuse, and discrimination – she drew anger from conservatives, such as the racist right-wing senator Jesse Helms. She once spoke out about Helms's criticism of her work, saying, 'Jesse Helms' objection to my work is not about obscenity... or even about sex. It is about revolution and change... Helms knows that my writing is aimed at his destruction, and the destruction of every single thing he stands for.'

HER LIFE STORY

Raised in Harlem during the Great Depression by West Indian immigrant parents, Lorde was born so nearsighted that she was considered legally blind. Still, her mum managed to show her how to read and write by the wee age of four, and Lorde inherited some of her love for writing and poetry from her mother. While she was still in high school, she had her first poem published, in *Seventeen* magazine. Lorde experienced racism at the Catholic schools she attended as a youth, and poetry was a refuge from the pain she dealt with there. She said her poems were 'very important to [her] in terms of survival, in terms of living'.

After getting a bachelor's degree from Hunter College and a master's in library science from Columbia University, Lorde worked as a librarian in New York City public schools from 1961 to 1968. She married a man (they later divorced), had two kids, and grew active in the gay scene in Greenwich Village. Her first book of poetry, *The First Cities*, was published in 1968. That same year, she moved to Louisiana to be a writer-in-residence at Toogaloo College, where she met her long-time partner, Frances Clayton, and began her interest in teaching.

Most of Lorde's early poems focused on the complexities of love, but as the social turmoil of the sixties began to sweep the country, her work grew more politically driven. Jerome Brooks reported in *Black Women Writers (1950–1980): A Critical Evaluation*, 'Lorde's poetry of anger is perhaps her best-known work.' Lorde opened up about her sexual identity as a lesbian in her second book of poems, *Cables to Rage*, in a piece called 'Martha'. *Cables to Rage* was different from her first book because of its broadened political scope: by then, Lorde had seen Martin Luther King Jr get assassinated and had endured a number of other personal and cultural hardships. She felt she couldn't stay silent about her rage anymore.

Lorde wasn't just angry about racism and sexism – though she was rightfully pissed about both. She didn't always see eye to eye with white feminists, who had a history of trivialising or ignoring black women's struggles and their critical role in women's rights. But Lorde made it a personal goal to '[meet] across our differences' when it came to working with feminists of different cultures and backgrounds, striving to band together for common aims.

In the eighties Lorde moved to the Virgin Islands with her partner, where in 1992 she died of breast cancer after a fourteen-year struggle. She chronicled her illness and her feelings about confronting death in a book titled *The Cancer Journals*.

HER COOL CREDENTIALS

★ From 1991 to 1992, Lorde had the distinction of being the poet laureate of New York.

★ Lorde's powerful and much-loved collection *Sister Outsider: Essays & Speeches* (1988) is considered essential feminist reading, both in and out of academia.

★ As an activist, Lorde helped found Kitchen Table: Women of Color Press in 1980, which first published the canonical *This Bridge Called My Back: Writings by Radical Women of Color* and *Home Girls: A Black Feminist Anthology*.

★ She was an avid player in the anti-apartheid movement as a founding member of a group called Sisters in Support of Sisters in South Africa.

QUOTABLES

'You cannot, you cannot use someone else's fire. You can only use your own. And in order to do that, you must first be willing to believe that you have it.'

'If I didn't define myself for myself, I would be crunched into other people's fantasies for me and eaten alive.'

'I have a duty to speak the truth as I see it and to share not just my triumphs, not just the things that felt good, but the pain, the intense, often unmitigating pain.'

'When I dare to be powerful, to use my strength in the service of my vision, then it becomes less and less important whether I am afraid.'

'Your silence will not protect you.'

'The language by which we have been taught to dismiss ourselves and our feelings as suspect is the same language we use to dismiss and suspect each other.'

'I have come to believe that caring for myself is not self-indulgent. Caring for myself is an act of survival.'

17.
JANE GOODALL

NÉE VALERIE JANE MORRIS-GOODALL (1934–)

*'Only if we understand, can we care. Only if we care,
we will help. Only if we help, we shall be saved.'*

Claim to Fame	Country of Origin
Primatologist, anthropologist	England

HER LEGACY

Jane Goodall is one of the leading scientists, conservationists, and animal educators of our time. With her pioneering studies of chimpanzees – she lived in Africa for years to do in-depth field research and form relationships with the animals – Goodall discovered many things no one else had before, such as chimpanzees' capability for emotional relationships. She also revealed a four-year-long war between two chimp communities in Gombe, unveiled new insights into the bond between mothers and infants, and learned they had a primal language with more than twenty individual sounds. With each of Goodall's new discoveries, we learned more about the intimate connection between animals and humans, and how similar we truly are.

HER LIFE STORY

Goodall grew up in England in a middle-class family, where she had a beloved stuffed chimp named Jubilee – not to mention some big dreams. As she remembered it, 'I had this dream of going to Africa.

We didn't have any money and I was a girl, so everyone except my mother laughed at it.' A major animal lover, she said that her relationship with a dog named Rusty helped wake her up to the idea that animals can have feelings and personalities of their own, and when she was twelve, she started a nature club, the Alligator Society, that worked with animals.

Even then, Goodall was a budding scientist, always down in the dirt examining creatures and trying to figure out how they worked (she once hid out in a henhouse for hours to learn how hens lay their eggs). After high school, she wanted to go to college, but her family didn't have the funds, so she enrolled in the more affordable secretarial school.

Despite downgrading her dreams to attend secretarial school, Goodall finally made it on that trip to Africa. She first went to Kenya in 1957 to visit a friend's farm, and while she was there, she landed a job as an assistant and secretary for famous anthropologist Louis Leakey, then curator of a Nairobi museum. She began helping Leakey on his anthropological digs and was sent out to study the vervet monkey. Even though Goodall didn't have formal scientific training – or a college degree! – Leakey decided she was the right candidate for a long mission out in the wild to study chimps, the second-smartest primate in the world. The reason he picked Goodall was because he thought her temperament was well suited to being alone in nature for extended stretches. Fortunately, it turned out he was right. At age twenty-six, Goodall journeyed to the Gombe Stream in Tanzania to study chimps. She was required to bring a companion with her, so she took her mother along.

Though the chimps were initially shy and took a while to emerge from the forests and trust her, they eventually did, and Goodall formed bonds with them by imitating their actions, hanging out with them in trees, and eating their foods. She made two groundbreaking discoveries. Chimps eat meat; it was previously thought that they were all vegetarian. And they build and use tools, something believed only to be done by humans (she saw a chimp use a twig to hunt for termites in the ground). She also noted that they had a caste system, used touch to comfort each other, and wielded rocks as weapons.

In 1965 she returned to England and attended Cambridge University to obtain a PhD in ethology. She was only the eighth person ever permitted to pursue a PhD there without getting an undergrad degree first. Her colleagues looked down on her because they felt her research methods were too 'emotional' and unscientific. For example, she gave chimps names instead of ID-ing them by number.

Goodall started the Jane Goodall Institute in 1977 to further her research, all the while becoming a minor celebrity. But after attending a conference in Chicago in the 1980s where the growing threats to chimps' natural habitats were discussed, her life's purpose shifted from scientific exploration to wildlife conservation and education. Now she spends three hundred days per year travelling to educate people about chimps' disappearing habitats and the cruelties committed against them in the name of research.

Today, Jane's work continues to centre on endangered species, especially chimpanzees, encouraging people to pitch in and take action to make the world a healthier place for people, animals, and the environment. She concentrates her efforts on spreading awareness and educating the next generation on conservation and how they can help.

HER COOL CREDENTIALS

★ In April 2002 Secretary-General Kofi Annan named Goodall a United Nations Messenger of Peace. She was reappointed to this position by Secretary-General Ban Ki-Moon in June 2007. She has won numerous awards, such as the Gold Medal of Conservation from the San Diego Zoological Society and the J. Paul Getty Wildlife Conservation Prize. In 2004 she was named a Dame of the British Empire.

★ Like most authors, Goodall is usually the one being paid for her books, but Goodall herself paid to have her children's book, *The Chimpanzee Family*, translated into Swahili and distributed in Africa.

★ She launched Roots & Shoots, an organisation that helps young people work together to develop ways to find direct solutions to problems in their communities.

QUOTABLES

'The least I can do is speak out for those who cannot speak for themselves.'

'The greatest danger to our future is apathy.'

'You can have millions of face lifts and all these different things that women have done to their bodies… but personally, well: A) I haven't the money for that, and B) I haven't got the time for it, and C) I mean, there are more important things to me than how you look.'

'There is not much you can do singly, but if we can involve young people, especially at… [age] eighteen through twenty-four, going out in the world as the next politicians, the next lawyers, the next doctors, the next teachers, the next parents – then perhaps we get a critical mass of youth that has a different kind of values.'

18.
JUDY BLUME

NÉE JUDY SUSSMAN (1938–)

'I can't let safety and security become the focus of my life.'

Claim to Fame	Country of Origin
Author	USA

HER LEGACY

Judy Blume is a beloved bestselling author of more than thirty young adult (YA), children's, and adult books. She was one of the first YA and tween-oriented authors to write explicitly about the ins and outs of puberty and of adolescent sexuality in its raw, gritty, sometimes painful glory – all from a young woman's perspective. This was considered quite forward thinking, and her books have sold more than eighty-five million copies and been translated into more than thirty languages.

Other than sex, some of the topics Blume has explored in her books – such as *Are You There, God? It's Me, Margaret*; *Deenie*; *Blubber*; and *Forever* – include menstruation, masturbation, racism, body image, divorce, and friendship. Blume has been a target of censors because of her candour in tackling these sometimes taboo subjects, but she hasn't let that slow down her (extremely prolific) output. She became an anti-censorship activist in part to fight against the critics who were attempting to ban her books, especially from school libraries.

HER LIFE STORY

Growing up in New Jersey, Blume said that even though she loved to read and 'make up stories' in her head, she never wanted to be a writer. Instead, she said, 'I dreamed about becoming a cowgirl, a detective, a spy, a great actor, or a ballerina. Not a dentist, like my father, or a homemaker, like my mother.' She didn't begin writing until adulthood, when she was married and her two kids were in preschool, and she was 'desperate for a creative outlet'.

Blume attended New York University, where she earned a BS in education in 1961. She published her first book in 1969, *The One in the Middle is the Green Kangaroo*, and released a rapid succession of new books over the next ten years, including some of her most popular works, such as *Blubber* and *Are You There, God? It's Me, Margaret*. Though her work touched many readers from the beginning, her books were controversial. One woman reportedly called Blume on the phone and accused her of being a communist for writing *Are You There God? It's Me, Margaret*. The book, however, has nothing to do with politics.

Blume has been married three times and is open about personal struggles she went through in her life. After she divorced her first husband, lawyer John M. Blume, she remarried quickly, admitting she 'didn't know how to be unmarried'. Her second marriage didn't fare well either, and she remembered that relationship as 'a disaster, a total disaster. After a couple years, I got out. I cried every day. Anyone who thinks my life is cupcakes is all wrong.' She credited her work with helping her get through those tough times, saying, 'Work really saved me. I've always been able to write, even when everything else was falling apart.' Later in life, Blume successfully conquered breast cancer and cervical cancer diagnoses.

FIVE OF JUDY BLUME'S
MOST BANNED BOOKS

More than a few of Judy Blume's books have made an appearance on the American Library Association's list of 100 Most Frequently Challenged Books. These five classic Blume books earned this dubious distinction between 1990 and 1999.

Forever (1975)
Katherine, a teen girl, loses her virginity to her first love, Michael. (And miraculously, they don't get punished for their wanton teen ways!) Soon she navigates the murky waters of falling for another boy while she's still kind of involved with Michael. *Forever* is frank in its coverage of teen sexuality, and many girls (this one included!) have fond, vivid memories of devouring the dirty passages under their covers by flashlight while their parents were asleep. Oh, and Michael's penis is nicknamed Ralph, if you care about that sort of thing.

Blubber (1974)
Jill, the narrator, is a Pennsylvania fifth-grader who participates in the bullying of an overweight kid in her class named Linda. She doesn't buy into the bullying because she's a bad person or because she truly believes Linda deserves it – she does it to fit in with her peers, especially Wendy, the requisite horrible Mean Girl who dominates the girls' class. Wendy doesn't get hers in the end, and apparently this bothered some adult readers. Blume wrote in 2013 that *Blubber* was 'banned in Montgomery County, Maryland, for "lack of moral tone" and, more recently, challenged in Canton, Ohio, for allowing evil behaviour to go unpunished'. Ugh.

Are You There, God? It's Me, Margaret (1970)
This work is, perhaps, Blume's most famous book — and it's one that helped girls everywhere through the roughest parts of their tween years. The book centres on Margaret, an eleven-year-old who just moved to New Jersey with her family. She befriends a crew of girls who candidly talk about their secret hopes and fears (buying their first bra, getting their period, kissing boys). Margaret is different from them, though, because her mum is Christian and her dad is Jewish... and apparently this was scandalous way back when.

Deenie (1973)
This book doesn't, on the surface, sound remotely controversial. It's about a thirteen-year-old wannabe model who finds her life upended when she's diagnosed with scoliosis and is forced to wear a back brace. She's a normal pubescent girl in every other respect, confronted with the usual insecurities. What Blume dares to, ahem, touch on – and what got this book in trouble – is its references to Deenie getting a 'very nice feeling' from touching her 'special place'.

Tiger Eyes (1981)
The protagonist is a fifteen-year-old girl named Davey who's reeling after her father was shot dead in a holdup. Soon her mum decides to relocate the family to New Mexico to move on, and her world is rocked even more. Thankfully Davey meets a new friend named Wolf who helps her navigate the murky new life she's been thrust into. This book reportedly ended up on the American Library Association list due to its portrayals of underage drinking, depression, and death.

HER COOL CREDENTIALS

★ Blume has won more than ninety awards, including a Library of Congress Living Legends Award and the 2004 National Book Foundation's Medal for Distinguished Contribution to American Letters.

★ In 1996 she won the American Library Association Margaret A. Edwards Award, which recognises a writer's unique body of work for its 'significant and lasting contribution to young adult literature' and work that helps 'adolescents become aware of themselves and in addressing questions about their role and importance in relationships, society, and in the world'. Her 1975 book *Forever* was specifically noted in the citation: 'She broke new ground in her frank portrayal of Michael and Katherine, high school seniors who are in love for the first time. Their love and sexuality are described in an open, realistic manner and with great compassion.'

★ She founded the Kids Fund, a charitable and educational foundation that gives about $40,000 per year to various non-profits offering a range of children's programmes from workshops on divorce to teen-mum support groups.

★ The seventeenth of June is a holiday called Judy Blumesday, started by two Blume fans who wanted to riff on Bloomsday, the annual holiday when James Joyce fans celebrate his book *Ulysses*.

QUOTABLES

'Hate and war are bad words. Fuck isn't.'

'Each of us must confront our own fears, must come face to face with them. How we handle our fears will determine where we go with the rest of our lives. To experience adventure or to be limited by the fear of it.'

'It's all about your determination, I think, as much as anything…
I would cry when the rejections came in – the first couple of
times, anyway – and I would go to sleep feeling down, but I
would wake up in the morning optimistic and saying, "Well,
maybe they didn't like that one, but wait till they see what I'm
going to do next." And I think you just have to keep going.'

'When you ask, "Did writing change my life?" It
totally changed my life. It gave me my life.'

19.
JUDY CHICAGO
NÉE JUDITH SYLVIA COHEN (1939–)

'I didn't make myself an outsider. The art world made me an outsider.'

Claim to Fame	Country of Origin
Artist	USA

HER LEGACY

Judy Chicago is an artist, writer, and feminist pioneer who has devoted her career to helping advance women's voices in the art world. One of the core leaders of the feminist art movement that emerged in the seventies, Chicago made it her personal mission to ensure that women's creative achievements not be erased from history. Though her work embraces stereotypically 'feminine' art forms, like needlework and textile arts, it has also incorporated traditionally male ones, such as pyrotechnics and welding. Chicago is best known for her massive installation 'The Dinner Party' (1979), which painstakingly depicts a giant banquet on a triangular table with a total of thirty-nine place settings, each designated for a pivotal female figure from history, including Virginia Woolf, Sojourner Truth, and Susan B. Anthony.

HER LIFE STORY

The artist (who changed her last name in the seventies as a feminist statement on personal identity) grew up in, yes, Chicago, in a family that, she said, 'believed in equal rights for women, which was very unusual for that time. The bad news was they never bothered to tell me that not everyone else believed in that, too.' Her father Arthur's activism helped shape his daughter's burgeoning political and social worldviews, which played a huge role in the artwork she would later create. Arthur was a Marxist labour organiser who was deeply involved in the Communist Party and was investigated by a nation then in the throes of McCarthyism. May, Chicago's mother, was a dancer and helped pass down some of her love for artistic pursuits to her daughter, who knew by age five that she 'never wanted to do anything but make art'. Chicago went off to college at the University of California, Los Angeles, for a bachelor's degree in art in 1962 and a master's degree in painting and sculpture two years later.

In college she began designing posters for the National Association for the Advancement of Colored People and went on to work as the NAACP's corresponding secretary. As a young artist, Chicago started out making works that were more abstract than the art she would go on to create later. In grad school, while reeling from the death of her husband in a car crash, she created a series called *Bigamy*, which featured male and female sex organs, but that was as pointedly gendered as her work got during that time. She described her early work as minimalist, but she also noted that in school she started to feel that she 'could no longer pretend in [her] art that being a woman had no meaning'.

While her work was beginning to attract attention, Chicago began feeling increasingly inspired by the launch of the women's movement. She co-founded the Feminist Art Program at California State University, Fresno, to help young women artists. She taught the students carpentry skills so they could build their own studios and urged them to use their own lives as the basis for the works they created.

In 1974 Chicago began work on her biggest piece, 'The Dinner Party', recruiting hundreds of women to help her create the super-intricate work. Each of the thirty-nine place settings contains a hand-painted china plate, a ceramic chalice with flatware, and a napkin with an embroidered gold edge. Each plate bears an ornate image of a vagina. Though the installation received mixed reviews when it was first shown at the Museum of Modern Art in San Francisco in 1979, it drew huge audiences throughout the United States and Western Europe, thanks largely to the power of passionate women spreading the word. Enthusiasts even raised money to show it in cities where museums had rejected it. 'The Dinner Party' also sparked controversy. Some black women said they felt underrepresented in the admittedly less-than-diverse piece, which primarily highlights white women's contributions to history. They also pointed out that Sojourner Truth's plate is the only one without a vagina image. Some saw this as a dismissal of Truth's womanhood.

'The Dinner Party' seemed to gain more appreciation over time – art critic Arthur Danto called it 'one of the major artistic monuments of the second half of the twentieth century' – as did Chicago's place in the art canon. She still uses feminist concepts to bring women's stories to the forefront of cultural consciousness and to help combat the enduringly male-centric art world.

HER COOL CREDENTIALS

★ Chicago's work has been shown and celebrated all over the world, and she has lectured widely and has written many books about art, feminism, and life.

★ In 1985 she unveiled a huge work, 'The Birth Project', an ambitious undertaking that uses macramé, quilting, embroidery, and other traditionally female handicrafts to reinterpret the Bible's Genesis creation myth. Possessing an unshakable faith in her talent and her work, she has always been super-confident, using words like monumental and major to describe her work. She said she knows it has changed people's lives. (Hey, if you don't believe in you, who will?)

QUOTABLES

[On why she began making less sexually driven work:] 'I guess you could say that my eyes were lifted from my vagina.'

'There was no way on this earth I could have had children and the career I've had. But you know what? I don't care how much I had to give up. This was what I wanted.'

'Starting out, several things sustained me. One was my burning desire to make art. Another was when I realised what women before me had gone through in order for me to have the opportunities that I had.'

20.
FRANCES M. BEAL

(1940–)

'A number of the young girls today that are projected as beautiful are all these black girls that have all these white features. Straight, straight hair: there is nothing African about it, you know, at all. And it shows the kind of rejection, once again, of our own cultural background.'

Claim to Fame	Country of Origin
Activist, writer	USA

HER LEGACY

Frances M. Beal is a feminist activist and civil rights superstar whose tireless mission was to fight, in her words, the 'grave misconceptions, outright distortions of fact, and defensive attitudes' that plagued black women in America. She broke from the traditional cliquey white mould of sixties and seventies feminism to demand that the women's movement and the world at large be way more inclusive of women of colour. Believing that capitalism, race, and class were the primary elements still holding women down, she was bothered that no one – especially white feminists – was talking about these ideas. Her refusal to stop challenging commonly held feminist beliefs had a powerful reach, and the issues she raised are still lightning rods in the movement today.

HER LIFE STORY

Born to an African American father and a Russian Jewish mother in Binghamton, New York, Beal grew up naturally sensitive to her parents' personal struggles with anti-Semitism and racism. This helped fire up Beal's lifelong commitment to working for justice. When Beal's father died, her mum moved their family to Queens, New York. Beal was inspired by her mother's lefty activism and was deeply stricken by the 1955 murder of Emmett Till. Till was a fourteen-year-old African American boy in Mississippi who was killed by two racist white men after he supposedly 'flirted' with a white woman in a store. The men who murdered him were eventually acquitted. Beal later recalled, 'He was [around] the same age as I was. And it was… some sort of an awakening… That could happen to me.'

After graduating from high school, Beal went off to college in Wisconsin, where she became taken with civil rights and socialist causes. While living in Paris to attend the Sorbonne, she met Malcolm X. It was in Paris that she also reportedly became acquainted with the influential works of feminist philosopher Simone de Beauvoir (see page 39).

When Beal returned to the US in 1966, she began a job at the National Council of Negro Women, where she worked for ten years. In 1968 she co-founded the Black Women's Liberation Committee of the civil rights organisation the Student Nonviolent Coordinating Committee. The committee later morphed into the Third World Women's Alliance (TWWA) – a feminist organisation that centred on intersectionality as one of the most critical aspects of feminism. Intersectional feminism is grounded in the belief that there are many other factors beyond sex and gender – such as race and class – involved in women's oppression.

That same year, Beal wrote a groundbreaking essay (first published as a pamphlet), 'Double Jeopardy: To Be Black and Female', which went on to be published in anthologies like the classic second-wave feminist tome *Sisterhood is Powerful*. In her essay, Beal tried to reconcile black feminism and Marxist ideals. Writer Winifred Breines noted that Beal's essay 'announced that any feminists who did not have an anti-racist and anti-imperialist ideology shared nothing with the black woman's struggle'. 'Double Jeopardy' is still considered a seminal work today.

In the seventies, as a member of the New York TWWA branch, Beal began to focus on abortion rights and sterilisation abuse. Forced sterilisation was prevalent then, especially for low-income and minority women.

Beal later moved to Oakland, California. She retired in 2005 but is still very socially active via her support of the Women of Color Resource Center, a group that stemmed from the TWWA. She's also an adamant peace activist and has been outspoken about protesting the war in Iraq and war in the Middle East in general.

HER COOL CREDENTIALS

★ Beal was fearless in speaking her mind, even if some of her ideas were less than popular. In 'Double Jeopardy' she wrote, 'A woman who stays at home caring for children and the house often leads an extremely sterile existence. She must lead her entire life as a satellite to her mate. He goes out into society and brings back a little piece of the world for her... This kind of woman leads a parasitic existence that can aptly be described as legalised prostitution.'

★ She advocates for challenging traditional (white) notions of beauty. In her oral history contribution at Smith College, she said, 'Now we challenged the whole question of femininity equals a physical type of beauty, because we thought it was oppressive, particularly to black woman.' Beal spoke out about what she saw as the government disproportionately trying to sterilise women of colour. As she wrote in 'Double Jeopardy', '[P]erhaps the most outlandish act of oppression in modern times is the current campaign to promote sterilisation of non-white women in an attempt to maintain the population and power imbalance between the white haves and the non-white have nots.'

QUOTABLES

'If the white [women's] groups do not realise that they are in fact fighting capitalism and racism, we do not have common bonds.'

'When you look around today, and you see the assaults on young black men, and white men getting away with it, you realise we have not advanced very far. Black lives matter.'

'What does it mean when beauty is defined by white, blue-eyed, blond, you know... blah, blah, blah.'

'Black women's liberation is not just the skin analysis. It's not just the class analysis. It's not just the racial analysis. It's how those things operate in the real world in an integrated way, to both understand oppression exploitation and to understand some methods by which we might kind of try to deal with them.'

21.
WANGARI MAATHAI

NÉE WANGARI MUTA MAATHAI (1940–2011)

'Until you dig a hole, you plant a tree, you water it and make it survive, you haven't done a thing. You are just talking.'

Claim to Fame	Country of Origin
Activist	Kenya

HER LEGACY

Revered for the seamless way she interwove feminist issues with environmental ones, Wangari Maathai was a trailblazing figure in the environmental rights scene – a scene that has often failed to recognise its female leaders. Born and raised in Kenya, Maathai was the first African woman to win the Nobel Peace Prize, in 2004, for 'her contribution to sustainable development, democracy and peace'. The recognition became a huge boon for Kenya. Though she was a devout Catholic and was anti-abortion, Maathai did a lot of pioneering work for women and also worked with key leaders around the world.

In her home country of Kenya, Maathai's work was misunderstood and sometimes derided because of its subversive nature – she was seen as overstepping the traditional boundaries of African women's roles. One of her biggest accomplishments was launching the Green Belt Movement. The organisation gives stipends to Kenyan women to plant trees in their communities in an effort to help fight deforestation and preserve the environment.

HER LIFE STORY

Maathai was raised in a small Kenyan village when it was still a British colony, and her family took the unusual step of sending her to school when it was still not common for girls to be educated. Maathai was a talented student, and in 1960 she was one of 300 Kenyan students to win a scholarship from then Senator John F. Kennedy to study in the US. She earned a biology degree from Mount St. Scholastica College in Kansas and a master's degree in biology at the University of Pittsburgh. Later, she looked back fondly on these years, saying that watching American anti-war demonstrations – this was during the Vietnam War – helped her realise that people need to stand up for what they believe in. In 1971 Maathai earned a doctorate from the University of Nairobi, becoming the very first woman in both east and central Africa to do so!

In 1976, while working in the National Council of Women of Kenya, she came up with the idea that village women should be paid to help plant trees and improve the environment. The benefits were twofold: the

women earned a few shillings for their work, which helped support them financially, and the planted trees provided a fuel source while hindering deforestation and desertification. This effort, the Green Belt Movement, led to more than thirty million trees being planted in Africa. According to the United Nations, the campaign helped support almost 900,000 women. When describing why she focused specifically on helping women, Maathai said, 'In that part of Africa, it's the women who actually are the first victims of environmental degradation, because they are the ones who fetch water, so if there is no water, it is them who walk for… hours… looking for [it]. They are the ones who fetch firewood. They are the ones who produce food for their families. So it's easy for them to explain when the environment is degraded and to persuade them to take action.'

Leaders of the Green Belt Movement formed the Pan African Green Belt Network in 1986 to educate world leaders about conservation and bettering the environment. Green Belt also spurred similar campaigns in a slew of other African countries, including Ethiopia, Tanzania, and Zimbabwe.

Maathai frequently protested against the Kenyan government's ecological practices and the way it handled the country's land. Dictator Daniel arap Moi – of whom she was an outspoken critic – labelled the Green Belt Movement 'subversive' during the eighties. One of her best-known actions against Moi's policies took place in 1989, when Green Belt staged a protest in Nairobi's Uhuru Park to try to stop a skyscraper from being erected. Though the campaign got attention from all over the world and the skyscraper project ended up falling through, Maathai was punished and beaten unconscious afterward for protesting. The spot where she demonstrated became known as Freedom Corner.

Maathai was loud and proud in her opposition to the Kenyan government all the way up until Moi's political party lost control in 2002. That year, Maathai won a seat in the country's parliament. In 2003 she was appointed assistant minister of environment and natural resources. The following year, when she won the Nobel Prize, the committee praised her 'holistic approach to sustainable development that embraces democracy, human rights, and women's rights in particular'.

Beyond her passion for conservation, Maathai also worked on AIDS prevention, human rights, and women's issues. She was not shy about standing up for these concerns at meetings of the United Nations

General Assembly. As the Nobel committee said about Maathai, 'She thinks globally and acts locally.'

HER COOL CREDENTIALS

★ People from various fields deeply admired her. Adam Steiner, the executive director of the UN's environment programme, once called her 'a force of nature'. Feminist writer Jessica Valenti called her an 'amazing leader', and John Githongo, an anti-corruption campaigner in Kenya, noted that she 'blazed a trail in whatever she did'.

★ In 2005 Forbes named her one of the hundred most influential women in the world.

★ In honour of Maathai's contributions to the environment, the Wangari Maathai Award was created a year after her death to commemorate 'an extraordinary woman who championed forest issues around the world'.

QUOTABLES

'You must not deal only with the symptoms. You have to get to the root causes by promoting environmental rehabilitation and empowering people to do things for themselves. What is done for the people without involving them cannot be sustained.'

'It was easy to persecute me without people feeling ashamed. It was easy to vilify me and project me as a woman who was not following the tradition of a 'good African woman' and as a highly educated elitist who was trying to show innocent African women ways of doing things that were not acceptable to African men.'

'I don't really know why I care so much. I just have something inside me that tells me that there is a problem, and I have got to do something about it.'

22.
WILMA RUDOLPH

NÉE WILMA GLODEAN RUDOLPH (1940–94)

'My doctors told me I would never walk again. My mother told me I would. I believed my mother.'

Claim to Fame	Country of Origin
Athlete	USA

HER LEGACY

Wilma Rudolph was an award-winning runner who made history in 1960 when she became the first American woman to win a whopping three gold medals at the Olympic Games. She's one of the fastest women runners in history, an idol to sports lovers everywhere for the inspiring way she triumphed over all kinds of adversity, both personally and professionally. She didn't just transcend the perceived limitations of her race and gender – being an African American woman in the sixties – but she triumphed over poverty and a host of major health issues as well.

HER LIFE STORY

Rudolph didn't have an easy start. During her childhood in Tennessee, she was plagued with serious health problems. These began at birth, when she wasn't expected to survive. Rudolph was born premature, at only four and a half pounds, and because of segregation, her mum was turned away at the hospital door when she arrived to give birth. As a child,

Rudolph developed double pneumonia, scarlet fever, and then polio, and was forced to stay in bed most of the time. She lost the use of her left leg when she was six and had to wear a leg brace, but physical therapy and lots of determination, plus regular massages from her siblings, helped her walk again. By age nine, she was able to dump the brace.

The twentieth of her father's twenty-two children, Rudolph grew up poor when segregation was still legal. At her all-black high school, her basketball coach gave her the nickname Skeeter (short for Mosquito) for her agility on the court and her propensity for 'buzzing around' the team. A few years later she participated in a track meet where she lost every race, but she clearly showed the spark of major promise because she drew the attention of track coach Ed Temple from Tennessee State University. He decided to recruit her to his summer track camp at TSU.

At the precocious age of sixteen, Rudolph qualified as a runner to enter the 1956 Olympic Games in Australia, making her the youngest person on the US team that year. She won a bronze medal in the 4x100-metre relay. She later attended Tennessee State University, where she studied education and continued to train her butt off as a runner. Her life wasn't all picnics and roses, though. At age seventeen, while still in high school, she gave birth to a baby, so she couldn't run (or do any other sports) throughout her senior year in high school.

Rudolph's sister began taking care of the baby so that Rudolph could attend college and continue chasing her passion for track. At the 1960 Olympic Games in Rome, Rudolph was officially deemed 'the fastest woman in the world', winning the 100- and 200-metre races and helping to bring the US team to victory in the 4x100-metre relay. After this accomplishment, she rocketed to international stardom. The media took to calling her 'The Black Pearl' and 'The Black Gazelle'.

Tennessee Governor Buford Ellington, a segregationist, intended to spearhead her welcome home festivities following the Olympics. Rudolph said she refused to take part in a racist, segregated event – which led to her parade being the first racially integrated event in her Clarksville hometown.

She devoted much of her life to family and chose not to run in the 1964 Olympics. By that time she had become a teacher at her former elementary school, and then went on to work as a coach on Indiana's DePauw University track team. She served as a US goodwill ambassador to French West Africa and was voted into both the Black Athletes Hall of Fame and the National Track and Field Hall of Fame. But Rudolph said her life's highest achievement was forming the Wilma Rudolph Foundation, a community-centred, non-profit amateur sports programme.

Rudolph died of brain cancer at age fifty-four in Nashville. Her legacy in the sports world lives on. She helped elevate women's track to a major sport, and she is still a source of inspiration for female athletes everywhere.

HER COOL CREDENTIALS

★ Rudolph twice won the Associated Press Woman Athlete of the Year Award, in both 1960 and 1961.

★ Her autobiography, *Wilma*, was later turned into a made-for-TV movie.

★ In 2004 the United States Postal Service honoured the Olympic champion by featuring her likeness on a twenty-three-cent stamp.

★ Rudolph was inducted into the US Olympic Hall of Fame in 1983.

QUOTABLES

'I believe in me more than anything in this world.'

'Never underestimate the power of dreams and the influence of the human spirit. We are all the same in this notion: the potential for greatness lives within each of us.'

'The triumph can't be had without the struggle.'

'[Black women] don't go to work to find fulfilment, or adventure, or glamour and romance, like so many white women think they are doing. Black women work out of necessity.'

23.
ANGELA DAVIS

NÉE ANGELA YVONNE DAVIS (1944–)

'We have to talk about liberating minds as well as liberating society.'

Claim to Fame	Country of Origin
Activist, author	USA

HER LEGACY

Angela Davis, an author and revolutionary known for kicking ass, taking names, and never backing down, was an international powerhouse in the Black Power Movement of the sixties and seventies. A formidable figure in feminist history, Davis has had an inspiring range of cool and sometimes crazy experiences – from serving as a high-ranking Communist Party leader, to getting slapped onto the FBI's Ten Most Wanted list, to sparking a worldwide 'Free Angela Davis' campaign after she was imprisoned on false charges of kidnapping and murder. She is a vocal critic of the U.S. criminal justice system, and has done crucial work on prison reform (she wrote a book called *Are Prisons Obsolete?*). However, Davis did not always align herself with other feminists. In a 2010 speech, she recalled, 'Everyone started calling me a feminist. My response was, "Who, me? I'm not a feminist! I'm a revolutionary black woman who identifies with working class people's struggles all over the world! How could I be a feminist!?"'

HER LIFE STORY

Davis is perhaps most famous for her trailblazing book *Women, Race, and Class*, which is read in women's studies college departments far and wide. It deserves a place on every feminist bookshelf because it helped set a new standard in articulating the importance of intersectionality. In her impeccably researched, historically centred book, Davis shatters myths about the experience of black female slaves and seamlessly traces the separate but unequal histories of black and white women.

Davis's parents were members of the National Association for the Advancement of Colored People. Her mum was an organiser and national officer of the Southern Negro Congress, a group influenced by the Communist Party, which championed an anti-capitalist economic system. Davis found herself surrounded by communist thinkers, who played a big role in her intellectual development as a young woman.

Her political activism was also sparked from being raised in the then segregated city of Birmingham, Alabama, in a neighbourhood called Dynamite Hill, where the Ku Klux Klan would often bomb the homes of African Americans.

Davis studied French on a full scholarship at Brandeis University, where as one of only three black students in her class she felt lonely and alienated. As a grad student in San Diego in the sixties, she became involved with the Black Liberation movement, joined the Communist Party, and was active with the Black Panthers and the Student Nonviolent Coordinating Committee. She also started the first Black Student Union on her grad school campus! But it wasn't until 1969 that Davis became publicly known when she was yanked from her teaching position in the philosophy department at UCLA because of her communism-centred political beliefs. She fought to get her job back – and won.

In 1970 Davis got even more famous when she was arrested as a suspected conspirator in a California courthouse shootout that left four people dead. The guns used were registered in her name. She was put on the FBI's Ten Most Wanted list and received a death sentence in 1972 for her alleged participation in the shooting. After she gained an international wave of support through the Free Angela Davis campaign, she was finally acquitted of all charges. It was, she said, the 'happiest day of my life'. She had been incarcerated for eighteen months. Davis soon became a well-known beacon of African American resilience and resistance.

In 1981 Davis published her classic tome *Women, Race, and Class*, which cemented her reputation as a brilliant scholar and feminist treasure. In the book, Davis traces the birth of the US women's rights movement, noting that perhaps its biggest flaw was how most of its leaders suppressed or overlooked the voices of black and working-class women.

Davis believes that for women to be truly liberated, the issue of violence against women must be addressed once and for all. She doesn't just feel that violence is restricted to rape and assault. It also includes affronts against women's reproductive freedoms, such as bombing abortion clinics and restricting abortion access, and sexuality, like prohibiting gay women from having kids.

A prolific author, a frequent lecturer, and a super-active presence in the feminist, anti-racist, and prison reform worlds, Davis shapes a new generation of activists. During the last twenty-five years, she has lectured in all fifty states of the United States, as well as in countries around the world.

HER COOL CREDENTIALS

★ In 1972 John Lennon and Yoko Ono wrote a song about Davis's wrongful incarceration, called 'Angela'.

★ In 1980 Davis ran for US vice president on the Communist Party ticket, though she didn't win.

★ She is affiliated with Sisters Inside, an Australian abolitionist group that works in solidarity with women in prison.

★ Davis is a founding member of Critical Resistance, a national organisation dedicated to dismantling the prison industrial complex.

QUOTABLES

'I can't imagine a feminism that is not anti-racist.'

'Rape bears a direct relationship to all of the existing power structures in a given society. This relationship is not a simple, mechanical one, but rather involves complex structures reflecting the interconnectedness of the race, gender, and class oppression that characterise the society.'

'We have accumulated a wealth of historical experience which confirms our belief that the scales of justice are out of balance.'

'You cannot think about liberation without education.'

'We know the road to freedom has always been stalked by death.'

24.
ALICE WALKER

NÉE ALICE MALSENIOR WALKER (1944–)

'The most common way people give up their power is by thinking they don't have any.'

Claim to Fame	Country of Origin
Novelist, poet	USA

HER LEGACY

For her beloved book *The Color Purple*, Alice Walker was the first African American woman to receive the Pulitzer Prize for fiction – but, in fact, her legacy goes even deeper. Indeed, she's one of the most admired – and censored! – black women writers of all time. She's a literary icon in part because of the vast scope of her work. Her writing touches on many raw, painful, yet ultimately transcendent hot spots that lots of people can relate to. However, not everyone appreciates her unabashedly fiery language and determination to always 'go there'. One critic of her 1989 novel *The Temple of My Familiar* called it 'pantheistic plea, lesbian propaganda, a hootchie-cootchie dance to castration'.

Throughout her writing and speaking, Walker has tackled a range of important issues, from the scars of slavery to anti-war activism, from sexuality – she has had relationships with both men and women, and refuses to label herself – to Buddhist meditation. As Alex Clark in *The Guardian* once put it, she has 'done so many different things in so many different places with so many different people'.

In 1983 she came up with the term 'womanism', an inclusive feminist sub-sect for women of colour. She once said, 'Womanist is to feminist as purple is to lavender.' When Walker coined the term, big-box feminism was rife with racial divisions and a general neglect of issues that didn't affect middle-class straight white women. Walker helped expose those rifts, and wanted black feminists to have a separate identity and a 'word of our own'. Walker explained the meaning of womanism: 'A black feminist or feminist of colour… A woman who loves other women, sexually and/or non-sexually. Appreciates and prefers women's culture, women's emotional flexibility (values tears as natural counterbalance of laughter), and women's strength.'

HER LIFE STORY

Walker grew up poor in a rural Georgia town as the youngest of eight children. She attended segregated schools and was exposed to the racist terror rampant in the South then. When she was only eight years old, one of Walker's brothers accidentally shot her in the eye with a BB gun, badly damaging her sight in that eye. She shut herself off from other kids, mainly spending time writing and reading, because, she said, the accident made her 'shy and timid, and I often reacted to insults and slights that were not intended'. She was later able to get the scar tissue in her eye removed. In high school, Walker became much more confident and outgoing: she was the class valedictorian and prom queen.

Another childhood event had a profound impact on Walker, searing itself into her consciousness forever. At thirteen, she saw the body of a woman who had been shot in the face by her husband. (One of Walker's sisters was a cosmetologist who did the make-up for dead people before their funerals.) Walker said that the experience changed her and truly hammered home the idea that 'brutality against women is endemic'.

When she was in college, Walker began engaging with the civil rights movement and attended the 1963 March on Washington to support political and social equality for black people. While enrolled at Sarah Lawrence College, Walker spent a year abroad in Uganda. When she returned, she learned she was pregnant. She was twenty-one and not ready for a child. She decided she would kill herself if she wasn't able to obtain an abortion, which was illegal at the time. 'It was me or it,' she wrote. Fortunately, a friend helped her procure an abortion.

After college, Walker kept writing and stayed active in civil rights – she was even invited to Martin Luther King Jr's home once. She worked on African American voter drives in Georgia and became a contributing editor at *Ms.* magazine.

Walker published a good deal of work before hitting it big. Some of her more pervasive themes were racism, sexism, folk wisdom, violence, and family dynamics. Then her 1982 novel, *The Color Purple*, propelled her to major fame, selling five million copies and establishing Walker as one of the leading voices in African American feminist fiction. The film version was directed by megastar Steven Spielberg and garnered eleven Academy Award nominations and drew even more fans into Walker's orbit. Of course, there were critics, too, and some deemed the film to be man-bashing.

Walker's list of bestsellers extends beyond *The Color Purple*. *Possessing the Secret of Joy* (1992) detailed the abominable consequences of female genital mutilation. She also did a documentary on the subject with the Indian British filmmaker Pratibha Parmar, called *Alice Walker: Beauty in Truth*.

After forty-plus years as a writer and activist, Walker doesn't seem to be pausing for a breather anytime soon.

HER COOL CREDENTIALS

★ *The Color Purple* was adapted into a Broadway show in 2005 and earned eleven Tony awards nominations and a Grammy nomination.

★ Walker's work has been translated into more than twenty-four languages, and her books have sold upward of fifteen million copies.

★ After *To Hell With Dying* was published in 1988, Langston Hughes sent her a handwritten note of praise and encouragement.

QUOTABLES

*'Don't wait around for other people to be
happy for you. Any happiness you get
you've got to make yourself.'*

*'Is solace anywhere more comforting
than that in the arms of a sister?'*

*'Clearly older women... have so much to teach
us about sharing, patience, and wisdom.'*

*'I'm not lesbian; I'm not bisexual;
I'm not straight. I'm just curious.'*

25.
WILMA MANKILLER

NÉE WILMA PEARL MANKILLER (1945–2010)

*'I want to be remembered as the person who
helped us restore faith in ourselves.'*

Claim to Fame	Country of Origin
Chief of the Cherokee Nation; activist	USA

HER LEGACY

Wilma Mankiller was the first female chief of the Cherokee Nation, a position she held for ten years. That is a huge feat – Cherokees are the second-largest Native American tribe in the US. And Mankiller accomplished more in those years of service than many dreamed possible: she helped upgrade the Cherokee Nation's housing, education, and healthcare systems, and greatly strengthened the tribe's internal government. She also helped swell the nation's population from 68,000 to 170,000 people.

Beyond that, Mankiller is remembered for her pioneering feminist spirit and dedication to helping her tribal comrades, both male and female. She mobilised and encouraged them, helping them seize the power to reform their communities from within.

HER LIFE STORY

Mankiller spent her childhood in the community of Mankiller Flats in Oklahoma, where her family had been forced to relocate following the

Trail of Tears. The Trail of Tears was a horrific mass trek from 1838 to 1839, when the US government made the Cherokee people give up all their land east of Mississippi and march to what is now known as Oklahoma. This move caused 4,000 Cherokees to die along the way.

When she was twelve, Mankiller's dad moved the family again as part of a government relocation programme sponsored by the Bureau of Indian Affairs. This time they were headed to San Francisco, where he was promised awesome economic opportunities; unfortunately, those didn't quite pan out as hoped. Her family was often the sole Native American one in the neighbourhoods they lived in, and Mankiller missed her home, her tribe, and her community. She even said that her experience in San Francisco was her 'own little Trail of Tears'.

In 1969, Mankiller became deeply inspired by a group of young protesters fighting for Native American rights. The protesters had taken control of Alcatraz, the famous abandoned prison island in the

San Francisco Bay, to bring attention to the government's mistreatment of Native Americans. Mankiller went there to visit them often, later recalling, 'It was on Alcatraz... where at long last some Native Americans, including me, truly began to regain our balance.'

Mankiller got married at age seventeen. When her marriage ended in divorce, she moved back to Oklahoma with her two kids. She started volunteering for her tribe and then working for the Cherokee Nation government as an economic stimulus coordinator. But after surviving a brutal head-on car crash that claimed the life of a friend, Mankiller was unable to work for eighteen months (she required seventeen surgeries, mostly on her legs). In 1983 she returned to work and was excited when the Cherokee Nation's principal chief, Ross Swimmer, asked her to run in the upcoming election alongside him as his deputy chief. Then in 1985 Mankiller landed the position of principal chief, the first woman with that title.

Mankiller used her newfound platform to help her tribe in innumerable ways. One of her primary goals was to empower her people to achieve new levels of self-sufficiency. She helped get cleaner water, created a job centre, improved adult literacy, created summer programmes for kids, and increased the number of health clinics on the nation's land. Also concerned with women's rights, she worked on mentoring programmes to help strengthen Native American girls' self-esteem. Mankiller was passionate about combating harmful, negative cultural stereotypes. As she explained, 'Western movies always seemed to show Indian women washing clothes at the creek and men with a tomahawk or spear in their hands, adorned with lots of feathers... Many think we're either visionaries, "noble savages", squaw drudges or tragic alcoholics. We're very rarely depicted as real people.'

Mankiller proved to be one of the most effective leaders her tribe has ever seen. She did it all while battling lame preconceptions about women's ability to lead – and she did it while battling severe health issues, from kidney failure to multiple bouts of cancer to a grave neuromuscular condition. She was a die-hard optimist even in the face of terrible luck and tragedy.

As she once wrote, 'How can I be anything but positive when I come from a tenacious, resilient people who keep moving forward with an eye toward the future even after enduring unspeakable hardship?

How can I not be positive when I have lived longer than I ever dreamed possible and my life plays itself out in a supportive community of extended family and friends? There is much to be thankful for.'

HER COOL CREDENTIALS

★ After Mankiller died in 2010, President Barack Obama released a moving statement about her: 'She served as an inspiration to women in Indian country and across America. Her legacy will continue to encourage and motivate all who carry on her work.'

★ While she served as principal chief, President Bill Clinton appointed her as an adviser to the federal government on tribal affairs.

★ Mankiller received many honours and awards for her activism and work leading the Cherokee Nation, including the 1998 Presidential Medal of Freedom, one of the US top civilian awards.

QUOTABLES

'Prior to my election, young Cherokee girls would never have thought that they might grow up and become chief.'

'Growth is a painful process.'

'I've run into more discrimination as a woman than as an Indian.'

'Suddenly you hear young Cherokee girls talking about becoming leaders. And in Cherokee families, [now] there is more encouragement of girls.'

26.
SHIRIN EBADI
(1947–)

'How can you defy fear? Fear is a human instinct, just like hunger. Whether you like it or not, you become hungry. Similarly with fear. But I have learned to train myself to live with this fear.'

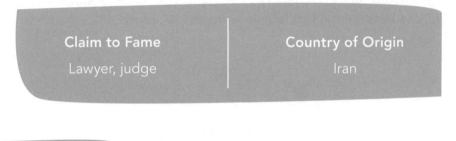

Claim to Fame	Country of Origin
Lawyer, judge	Iran

HER LEGACY

Shirin Ebadi, a famous Iranian judge, activist, and civil rights lawyer, was the first Iranian and the first Muslim woman to win the Nobel Peace Prize. Dubbed a 'new suffragette' by the UK's *Independent*, she's a powerful spearhead for international women's rights and is widely extolled for her bravery and honesty in the face of death threats, exile, and constant disparagement. Human rights activist Hadi Ghaemi said it was Ebadi who singlehandedly gave 'birth to the human rights movement in Iran in the 1990s'.

Ebadi is also active in the fight for the rights of children, survivors of violence, censored journalists, and students. A practicing Muslim, she believes in Islam, but she's against the patriarchal traditions that dominate Iran. She believes women have the power to change all that. As she said, 'My hopes for Iran's future lies with women first and foremost. This is currently the strongest women's movement in the Middle East.'

Ebadi was born into a loving, well-educated family. As she was growing up, her parents taught her that she was an equal to her brothers, and they helped instil confidence and self-reliance in her. She said her father's faith in her was her 'most valued inheritance'. Not until later in life did she come to the sad realisation that, in general, Iranian girls and boys were treated quite differently – with girls on the losing end – even though the country's 1906 constitution was supposed to grant equal rights to everyone. Ebadi did well in school and earned a law degree from Tehran University's Faculty of Law. When she was twenty-two, she became the first female judge in Iran, and in 1975 she became

the president of Bench 24 of the Tehran City Court. But in 1979, after the Iranian Revolution and the introduction of the Iranian Penal Code, Ebadi and other women were stripped of their positions as judges because they were female, and their jobs were downgraded to 'clerical duties'. She and the other women protested, and they got promoted to 'experts' for the Justice Department. Ebadi said that 'the laws, in short, turned the clock back 1,400 years'.

In 1992 Ebadi was finally able to get a lawyer's licence. She established a private practice and began taking on pro bono cases that challenged the inequity of Islamic Republic laws. Many cases were controversial and helped win justice for people unfairly persecuted by the government. Among her most widely known cases, she represented the mother of Arian Golshani, a nine-year-old Iranian girl who was tortured and beaten to death. She also represented the families of serial murder victims Dariush Forouhar and Parvaneh Forouhar, and Ezzat Ebrahim-Nejad. (On a ridiculous note, Ebadi and three other female Iranian activists were nicknamed the four mares of the apocalypse by their haters.)

Ebadi was jailed for three weeks in 2000 after discovering and disseminating proof that government officials participated in a calculated spate of murders of local students and intellectuals. Reading through pages and pages of secret government documents, she saw that she herself was a target on the government's 'kill list'! Thankfully she wasn't killed, though she was fined, sentenced to prison for 'disturbing public opinion' and banned from practising law for five years.

She has also helped launch important Iranian feminist organisations such as the One Million Signatures Campaign, which aims to get one million signatures to petition the Iranian government to end legal discrimination against women.

Ebadi self-exiled to London in 2009 after her husband was beaten and she received threats to stop her work. But she remains dedicated to her work in making Iran a safer place for women and girls and continues fighting her home country's outdated, patriarchal traditions. In her autobiography, *Iran Awakening: A Memoir of Revolution and Hope*, she described her mission to 'help correct Western stereotypes of Islam, especially the image of Muslim women as docile, forlorn creatures'.

HER COOL CREDENTIALS

★ In 2004 Ebadi sued the US Treasury Department for trying to stop US publication of her book *Iran Awakening* under anti-Iranian embargo laws. She won the suit, and two years later Random House released her autobiography.

★ Ebadi has done tons of work on behalf of kids. She co-founded an organisation, the Society for Protecting the Rights of the Child, and is generally considered the creator of Iran's landmark 2002 law outlawing the physical abuse of children. She has also provided free tuition to Iranian kids who didn't have the financial means to attend school.

★ In 2004 Forbes dubbed Ebadi one of the hundred most powerful women in the world.

QUOTABLES

'Whenever women protest and ask for their rights, they are silenced with the argument that the laws are justified under Islam. It is an unfounded argument. It is not Islam at fault, but rather the patriarchal culture that uses its own interpretations to justify whatever it wants.'

'Human rights is a universal standard. It is a component of every religion and every civilisation.'

'I maintain that nothing useful and lasting can emerge from violence.'

'What is important is that one utilises one's intellect and not to be 100 per cent sure about one's convictions. One should always leave room for doubt.'

'It's not just about hope and ideas. It's about action.'

27.
HILLARY CLINTON

NÉE HILLARY DIANE RODHAM (1947–)

'The harder they hit, the more encouraged I get.'

Claim to Fame	Country of Origin
Politician	USA

HER LEGACY

Hillary Clinton has been called names. Lots and lots of names, from Saint Hillary to the hildebeest to Hilla the Hun. She has always had the power to stir up colourful opinions, both positive and, well, way less than positive. One thing is undisputed: Clinton has had an unassailable impact on American women's health, security, and overall well-being.

She's a die-hard advocate for women in nearly every aspect of their lives, from motherhood to abortion rights to equal pay. A political powerhouse who has made many strides that no other female politician has before, she puts her money where her mouth is when it comes to supporting legislation that supports women.

HER LIFE STORY

On her WhiteHouse.gov website, Clinton writes that she had a happy upbringing in suburban Illinois, though her father could be tough, sarcastic, and combative, as well as prejudiced. She doesn't talk about him much publicly, though Bill Clinton once described him as 'tough and gruff'. Her dad was a staunch republican while her mother was a closet democrat who tried to instil self-confidence and resilience in her daughter, encouraging her to stand up for herself against bullies. Clinton was active in her church and in sports, and she excelled academically. Her parents encouraged her to pursue any future career that might float her boat.

The turbulent sixties helped open Clinton's eyes to new political ideas and issues. Though she started out her years at Wellesley College leading the Young Republicans Club, her politics shifted. Soon she was supporting Democratic candidates and organising teach-ins to get more black teachers into schools in the tragic wake of Martin Luther King Jr's assassination, which affected her deeply. She had gone to see King speak when she was younger, and later she wrote that she was 'transfixed' and that his 'grace and piercing moral clarity left a lasting impression on me'. After graduating from Yale Law School, Clinton joined the staff advising the Judiciary Committee of the House of Representatives during the hearing to impeach President Richard Nixon for the Watergate investigation, a scandal that involved the President's attempted cover-up of a break-in at the Democratic National Committee office. She then moved to Arkansas with Bill Clinton, got married, and ended up becoming Arkansas's first lady after Bill was elected governor in 1978. During that time, she co-founded the Arkansas Advocates for Children and Families and served on the boards of the Children's Defense Fund, Arkansas Children's Hospital, and Legal Services Corporation.

After her husband became president in 1993, Clinton's hard work continued. She became chair of the Task Force on National Health Care Reform and played a major role in pushing for the creation of the State Children's Health Insurance Program, which provides for kids whose parents cannot afford health coverage. In 1994 she created the Office on Violence Against Women at the Department of Justice.

BEST MOMENTS FROM HILLARY'S ICONIC 'WOMEN'S RIGHTS ARE HUMAN RIGHTS' SPEECH AT THE UN FOURTH WORLD CONFERENCE ON WOMEN IN BEIJING, 1995

'What we are learning around the world is that, if women are healthy and educated, their families will flourish. If women are free from violence, their families will flourish. If women have a chance to work and earn as full and equal partners in society, their families will flourish.'

'We need to understand that there is no formula for how women should lead their lives. That is why we must respect the choices that each woman makes for herself and her family.'

'Tragically, women are most often the ones whose human rights are violated... It is time for us to say here in Beijing, and the world to hear, that it is no longer acceptable to discuss women's rights as separate from human rights.'

'It is a violation of human rights when babies are denied food, or drowned, or suffocated, or their spines broken, simply because they are born girls.'

'It is a violation of human rights when women and girls are sold into the slavery of prostitution.'

'It is a violation of human rights when women are doused with gasoline, set on fire and burned to death because their marriage dowries are deemed too small.'

'It is a violation of human rights when young girls are brutalised by the painful and degrading practice of genital mutilation.'

'It is a violation of human rights when women are denied the right to plan their own families, and that includes being forced to have abortions or being sterilised against their will.'

'If there is one message that echoes forth from this conference, it is that human rights are women's rights... And women's rights are human rights.'

When she got elected to the US Senate in 2000, Clinton became the only American first lady to hold national office, as well as the first woman elected statewide in New York. She lost in a 2008 presidential run, though she won more primary victories and delegates than any of her female predecessors. From 2009 through 2013, Clinton served as the sixty-seventh secretary of state under President Barack Obama. One of her big initiatives was to champion gender equality, a hallmark of her political career that stretches back to her days as first lady. In 1995 she gave an iconic speech known as the 'Women's Rights are Human Rights' speech at the UN Fourth World Conference on Women.

As secretary of state, Clinton visited 112 countries in an effort to help repair the badly damaged US reputation from involvement in the Middle East. In her own words, she wanted to ensure that the US has 'a seat at every table that has the potential for being a partnership to solve problems'. As Clinton geared up for her 2016 presidential run, her popularity surged, especially among female voters. Unfortunately the election didn't work out in her favour (sob), but we have no doubt there will be tons more exciting news from her on the horizon.

HER COOL CREDENTIALS

★ In 2015 Google Trends showed a rising level of Internet users' interest in the former secretary of state, though she'd been in the national spotlight since 1992.

★ Clinton has spent the last thirteen years as the Gallup poll's most admired woman.

★ In her book *Hard Choices*, Clinton did what many politicians won't: admitted to past mistakes. She wrote that she 'got it wrong, plain and simple' when she voted to authorise war in Iraq in 2002.

QUOTABLES

'I have always believed that women are not victims, we are agents of change, we are drivers of progress, we are makers of peace – all we need is a fighting chance.'

'There is no doubt in my mind that without the involvement of women in the economy, in politics, in peace-making, in every aspect of society, you can't realise [a country's] full potential.'

'To all the little girls who are watching this, never doubt that you are valuable and powerful and deserving of every chance and opportunity in the world to pursue and achieve your own dreams.'

28.
KATE BORNSTEIN

NÉE AL BORNSTEIN, NOW KATHERINE VANDAM BORNSTEIN (1948–)

'I am a queer and pleasant danger, and my time is coming.'

Claim to Fame	Country of Origin
Author	USA

HER LEGACY

Kate Bornstein is a world-renowned transgender author, activist, and self-proclaimed 'gender outlaw' with a lasting legacy in the feminist world for her pioneering work in the lesbian/gay/bisexual/transgender/queer/inter-sex (LGBTQI) community. She was originally born a boy named Al but had sexual reassignment surgery in 1986, though she's written, 'I identify as neither male nor female... I'm neither straight nor gay.'

Bornstein is famous for her belief that – for herself, at least – there is no binary when it comes to gender. Her influential book *Gender Outlaw: On Men, Women and the Rest of Us* helped lay the foundation for the idea that gender is a cultural and social construct – a creation – more than an innate trait ordained at birth. Her ideas were an early part of the current cultural shift in how we think about the construct of gender, as well as how we view transgenderism and trans folks in general.

HER LIFE STORY

Raised in New Jersey, Bornstein was part of a secular Jewish family with a loving mother and a 'macho, macho man' for a father. Growing up, she felt trapped in the wrong body and had dreams of looking like Audrey Hepburn: 'I wanted to grow up to be Audrey Hepburn: skinny, graceful, charming, delightful, smart, talented, a star and a lady.' Bornstein didn't necessarily feel that comfortable in her skin. She became anorexic and got involved in theatre so she could try on different people's lives.

The controversial religion of scientology called to Bornstein after she left theatre school at age twenty-two. She was attracted to the church's concept of 'thetans', genderless spirit beings considered to be made solely of thoughts. 'They said I was not my body, not my mind… [That] I am an immortal soul,' she explained later on.

Still known as Al back then, Bornstein began to climb the ranks within the Sea Org, the Church of Scientology's inner sanctum, and lived on founder L. Ron Hubbard's personal yacht. She married a scientologist and had a daughter, but after twelve years, she was forced out of the church and labelled a 'suppressive person', which indicated to other members that they should not associate with her. Even her daughter was instructed to cut contact with her.

Diagnosed with PTSD after leaving the church, Bornstein went through a lot of difficult experiences before finally learning to feel comfortable with herself. She decided to have sexual reassignment surgery, changed her name to Kate, and came out. After that, she began speaking and writing about her perspectives on gender – for example, that gender isn't a two-item checkbox – and made waves with her seminal book *Gender Outlaw*.

Four years later, she followed that book up with *My Gender Workbook: How to Become a Real Man, a Real Woman, the Real You, or Something Else Entirely*. She has also written about bullying and teen suicide. Her book *Hello, Cruel World: 101 Alternatives to Suicide for Teens, Freaks, and Other Outlaws* is a quirky compendium of ideas about how 'freaks', teens, and anyone else can avoid succumbing to suicidal depression.

Bornstein is an important figure in part because she celebrates her own 'freak' status with aplomb. Incredibly candid and raw in her work, she shares very personal titbits about her life with readers, including her ongoing struggle with anorexia and her penchant for S&M. Bornstein vehemently wants her fans to define themselves for themselves – never to allow themselves to be shoved into a tiny box by society's bullshit cultural mores.

HER COOL CREDENTIALS

★ Bornstein's books are taught in five languages in more than 120 colleges and universities around the world.

★ For her work against bullying, she earned two citations of honour from the New York City Council.

★ Instead of identifying as a lesbian, she sometimes refers to herself as a 'tranny dyke'. Tranny dykes, she said, are 'like Pippy Long Stocking – like Willow from *Buffy*, with a good sense of humour'.

QUOTABLES

'I really don't get how there's only two choices. There's no two of anything else in the entire universe; why should there only be two genders? I don't get it.'

'Please, stay alive. Have good sex, have fun with gender, and write great stuff about that.'

'Let's stop pretending that we have all the answers, because when it comes to gender, none of us is fucking omniscient.'

'Let's stop "tolerating" or "accepting" difference, as if we're so much better for not being different. Instead, let's celebrate difference, because in this world it takes a lot of guts to be different and to act differently.'

'It's simple: do whatever it takes to make your life more worth living. And there's only one rule you need to follow to make that kind of blanket permission work: don't be mean.'

29.
PAM GRIER

NÉE PAMELA SUZETTE GRIER (1949–)

'People see me as a strong black figure, and I'm proud of that.'

Claim to Fame	Country of Origin
Actor	USA

HER LEGACY

Pam Grier revolutionised the way African American women were seen in movies in the 1970s and beyond. She was sexy, sure, but she was also one of the biggest, baddest film icons of the disco era at a time when black women were typically portrayed as, well, far less empowered. She has been called 'the action hero who got a lot of action', and her roles stood out like a gaping wound for the way they fused, as Mia Mask of NPR put it, 'feminist sensibilities, black nationalist radicalism, [and] vigilante justice.'

Grier is notorious – in a good way – for the joyful verve she seemed to bring to killing and maiming shady dudes on screen. Her characters were smart, and they knew men would routinely dismiss her as a sexual plaything. She didn't care because she always got the last laugh, showing them who was boss by any means necessary, including shooting their balls off, karate chopping them, and dousing them in tubs of chlorine.

Black female characters with personal agency weren't commonly seen on film then (and still aren't!). And through Grier's work in 'blaxploitation' films like *Foxy Brown* and *Coffy*, she became living proof that women of colour could be many things at once: strong, smart, beautiful, and fearless. (The blaxploitation film genre, catering chiefly to African American audiences, was campy and controversial, but also incredibly popular, with strong anti-establishment and political undertones.) Grier has starred in a long roster of roles that solidified her place in the feminist film canon and earned her millions of fans along the way.

HER LIFE STORY

Grier was born in Winston-Salem, North Carolina, to a black father and a Cheyenne Indian mother (she has Chinese, Filipino, and Hispanic roots as well). Mainly growing up in Colorado during a time of racial segregation, Grier learned from her family how to take care of herself – especially from her grandfather, 'Daddy Ray', whom she described as 'the first feminist'. She said that her family taught her to 'sleep in a tent at night in the rain and go fish for your food in the morning'.

When Grier was only six years old, she was alone at her aunt's house when she was raped by two older boys. That experience prompted her to turn inward and become quiet and self-protective. She also developed a stutter that stuck with her until she was twelve. She wrote in her autobiography, 'I never told a soul about what happened to me… I was so afraid and silent after the rape, I hid in my bedroom closet when people came over to visit.'

After enrolling in Denver's Metropolitan State University (she was pre-med and wanted to become a veterinarian or an anaesthesiologist), Grier was approached by a Hollywood agent named David Baumgarten at a beauty pageant. Grier's career slowly took off when she relocated to Los Angeles and signed on to work with him.

She landed some smaller roles in films including *Beyond the Valley of the Dolls*, and people started to stand up and take note with her work in movies like *Black Mama White Mama* and *Coffy*. Those movies led to her star-making role in *Foxy Brown*, a film that came to define both Grier's career and the blaxploitation era in general. Grier said that she modelled both Coffy and Foxy on female relatives — her mum was Coffy, and her aunt was Foxy Brown. She described her relatives as 'pioneer women. They could ride a horse and drive a wagon and shoot and hunt.'

Grier believes her films resonated because she 'attached a political voice to sexuality for women'. She also thinks that men were often freaked out by her work, feeling threatened by such strong images of a black woman. 'A lot of men were afraid I was telling women to castrate them,' she said. (Some women were probably alarmed, too. After all, Grier was pushing the envelope in brand-new ways.)

Grier eventually decided to move on and try other parts, including the title role in Quentin Tarantino's 1997 hit, *Jackie Brown*, which pushed her back into the limelight after a quiet period. Despite all her great work, she said that her life's biggest feat was beating cervical cancer, in 1988.

HER COOL CREDENTIALS

★ Director Quentin Tarantino reportedly dubbed Grier cinema's first female action hero.

★ She knows her own mind and follows her heart. She turned down her famous basketball-player boyfriend, Kareem Abdul-Jabbar, when he said he would only marry her if she converted to his recently adopted religion, Islam.

★ Grier was the first African American woman to appear on the cover of *Ms.* magazine in 1975. The headline? 'Super-sass.'

★ Grier said that Gloria Steinem was a mentor to her.

QUOTABLES

'My life is probably more interesting and dangerous than some of the movies I've done.'

'It isn't just about jobs and pay. It's expectations, mores and values. Women aren't supposed to be strong. Women are supposed to be married.'

'A woman can still wear her high heels
and still fix the plumbing.'

'People weren't used to seeing a female lead in an
action movie, and I think a lot of them related to
the independence my characters showed.'

'Nothing could sway me from my belief that
the more educated the woman, the more
liberated and powerful she could become.'

30.
LESLIE FEINBERG
(1949–2014)

'Hasten the revolution!'

Claim to Fame	Country of Origin
Writer, activist	USA

HER LEGACY

Leslie Feinberg was a revolutionary, a Marxist/communist activist, and a radical transgender icon beloved all over the world for her boundary-smashing, gender-bending work. She initiated the practice of using gender-neutral pronouns like ze (instead of he or she) and hir (instead of him or her) because she didn't believe in using umbrella terms for something as individual and complex as gender identity. For this and other reasons, she's been described as a 'founding figure of contemporary transgender studies'.

One of the biggest elements of her legacy is her kickass commitment to speaking the truth at all costs – even when it was painful, inconvenient, or unpopular. She didn't just use her platform to advocate for people like herself – she also mobilised on behalf of many other oppressed groups, like the poor, because as journalist Paisley Currah explained, 'for her, radical queer and gender politics couldn't be isolated from the fight against class oppression.'

Feinberg might not have been particularly well understood by the cisgender masses. She was born a woman but had surgical and hormonal interventions to present as a man. She once said, 'There are no pronouns in the English language as complex as I am.' But her writing gave hope to a growing population of marginalised people who have yet to see themselves represented in pop culture. Feinberg became a household name in the LGBT community, especially after the publication of her acclaimed 1993 lesbian coming-of-age novel, *Stone Butch Blues*, which won the 1994 Stonewall Book Award and is the work she was most famous for.

HER LIFE STORY

Feinberg – who described herself as 'an anti-racist white, working-class, secular Jewish, transgender, lesbian, female, revolutionary communist' – grew up in Buffalo, New York, in a working-class Jewish family. As a young butch, she grew up in gay bars, hanging out with other people on the LGBT spectrum. Her family wasn't supportive of anything having to do with her sexuality or the way she expressed her gender, and she left home and struck out on her own as a teenager. (Until the day she died, she carried legal paperwork indicating that they were not her family.)

Feinberg moved to New York City, where she began to find some success with writing. Still, her long-time partner Minnie Bruce Pratt said that Feinberg had mainly made her living through menial jobs like washing dishes and working in book binderies because she was discriminated against. She was a national leader in the radical socialist organisation Workers World Party and a managing editor of *Workers World* newspaper. Her communist foundation was a common thread connecting all she believed in: 'I do not separate out trans issues, or lesbian/gay/bi issues, queer issues, from that larger relationship of forces… they take place, like our lives do, within the context of a larger economic and social reality – including economic class struggle, the war being waged abroad and on the domestic front, daily battles against racism, immigrant-bashing, and misogyny, and deaf and disabled accessibility.'

Her first novel, *Stone Butch Blues* (1993), was a groundbreaking semi-autobiographical story of a young butch lesbian named Jess growing up working class in the 1950s. It won the American Literary Association Award for Gay and Lesbian Literature and the Lambda Small Press Literary Award, and was cherished by readers around the globe. It has been taught in countless women's studies classes and is beloved by people of all genders and sexualities for its sensitive but realistic take on the nuances of gender identity.

Before falling sick with a degenerative disease and passing away at age sixty-five, Feinberg spent more than thirty years as an advocate for everything from gay and lesbian rights to the rights of Native nations to the freedom of political prisoners in the US. Feinberg strove to 'build strong bonds of unity between these struggles and those of movements in defence of oppressed nationalities, women, disabled, and the working-class movement as a whole'. She proved that embracing being different is more than okay, and that being true to yourself is the absolute key to leading a passionate and fulfilled life.

HER COOL CREDENTIALS

★ *Curve* magazine named Feinberg one of the fifteen most influential people in the fight for gay and lesbian rights.

★ *Stone Butch Blues* has been translated into several languages, including Chinese, German, Italian, Dutch, Turkish, Slovenian, and Hebrew.

★ Her last words were pretty badass: 'Hasten the revolution! Remember me as a revolutionary communist.'

QUOTABLES

'Once you break the silence, it's just the beginning.'

'More exists among human beings than can
be answered by the simplistic question I'm hit with every
day of my life: "Are you a man or a woman?"'

'I have been referred to in my life as a butch,
as a he-she, as a passing woman, as a drag king.
None of those words were words that I chose.'

31.
SALLY RIDE

NÉE SALLY KRISTEN RIDE (1951–2012)

'For whatever reason, I didn't succumb to the stereotype that science wasn't for girls.'

Claim to Fame	Country of Origin
Astronaut	USA

HER LEGACY

Though Sally Ride never grew up dreaming of becoming an idol for young women across the globe, that is exactly what she went on to do – and at the relatively young age of thirty-two. In 1983 Ride crashed through the celestial glass ceiling to become the very first American woman astronaut as well as the youngest American in space. It was a huge coup that paved the way for women in the sciences for years to come. Her impact is still felt today, at a time when, finally, 50 per cent of contemporary astronauts are women.

Ride didn't just contribute to the expansion of the public's understanding about space travel; she was also a renowned physicist who encouraged girls to pursue careers in science when it was still discouraged as a man's field. That is, sadly, still true today – girls are mainly pushed toward professions in the arts or communications, while boys are believed to be better at maths and science. Ride explained back in 2006, 'If we want scientists and engineers in the future, we should be cultivating the girls as much as the boys.'

HER LIFE STORY

Growing up in Los Angeles, Ride experienced what she called a 'typical childhood'. Though fascinated by astronauts and space, she didn't think about becoming an astronaut. Instead, she thought she'd eventually be a physics professor (surprise, surprise – she did that too, among other things!). Fortunately her parents were open-minded when it came to their daughter's academic interests and career goals, and they didn't discourage her from pursuing her passion for science and maths. Though she was obviously very smart, she remembered being the kind of kid who hid in the back of the classroom, hoping the teacher wouldn't call on her.

Ride graduated from Stanford University in Palo Alto, California, with a bachelor's degree in physics and English, and then went on to get a master's and PhD from the same school. While preparing to defend her PhD thesis, Ride spotted a newspaper ad saying that NASA was on the hunt for new astronauts. 'The moment I saw that ad I knew that that was what I really wanted to do,' she later remembered. She was among more than 8,000 applicants and won one of the prestigious jobs even though, up until then, all of America's prior astronauts had been male. Her training included mastering fun-sounding activities like weightlessness, navigation, parachute jumping, water survival, and radio communications.

In 1983 she blasted off on the *Challenger* space shuttle from the Kennedy Space Center in Florida, officially sealing her legacy as a women's barrier-buster. Ride went out on the *Challenger* again the following year. She was later asked to join the special presidential commission that investigated what had caused the explosion of the *Challenger* in 1986 and also investigated the 2003 breakup of the Columbia shuttle. Ride eventually became the first director of NASA's Office of Exploration and was inducted into the Astronaut Hall of Fame.

After she retired from nine years with NASA, Ride began teaching physics as a college professor in California and wrote science books for children. She was passionate about researching and defending NASA and three other astronaut programmes in general: she advised two presidents and testified before Congress on these subjects. She also continued championing programmes that advanced opportunities for kids – especially girls – in the science world. Sally Ride may not be a household name today, but her mark on women's lives is undeniable.

WOMEN ASTRONAUTS YOU SHOULD KNOW ABOUT

Sally Ride wasn't the first, last, or only woman to journey to the stars. Check out these other notable names.

Kalpana Chawla

The first Indian American astronaut and first Indian woman in space was one of the seven people killed in the Columbia disaster in 2003, when the shuttle broke apart about fifteen minutes before landing, killing all seven on board. Chawla, who went by the nickname KC, was born in India and later moved to the US to continue her studies in aerospace engineering. After her first launch in 1997, she reportedly said, 'When you look at the stars and the galaxy, you feel that you are not just from any particular piece of land, but from the solar system.' After Chawla passed away, she was awarded the NASA Space Flight Medal, the Congressional Space Medal of Honor, and the NASA Distinguished Service Medal.

Mae Jemison

Jemison's dreams of going into space were bred partly from a long-time love of astronomy and partly from her obsession with *Star Trek*. She worked as a Peace Corps physician before applying to the Astronaut Corps and was thrilled to enter the hallowed halls of NASA in 1987. Jemison became the first black woman in space, in 1992, on the second flight of the space shuttle *Endeavour*, which lasted eight days. She went on to realise another dream when she was hired to make a guest appearance on *Star Trek: The Next Generation*!

Valentina Tereshkova
In 1963 the Russian cosmonaut, a.k.a. the 'First Lady of Space', became the very first woman to go into space. As a kid, she was into parachuting, which later led to an interest in astronomy. She was one of only four women recruited into the Soviet women's space programme – and was the only one to complete it. When Tereshkova headed out on the *Vostok 6* on 16 June 1963, she was only twenty-six years old. The craft orbited the earth a whopping forty-eight times in seventy hours! While on-board, she took photographs and conducted experiments to help show the effects of space travel on her body. She also manually piloted the ship on her own. She didn't fly again after that, but she got a doctorate in engineering and was granted the title 'Hero of the Soviet Union'.

HER COOL CREDENTIALS

★ Ride was the founder of a company, Sally Ride Science. Its mission is to make products that help kids – particularly girls – develop skills in the traditionally male fields of science and maths.

★ Though Ride became famous after her two space flights, she never cashed in on the flood of quick-money opportunities thrown at her. Those included book deals, movie contracts, and endorsement gigs.

★ She was a nationally ranked tennis junior player – eighteenth by the time she turned eighteen.

QUOTABLES

'It means a lot to me that my participation in that flight has meant so much to so many people. And I hadn't appreciated how much it did really mean to people, how much it touched particularly women, until after my flight.'

'For whatever reason, I didn't succumb to the stereotype that science wasn't for girls. I got encouragement from my parents. I never ran into a teacher or a counsellor who told me that science was for boys.'

'I never went into physics or the astronaut corps to become a role model. But after my first flight, it became clear to me that I was one... Young girls need to see role models in whatever careers they may choose, just so they can picture themselves doing those jobs someday. You can't be what you can't see.'

32.
BELL HOOKS

NÉE GLORIA JEAN WATKINS (1952–)

'Once you do away with the idea of people as fixed, static entities, then you see that people can change, and there is hope.'

Claim to Fame	Country of Origin
Author	USA

HER LEGACY

bell hooks is one of the most prolific feminist writers and thinkers of her generation – an intellectual giant revered for her contributions to the public dialogue about the relationships between gender, race, capitalism, and more. She believes these overlapping elements create ongoing systems of oppression in our culture, and her work both critiques these systems and tries to find ways to improve them. A lot of hooks' work also focuses on how black women are perceived – or, more often, misperceived – and the ways that feminist identities develop.

HER LIFE STORY

Born in Hopkinsville, Kentucky, in 1952, hooks grew up in a segregated town in the south, an experience that helped her be 'critically conscious since childhood'. In addition to being hindered by the overt racism, cruelty, and discrimination of the time, she felt neglected by her father and unsupported by her family in general, who believed women should live out traditional roles and aspire mainly to be wives and mums.

An insatiable reader, hooks believed critical thinking could help her transcend the pain she experienced as a youth, once noting that 'life-transforming ideas have always come to me through books'.

hooks started writing her first book, *Ain't I a Woman: Black Women and Feminism* – named after Sojourner Truth's famous 'Ain't I a Woman?' speech (see page 14) – at the age of nineteen. She decided to adopt a pen name inspired by her maternal great-grandmother because she loved her grandmother's feisty spirit and wanted to honour her African American female ancestors. By lowercasing her name, hooks was trying to escape the 'ego' that naturally tends to go along with people's names and identities. She also wanted readers to focus squarely on her work, not on her. Published in 1981, *Ain't I a Woman* was the result of eight years of research and rewriting and explored the biggest themes that persisted throughout hooks' life: the civil rights and suffragist movements, and the damaging impact of racism and sexism on black women's psyches.

In 1973 hooks graduated from Stanford University and eventually earned a PhD from the University of California, Santa Cruz. When she began teaching at schools including Yale, Oberlin, and the City College of New York, she was disturbed by the striking whiteness of women's studies departments and by the lack of diversity in mainstream (white) feminism in general. Some white feminists bashed her and her first book, criticising it for its unusual writing style and lack of footnotes. But hooks pressed on, writing about the importance of female solidarity instead of division.

Since then she has published more than thirty books on a range of topics, from feminism, racism, and class to love, masculinity, and sex. One of her most groundbreaking, classic works, *Feminism is for Everybody*, is a feminist primer that deftly explains why feminism should matter to, well, anyone and everyone. It touches on reproductive rights, beauty standards, patriarchal masculinity, women in the workplace, feminist parenting, and how 'sisterhood is still powerful'. The book is a must-read.

The recipient of many prestigious awards, hooks continues to write, speak, and work to advance feminist and anti-racist dialogues in American culture. An avid social media maven, she uses lots of different outlets to reach a new generation of women, preserving her presence as one of modern feminism's most significant voices.

HER COOL CREDENTIALS

★ hooks was named one of the most influential American thinkers by *Publishers Weekly* and *The Atlantic Monthly*.

★ hooks has more than 80,000 followers on Twitter.

★ She founded the bell hooks Institute, a centre at Kentucky's Berea College for 'critical thinking, contemplating, and dreaming'.

QUOTABLES

'Every act of violence brings us closer to death. Whether it's the mundane violence we do to our bodies by overeating toxic food or drink or the extreme violence of child abuse, domestic warfare, life-threatening poverty, addiction, or state terrorism.'

'The greatest movement for social justice our country has ever known is the civil rights movement.'

'I will not have my life narrowed down. I will not bow down to somebody else's whim or to someone else's ignorance.'

'It's in the act of having to do things that you don't want to that you learn something about moving past the self. Past the ego.'

'Any society based on domination supports and condones violence.'

33.
CINDY SHERMAN

NÉE CYNTHIA MORRIS SHERMAN (1954–)

'When I look at the pictures, I never see myself; they aren't self-portraits. Sometimes I disappear.'

Claim to Fame	Country of Origin
Photographer, artist	USA

HER LEGACY

Cindy Sherman is one of the most famous artists of the twentieth century and certainly one of the most famous artists working today. What makes her sometimes controversial art so special is the nuanced way she dissects the roles of women in society, often through her conceptual photographic portraits. Using herself as a subject in many of her works, Sherman explores elements of dress-up, fantasy, and play to mould herself into gritty alter egos, many based on female caricature and stereotypes.

One cool thing about her work is that almost all her portraits depict women deeply lost in their own thoughts. As critic Eleanor Heartney wrote, 'Sherman's heroines are always alone, nearly expressionless, and caught up in very private emotions. They seem to be women with impenetrable interior lives, caught in a moment of quiet contemplation.'

Sherman is striking for how malleable she is. She's like an actor, with an insanely wide range of characters she's comfortable playing. She once said she was 'more influenced by performance art than photography or art'. She looks totally different in each of these hundreds of personas, though she said that 'none of the characters are me… They're everything but me.' Each one seems to examine conflicting aspects of modern womanhood – what women today are expected to be, physically, emotionally, intellectually, domestically, and professionally. Sherman described her work this way: 'I like making images that from a distance seem kind of seductive, colourful, luscious and engaging, and then you realise what you're looking at is something totally opposite. It seems boring to me to pursue the typical idea of beauty, because that is the easiest and the most obvious way to see the world.'

HER LIFE STORY

As a kid growing up on Long Island, New York, Sherman was obsessed with dressing up. In college at the State University of New York at Buffalo, she began painting in a hyper-realist style in which paintings and sculptures look so true-to-life that they resemble photos. She decided

to switch from painting to photography as her preferred medium when she felt she had 'nothing more to say' via painting. (Interestingly, she failed her first photography exam!)

After college she moved to New York City to pursue her art. In 1977, at age twenty-three, Sherman began work on her most famous photographs: a series of sixty-nine black-and-white images, in the style of film noir, called *Untitled Film Stills*. She photographed herself playing different female clichés, like the 'luscious librarian', 'ice-cold sophisticate', and 'domesticated sex kitten', to painfully visceral effect. There were no men in any of the works. The Museum of Modern Art bought the collection for an estimated one million dollars in 1995.

Sherman's later work explored women's roles in society and culture, but in sometimes more violent and unnerving ways. She stopped using herself as a model in many of her works and began incorporating things like vomit, prosthetics, and doll parts in creepy photographs that evoked grotesque fairy tales and crime scenes. She also did explicit, sometimes shocking work around sex and anatomy. In one piece for her 1992 series known as *Sex Pictures*, a plastic doll-woman hybrid is seen lying back, pinup style, while wearing a gas mask. She has huge fake breasts, doll legs, and a vagina, but no torso.

Leaving most of her works untitled, Sherman never fully explains each piece for viewers, instead making them examine the images from their own perspectives and biases. Her work is clearly influenced by feminist concepts of artifice, objectification, and challenging the male gaze, but it's unclear if Sherman identifies as a feminist. She said, 'The work is what it is and hopefully it's seen as feminist work, or feminist-advised work. But I'm not going to go around espousing theoretical bullshit about feminist stuff.'

HER COOL CREDENTIALS

★ Sherman has received many prestigious awards, including the Guild Hall Academy of the Arts Lifetime Achievement Award for Visual Arts (2005), the American Academy of Arts and Sciences Award (2003), and the National Arts Award (2001).

★ An aficionado of horror movies, Sherman entered the male-dominated genre and directed her own scary flick, *Office Killer*, in 1997.

★ In the early 1990s, Sherman worked with the punk-rock all-girl band Babes in Toyland, creating cover photos for the albums *Fontanelle* and *Painkillers*. She also made a stage backdrop for the group's live concerts and acted in the promo video for the song 'Bruise Violet'.

★ One of her works from the *Untitled Film* series became the most expensive photo ever sold. At a Christie's auction in 2011, Sherman's piece went for approximately $3.9 million, a record then for the photographer and also, according to Daniel Kunitz, the 'highest price ever realised for a photograph'.

QUOTABLES

'I don't analyse what I'm doing. I've read convincing interpretations of my work, and sometimes I've noticed something that I wasn't aware of, but I think, at this point, people read into my work out of habit. Or I'm just very, very smart.'

'I was supporting myself, but nothing like the guy painters, as I refer to them. I always resented that actually. We were all getting the same amount of press, but they were going gangbusters with sales.'

'I can be fearlessly strong at times to protect an inner frailty.'

'There's a theory that there were so many women photographers at the time because we felt nobody else was doing it. We couldn't or didn't really want to go into the male-dominated painting world, so since there weren't any artists who were using photographs, we thought, "Well, yeah, let's just play with that."'

34.
OPRAH

NÉE OPRAH GAIL WINFREY (1954–)

*'Getting to the point where you are absolutely comfortable with yourself…
to have the kind of internal strength and internal courage it takes to say,
"No, I will not let you treat me this way" is what success is all about.'*

Claim to Fame	Country of Origin
Media mogul	USA

HER LEGACY

Oprah Winfrey, a.k.a. 'the queen of all media', is a worldwide mega-mogul who revolutionised the TV talk-show genre with *The Oprah Winfrey Show*, one of the highest-rated talk shows of all time.

She also conquered, well, pretty much everything else you could imagine. The first African American female billionaire, she has used her formidable platform to promote causes important to her, from her passion for reading to girls' education, to ending poverty, rape, and sex abuse. Winfrey's story has inspired women the world over – she grew up in a poor, troubled home, yet she rose up to become not only one of the wealthiest Americans but also one of the most powerful icons of the entertainment industry.

HER LIFE STORY

Until age six, Winfrey was raised by her grandmother on a farm in rural Mississippi. A natural communicator, Winfrey had a habit of reciting in church – starting at the precocious age of three – which earned her the nickname The Preacher among her peers. Her grandma taught her to read (reportedly by age three), a pastime that would become a lifelong passion and escape. She later went to live with her mother in Milwaukee. While in Milwaukee, however, she is reported to have suffered rape and sexual assault before she was eventually sent to live with her disciplinarian father in Nashville, Tennessee. She became an honours student, was elected to the student council, and was selected to attend the White House Conference on Youth.

From a young age Winfrey wanted to be an actor, and when she was still in high school she began working as a radio news reader – her voice was seen as a standout in the field. She later went on to work as a co-anchor at her local news channel while still in college at Tennessee State University, which she attended on a full scholarship. She eventually left college to become the first African American female news anchor in Nashville.

In 1984 Winfrey took over a low-performing talk show in Chicago, and within just a few weeks, its popularity surged and it became the highest-rated talk show in town. Because of this success, it became her show – The Oprah Winfrey Show – and was broadcast nationally beginning in 1986. Once she took the reins, her express mission, as she stated on the very first day of the show, was 'to validate women, to say "You matter. You matter if you've been divorced, you matter if you've been abused. You are not your circumstances."'

Winfrey's programme achieved such crazy success in part due to her warm personal demeanour and her ability to be vulnerable. Audiences felt close to her because she trusted them enough to share her personal highs, lows, and struggles along with discussing those of her guests. She once admitted, on air, to abusing crack cocaine in her twenties with an addicted boyfriend, a shockingly intimate confession that was very unusual (and very talked about) at the time.

The content and tone of Winfrey's globally syndicated show began to shift in the nineties as her interests moved toward more spiritual and philanthropic subjects. She launched her own women's magazine, *O*, in 2000, which *Fortune* magazine called 'the most successful start-up ever in the industry'. Her magazine is still operating – and still hugely successful – today, as is her accompanying website, which not only covers the usual women's lifestyle fare but also takes on difficult topics. The site once posted 'Oprah's Child Predator Watch List' to help track down accused child molesters. Within the first week of the list being online, two of the fugitives were captured.

Then, there's her influence in the literary world. In 1996 she launched Oprah's Book Club, and a ripple was felt in the entire publishing industry. Whenever she named a book as her pick of the month, readers took note, and some authors rocketed to fame, with their books almost instantly becoming bestsellers. Fifty-five million books were sold as a result of the club. Professor and author Kathleen Rooney wrote that Oprah's Book Club single-handedly changed 'the idea of what it's possible to do on TV'.

The Oprah Winfrey Show may no longer be around, but Winfrey is as busy as ever. Her striking ability to shift public opinion, especially consumer choices, has been dubbed 'The Oprah Effect'. *The New York Times* columnist Maureen Dowd once said Winfrey has 'more credibility than the president'.

HER COOL CREDENTIALS

★ In 2013 President Barack Obama awarded Winfrey the Presidential Medal of Freedom, one of the highest civilian honours.

★ She founded the Oprah Winfrey Leadership Academy for Girls, which offers a first-rate education to gifted but economically disadvantaged girls in South Africa. She conceived the idea while 'sitting in Nelson Mandela's living room' in 2002.

★ In 1985 Winfrey achieved her dream of becoming an actor. She earned an Oscar nomination for her supporting role as Sophia in the movie *The Color Purple*.

★ To drive home the power of her influence: by one estimate, Winfrey's support of Barack Obama in 2006–2008 secured him more than one million votes in the tight 2008 Democratic primary race.

QUOTABLES

'As long as I can be an influence and make a difference, that's what I want to do. But I also want to act because I think that it's very important to create work that… puts the black cultural experience on screen.'

'Education is what liberated me. The ability to read saved my life. I would have been an entirely different person had I not been taught to read when I was an early age. My entire life experience, my ability to believe in myself, and even in my darkest moments of sexual abuse and being physically abused and so forth, I knew there was another way. I knew there was a way out. I knew there was another kind of life because I had read about it.'

'I love being a woman, and I love being a black woman.'

'I am where I am because of the bridges that I crossed. Sojourner Truth was a bridge. Harriet Tubman was a bridge. Ida B. Wells was a bridge. Madame C. J. Walker was a bridge. Fannie Lou Hamer was a bridge.'

35.
GEENA DAVIS

NÉE VIRGINIA ELIZABETH DAVIS (1956–)

*'It's really important for boys to see that girls take
up half of the planet – which we do.'*

Claim to Fame	Country of Origin
Actor	USA

HER LEGACY

Geena Davis – who, along with the similarly kick-ass actor Susan Sarandon, made the film *Thelma & Louise* a feminist mainstay for all time – may not be doing a ton of acting these days, but that doesn't mean she's slacking off. Quite the opposite! A long-time feminist activist, especially when it comes to images of women in the media, Davis is ultra-vocal about her commitment to gender justice. She even started her own research, education, and advocacy non-profit, the Geena Davis Institute on Gender and Media, whose mission is to help fight gender bias in Hollywood as well as to 'reduce stereotyping and create diverse female characters in entertainment targeting children eleven and under'.

HER LIFE STORY

Davis grew up in Wareham, Massachusetts, where she suffered from self-esteem issues due to being six feet tall. After graduating from Boston University, where she majored in drama, she moved to New

York City to begin a modelling career (she was in the Victoria's Secret catalogue!) before landing a role in the seminal eighties film *Tootsie*. She then moved to Los Angeles, where her acting career flourished. She starred in well-received films such as *Beetlejuice* and *A League of Their Own*, as well as *Thelma & Louise*.

Davis launched her non-profit in 2004 partly because of something she noticed while watching cartoons with her daughter. She described it this way: 'My daughter was about two… and it really struck me how few female characters there seemed to be… I started counting the characters while we were watching. I knew there were far fewer parts for women in movies in general, but that we would be showing that to kids was sort of a revelation.' In response, Davis founded the institute that bears her name. The group is dedicated to transforming the offensive ways that women are often portrayed in mainstream media (if they're portrayed at all!). The institute commissioned the biggest research project ever done about gender in film and television, conducted by the USC Annenberg School for Communication and Journalism. The researchers' results weren't pretty: as it turned out, in family films made between 1990 to 2005, there is only one female character for every three male characters; in group scenes, only 17 per cent of the characters are female. Some of Davis's top goals for the institute are 'having more female representation as main characters, minor characters, narrators, and in crowd scenes; having more of that representation consist of people of colour; having more female characters with aspirations greater than romance.'

She has won many awards for her advocacy and activist work, and – fun fact – she did an ace job playing the first US female president on the TV show *Commander in Chief*. In 2013 she announced her own 'patented two-step fix' for Hollywood's gender issues: 'How can we fix the problem of corporate boards being so unequal without quotas? Well, they can be half women instantly, onscreen. How do we encourage a lot more girls to pursue science, technology and engineering careers? By casting droves of women in STEM jobs today in movies and on TV.'

HER COOL CREDENTIALS

★ Davis is a member of Mensa, a prestigious international high IQ society. Members score in the top 2 per cent on an IQ test. Davis hasn't attended any Mensa meetings, however.

★ Davis won an Academy Award for Best Supporting Actress for the film *The Accidental Tourist*. She won a Golden Globe Award for her role on *Commander in Chief* and was nominated for a Golden Globe for her work in the movie *A League of Their Own*.

★ In 2000 Davis launched the initiative Geena Takes Aim through the Women's Sports Foundation. Davis, who was an Olympic hopeful archer, wanted to help educate student athletes about their rights under Title IX, the federal civil rights law that prohibits sex discrimination in education. In 2015 she started the Bentonville Film Festival with the goal of promoting diversity in film.

QUOTABLES

'What if the plumber or pilot or construction foreman [in a movie role] is a woman? What if the taxi driver or the scheming politician is a woman? What if both police officers that arrive on the scene are women – and it's not a big deal?'

'I was attracted to complicated multi-dimensional women in charge of their own destiny. I wanted to play active parts. I've been fortunate to not just be a witness or the wife.'

[About her work with archery:] 'You're spending a lot of time alone with yourself practising. You get to know yourself, how calm you can be, how long you can focus. You have to be very self-motivated. You have to have faith in yourself and believe in your abilities. It was an area I had never delved into.'

36.
ANITA HILL

NÉE ANITA FAYE HILL (1956–)

*'When I think of what has happened in a larger sense,
beyond myself, then I would not change anything.'*

Claim to Fame	Country of Origin
Lawyer	USA

HER LEGACY

Anita Hill's name has long been synonymous with one thing: her groundbreaking 1991 testimony in Congress against conservative Supreme Court nominee (and now justice) Clarence Thomas. Hill was a law professor at the University of Oklahoma at the time, and Thomas was undergoing his confirmation hearings. All was moving along swimmingly until Hill was called to testify about the awful sexual harassment she had experienced while working for Thomas (the abuse had been leaked to the press).

Despite the awkwardness of having to describe graphic sexual harassment over and over in front of countless strangers, Hill maintained a steadily calm, confident, dignified demeanour, which resonated with the people watching, especially women. Her testimony helped launch a national conversation about workplace power dynamics and sexual harassment – and that conversation is still flourishing today. It shone a light on an issue that was hardly talked about at the time but desperately needed to be. It also encouraged more women to run for office and to speak out about their own harassment experiences.

HER LIFE STORY

Hill is the youngest of thirteen children, raised on a farm in rural Oklahoma. Her parents set very high standards for her and raised her in the Baptist faith. She was a rock star in school, making straight As and graduating as valedictorian and class secretary as well as a National Honor Society student. She went on to attend Oklahoma State University, where she graduated with a degree in psychology and, again, earned plenty of academic honours. She then got her law degree from Yale Law School in 1980, which was a feat in itself. In those days, there were so few women at law schools that many schools didn't even have women's bathrooms (during that time, 38 per cent of law students were female, as opposed to 50 per cent nowadays).

After graduating, Hill moved to Washington, DC, to begin her career as a lawyer. In 1981 Hill started working as a personal assistant to Clarence Thomas, who was then serving as the leader of the US Department of Education's Office of Civil Rights. Working under Thomas was reportedly a nightmare. Hill said as much in her testimony before the Senate Judiciary Committee during his confirmation hearing in 1991. That's when things became what *Time* magazine deemed 'an ugly circus'. In his autobiography, Thomas later described Hill as his 'most traitorous adversary'. In court, Hill vividly recalled Thomas's inappropriate comments, deeds, and suggestions, from talking about his penis size to making references to large breasts and pubic hair. The testimony escalated into a heated, vitriolic exchange, with Hill's credibility constantly being challenged. Thomas's supporters said she was upset because he had rejected her, despite her passing a polygraph test. When Thomas testified about the proceedings with Hill, he painted himself as the victim, describing the hearings as 'a high-tech lynching for uppity Blacks'.

In the end, the US House and Senate dismissed Hill's allegations, and Thomas still got a seat on the most powerful court in America. But Hill's testimony had sweeping cultural effects, and she didn't let the naysayers stop her. She once explained, 'I am not given to fantasy. This is not something I would have come forward with if I was not absolutely sure of what I was saying.'

During and after the court hearings, Hill survived death threats and bomb threats, plus a campaign to get her fired from her first teaching job in Oklahoma. Still, she went on to became a popular lecturer who spoke internationally about gender and race in the boardroom. She also wrote a variety of articles in major publications like *The New York Times* and *Newsweek*, and spoke out about sexual harassment on shows like *60 Minutes* and *Face the Nation*.

Hill's influence on the sphere of women in the workplace can't be overstated – her brave words helped pave the way for harassment laws and women speaking out about sexually inappropriate office behaviours.

HER COOL CREDENTIALS

★ Hill told her story in the book *Speaking Truth to Power*. A documentary was later made as well, called *Anita*.

★ Hill's testimony brought the popular phrase 'he said, she said' back into the national vernacular.

★ She has received lots of awards for her great work, including the Ida B. Wells Award, given to someone who worked to increase access and opportunities to people of colour in journalism, and she was named one of *Glamour* magazine's Ten Women of the Year in 1991.

QUOTABLES

'Being who we are is the only way to effectively convey the truth of our experiences.'

'I became the messenger who had to be killed.'

'We have a history of gender and racial bias on our court that continues to undermine the system.'

'The issue of sexual harassment is not the end of it. There are other issues – political issues, gender issues – that people need to be educated about.'

'The real problem is that the way that power is given out in our society pits us against each other.'

37.
POLY STYRENE
NÉE MARIANNE JOAN ELLIOTT-SAID (1957–2011)

'I'm a poseur and I don't care!'

Claim to Fame	Country of Origin
Singer	England

HER LEGACY

When the band X-Ray Spex hit it big in the late seventies, its frontwoman, Poly Styrene, burst onto the scene along with it. She quickly gained attention for her colourful stage presence; her songwriting – which tackled subversive subjects such as sexism, racism, and consumerism with both humour and seriousness – and her raw, singsongy vocals, offset by her distinctly adorable British accent. She was a punk-rock pioneer who paved the way for countless future icons, from Kim Gordon to Kathleen Hanna. The hallowed British music mag *NME* once dubbed her 'the original riot grrrl'.

Being mixed race (her mother was Scottish Irish and her father a Somali aristocrat), short, and not stick skinny – plus having a full mouth of metal braces – made Styrene's image fly in the face of the stereotypically beautiful frontwomen of the day (think movie-star types like Blondie). Styrene also stood out because she seemed effortlessly comfortable in her own skin. Oh, and her outrageously awesome fashion sense was another thing: she avidly embraced neon colours, a.k.a. Day-Glo, before they became THE BIGGEST THING EVER in the eighties.

HER LIFE STORY

As a kid, Styrene wanted to be an actor, fashion designer, or airline attendant. Like many who went through an incense/Birkenstocks/Phish phase, Styrene did the hippie thing as a teenager and then ran away from home at age fifteen with only a few English pounds to her name. She bounced from music fest to music fest before deciding to move to the big city of London, where she trained to be an opera singer. After catching a live performance by the legendary punkers the Sex Pistols, Styrene felt she absolutely had to form her own band. But first, she released her own ska-pop single in 1976, under the name Mari Elliott (her legit birth name was Marianne Elliott-Said, but she later picked Poly Styrene when she was looking for 'something plastic and synthetic' in the Yellow Pages telephone directory).

Soon Styrene placed an ad in an English music mag seeking 'young punx who want to stick it together' in a band. Eight months later, she was playing out as X-Ray Spex with fellow rockers Paul Dean, Jak Airport, BP Hurding, Rudi Thomson, and Lora Logic. In 1977 they became mainstays in the local punk scene, and they shook things up in both look and sound. Punk rock was extremely male dominated at the time, so Styrene's front-and-centre status as the face of the band, as well as the voice and writer of many of the group's in-your-face, often 'unfeminine' lyrics, was pretty revolutionary.

Though the band only released one album, *Germ Free Adolescents*, in 1978, and they broke up a year later, Styrene went on to record lots of new music under her own name. Her last album, *Generation Indigo*, came out just a month before she died of breast cancer in 2011, at the relatively young age of fifty-three. The music world still mourns her and celebrates her rock 'n' roll legacy.

The Times once noted that 'her unconventional style made her an inspirational figure to a generation of female pop singers,' and *The New York Times* wrote that the 'pioneering, braces-wearing frontwoman... made a place for feminine brashness in punk... She served as inspiration for other female musicians, prefiguring movements like riot grrrl.'

In the man's world of popular (and not so popular) music, Styrene was bold, fierce, and totally individual – a free-spirited rebel who managed to single-handedly change the punk landscape for women.

HER COOL CREDENTIALS

★ Styrene's songwriting and vocals inspired and influenced pretty much anyone who's anyone in the modern punk-rock world. Kim Gordon of Sonic Youth said of Styrene's sound, '[Her] voice on "Oh Bondage! Up Yours!" was the most exhilarating voice I ever heard – it was all body.' And Kathleen Hanna, punk feminist extraordinaire, wrote on her blog, 'Poly lit the way for me as a female singer who wanted to sing about ideas. Her lyrics influenced EVERYONE I KNOW WHO MAKES MUSIC.' Even legendary gay dance icon Boy George penned a moving remembrance of Styrene after her death, writing: 'Anyone who wants to experience the irreverent magic of punk should get hold of a copy. A vinyl copy, preferably scratched. It will make your soul smile and you'll want to rip holes in your tights and pogo.'

★ Even as she got older, Styrene didn't give a damn what people thought. At age fifty-one, she loved riding her scooter, ignoring any rude remarks from passers-by: 'I ride… along the St Leonard's promenade on my little manual chrome scooter. I've still got one as I haven't grown up. I used to ride it in London and someone shouted "supergran" at me.'

★ As a teenager, she used to frequent dinner parties with rock royalty, including members of Led Zeppelin and Pink Floyd. She was not especially impressed with their mainstream stardom shtick.

QUOTABLES

'I feel better for having been on stage, having been told I never could. I'm starting to think, maybe what I did then is working. Oh, I didn't waste my time. My youth wasn't misspent!'

'You remember that old song "Que Sera Sera, Whatever will be, will be, the future's not ours to see"? I've always felt that. It's been a rollercoaster ride, but I wouldn't change a thing.'

38.
SANDI TOKSVIG

NÉE SANDRA BIRGIT TOKSVIG (1958–)

'The one place women and men are absolutely equal is at the ballot box.'

Claim to Fame	Country of Origin
Comedian, actor, women's rights activist	Denmark

HER LEGACY

Sandi Toksvig is a pretty big deal when it comes to women's rights in the UK. Though she's best known for her work on TV and in comedy, Toksvig is also an avid, super-vocal feminist. In fact, she launched her own mini-revolution in 2015 when she founded the Women's Equality Party, campaigning to improve the lives of girls and women all across the country.

Though she's built her career on her dry wit, things weren't always rosy for Toksvig. After coming out as a lesbian in the 1990s, she faced hardship and hatred when she was vilified in the right-wing British press. But she used her detractors' vitriol as fodder to push herself even harder at work, helping transform her pain into a renewed sense of purpose. In 2016 she became the first woman to lead a prime-time panel show on British TV after taking over BBC2's comedy quiz show *QI* from Stephen Fry, and she's an outspoken crusader for women's equal pay and representation in all facets of life.

She's a beloved cultural figure among both women and men for the way she blends warmth and wit, levity and grit. She never takes herself too seriously, even when she's discussing the glass ceiling in STEM or the ridiculousness of people asking her if she, like, actually burns her bra. For these reasons, her social and feminist impact goes way beyond her being just another woman in entertainment.

HER LIFE STORY

Sandra Birgitte (Sandi) Toksvig gave her very first television interview when she was just six years old, and it was a harbinger of great things to come for the future TV star. The broadcaster, writer, and politician was born in Copenhagen, Denmark, in 1958. Because her father, Claus Toksvig, was one of Britain's top foreign correspondents, the family had to relocate somewhat frequently for work. She spent a good portion of her childhood in New York City, according to some reports.

Toksvig attended a girls' school when her family lived near London, and she did well academically. As a student, she earned a first-class degree in archaeology and anthropology at Cambridge University's Girton College, where she also won the Raemaekers Prize for Archaeology (in

addition to the Theresa Montefiore Memorial Award for outstanding academic achievement!). It was in college that Toksvig also first began dabbling in comedy – she performed in the Footlights' first all-women show, and wrote material for the Footlights Revue.

After graduating, Toksvig launched her comedy and acting career in earnest, starting out on children's shows while working the local comedy circuit. After a while she started appearing on popular British shows such as *Whose Line Is It Anyway?*, *QI*, *Mock the Week*, and *Have I Got News For You.*

Though Toksvig has said that she's always known she was gay, she decided to come out publicly about it in 1994. At that time, as she later described in a Fall 2016 TED talk, there was *not one* British female celebrity who was openly gay. Toksvig said that she decided to come out because she believes that secrets are toxic for the soul – but she never expected the type of extreme backlash she received. The right-wing press went into attack mode; it got so bad that her family began getting death threats and was forced to get police protection and go into hiding.

In 2015, Toksvig quit her job as a TV presenter to co-found a brand-new English political party: the Women's Equality Party. The party stands up for hugely important issues like equal pay, equal representation in business and politics, education, and ending violence against women. Within just one year of its inception, the party had spread to more than seventy branches across the country!

Currently, she lives on a London houseboat with her wife, Debbie Toksvig, a psychotherapist, whom she married in 2014 when gay marriage became legal in England. In keeping with her warm, open personality, Toksvig reportedly invited anyone and everyone to attend the celebration, and more than 2,000 people showed up to wish her well.

HER COOL CREDENTIALS

★ Toksvig isn't just a performer and political star – she is also an author. She's written more than twenty books (both fiction and non-fiction) for kids and adults.

★ With various honorary degrees under her belt, Toksvig is not only the Chancellor of the University of Portsmouth, but she's also the President of the Women of the Year Lunch. She also works with the Corporate Alliance Against Domestic Violence and, in 2014, the Queen made her an Officer of the British Empire.

★ In college, she studied with comedy and acting luminaries such as Hugh Laurie, Emma Thompson, and Stephen Fry.

QUOTABLES

'In that second I stopped to question almost everything I had been taught about the past. How often had I overlooked women's contributions?'

'I hope I can live by example and encourage anyone who still lives in the dark closet to open the door, but I can only encourage.'

'There is not now, nor has there ever been… a single country in the world where women have equality with men. Not one. 196 countries.'

39.
MADONNA

NÉE MADONNA LOUISE VERONICA CICCONE (1958–)

'I'm in charge of my fantasies… Isn't that what feminism is all about?'

Claim to Fame	Country of Origin
Singer	USA

HER LEGACY

In her late fifties at the time of this writing, Madonna has been a household name for more than thirty years. Since her self-titled debut album dropped in 1983, the power icon has become the bestselling female recording artist and sold an estimated 300 million records worldwide and toured nearly every inch of the globe. Everyone knows who Madonna is. But the weight of her legacy doesn't lie with her sales figures, her popularity, or even her music. What's always been most powerful about Madonna is her smarts (she has an IQ of 140, making her a certified genius), her die-hard ambition, and her relentless refusal to apologise for expressing herself, no matter how unconventional or risqué that expression has been. Oh, she's quite the fashion chameleon, too.

HER LIFE STORY

Let's start off with M's constantly evolving style (as we all know, she has a flair for re-invention). When she flounced onto the scene in the early eighties, Madonna looked nothing like the other pop stars on the Billboard charts. She was pretty, sure, but her look and attitude were darker and edgier than those of her contemporaries – she was essentially the anti-Debbie Gibson. She recalled to *Harper's Bazaar* in 2011, 'Straight men did not find me attractive… I think they were scared of me because I was different. I've always asked, "Why? Why do I have to do that? Why do I have to look this way? Why do I have to dress this way? Why do I have to behave this way?"'

FOUR PIVOTAL MADONNA PERFORMANCES YOU NEED TO WATCH RIGHT THIS SECOND

'Like a Virgin' at the 1984 MTV Video Music Awards

[https://www.youtube.com/watch?v=ud3pBKxudv8]

As the opening notes of her smash single 'Like a Virgin' rang out, Madonna emerged as the living, breathing topper on a towering three-level wedding cake. Wearing white lace and her famous 'BOY TOY' belt, Madonna was about to pull off the most talked-about performance of her career. She humped the floor and ripped her veil off, and began using it as a perfect prop. This was early Madonna at the height of her messy splendour. It doesn't get much better than this.

'Vogue' at the 1990 MTV Video Music Awards

[https://www.youtube.com/watch?v=lTaXtWWR16A]

This was a special performance in that Madonna decided to take a trip back in history and channel good ol' Marie Antoinette. With powdery white skin, boobs up to here, and a delicate pile of hair on her head, she got down with her usual massive bevy of backup as she lip-synced to her hit song 'Vogue'. She waved a fan to keep herself cool – bitch, it's Madonna, she'll always overexert herself, but only to an extent.

'Holiday' at Live-Aid 1985 in Philadelphia
[https://www.youtube.com/watch?v=E8pK_yOpas0]
This performance was notable for all the ways it wasn't overtly Madonna-y. It was a performance, but it wasn't overly rehearsed, and Madonna's exuberant young energy was palpable. It's cool seeing her a bit off-the-cuff every now and again, right? Also, her hair was an unassuming shade of brown, not rigorously styled, and she was wearing a modest, oversized white blazer. Modest? Madonna?!

Super Bowl Medley in 2012
[https://www.youtube.com/watch?v=W795W63n7mA]
Before the fact, Madonna said she intended to make her first Super Bowl performance 'the greatest show on earth'. Did she pull that off? Up to you to watch and find out. Personally, I thought she did pretty damn well – confident and sharp, and her moves were on point. See if you agree.

With her bleached, ratted hair (and inches-long, DGAF black roots), armfuls of punky rubber bracelets, lace gloves, and mesh tank tops, she turned the look of the day upside down, creating her own funky brand of ragamuffin chic. She radiated spunk, fire, and rebellion, and her brazen, 'I can do anything' attitude – which seemed to leak from every pore – instantly sparked the adulation of thousands of girls across the globe (including me).

She has accomplished pretty much every goal she put her mind to, and those goals are the opposite of small-scale stuff. In an interview on the show *American Bandstand* in 1984, host Dick Clark asked the then twenty-five-year-old rising star about her top goal. Her perfectly concise answer was 'to rule the world' – and she did.

Madonna's flair for rebellion only grew, and she has been incredibly controversial throughout her career. She didn't give a damn if you loved her or hated her. She just wanted you to notice her one way or the other, and her sexuality was one of the biggest ways she expressed her uniqueness. From almost being arrested for simulating masturbation onstage to hitch-hiking buck naked in her utterly NSFW coffee-table book *Sex* to licking milk from a saucer in the BDSM-tinged video for 'Express Yourself', Madonna used bold sexuality to help encourage other women and girls to feel okay about their own. She preached candour and lack of shame, which naturally extended to deciding whom to love. For instance, one of the bigger scandals of her career was when she kissed an icon of a black saint (the horror!) in her video for the 1989 song 'Like a Prayer'.

Though some critics dismissed her as exploiting her sexuality to get ahead, many feminists have long been in her corner, celebrating her profound impact on women. (I even released a book about it, called *Madonna & Me*!) And Madonna has always been adamant that her dramatic sexual proclivities are legit. In a 1990 *Nightline* interview with Forrest Sawyer, she explained, 'I'm in charge of my fantasies... Isn't that what feminism is all about?'

Madonna is also a super-smart, uber-confident, bona fide feminist icon with tons of thoughts about what's plaguing the world – and women – today. For instance, in a 2015 interview with *Refinery29*, she took

on ageism: 'As a man, you can date whoever you want. You can dress however you want. You can do whatever you want in any area that you want. But, if you're a woman, there are rules, and there are boundaries.' She talked about the importance of women supporting other women: 'Women need to embrace one another and be more vocally supportive of one another.' And she took on sexist beauty standards: 'The measure of one's worth has to come from the inside, and we don't live in a society that encourages that. We live in a society that encourages the opposite. That's why I think it's a scary time for women right now.'

HER COOL CREDENTIALS

★ The famous LGBT magazine *The Advocate* included Madonna on its '10 Celebrity Icons of HIV Activism' list. Madonna remained close with one of her early dance instructors, Chris Flynn, a gay man who came out as HIV positive. To support him, they appeared together at an AIDS Dance-A-Thon in 1989 to raise awareness and funds for the disease. Throughout the eighties and nineties, Madonna pushed for safer sex. She even put a condom in the packaging for her release of 'Like a Prayer'. In a culture that feared and misunderstood AIDS, she used her platform to raise awareness of the virus, publicly supporting the fight against the disease, which used to be considered a death sentence.

★ She's a major philanthropist on behalf of kids in Malawi. In 2006 Madonna co-founded a non-profit organisation Raising Malawi. Though the group weathered a mismanagement scandal in 2011, it continues to help provide kids and their families in the African nation with shelter, clothing, food, schooling, and medical treatment.

★ Camille Paglia once called her 'the future of feminism'. In a 1990 column for *The New York Times*, iconic author Paglia argued that Madonna was misunderstood by both mainstream media and big feminism as a whole. 'Madonna has a far profounder vision of sex than do the feminists,' Paglia noted. 'She sees both the animality and the artifice.'

QUOTABLES

'I'm strong, ambitious and I know exactly what I
want. Now, if that makes me a bitch, okay.'

'Don't tell me I can't be sexual and intelligent at the same time.'

'I won't be happy till I'm as famous as God.'

'I'd like to think I am taking people on a journey;
I am not just entertaining people, but giving them
something to think about when they leave.'

'If I weren't as talented as I am ambitious,
I'd be a gross monstrosity.'

40.
RENÉE COX

(1960–)

'The inner voice is your ancestors whispering in your ear.'

Claim to Fame	Country of Origin
Artist	Jamaica

HER LEGACY

Renée Cox is one of the most fearless and contentious African American feminist artists out there today. Reflecting her self-stated mission of 'the deconstruction of stereotypes and the empowerment of women', her work shocks you and makes you think. It's a combination of lofty anti-racist social critique and a celebration of black womanhood. Cox challenges people's biases about conventional female beauty, using her own (sometimes naked) body to help highlight the power of black female bodies. Some of her photos are modern feminist takes on stuffy white-dudes' artwork; she has even portrayed herself as Jesus, to much uproar.

HER LIFE STORY

Cox was born in Jamaica, but her family later moved to the ritzy New York City suburb of Scarsdale, New York. By age eight, she was snapping photos, and she started making short films when she was still in grade school. She pursued film studies at Syracuse University and also got a master's degree at the School of Visual Arts in New York City. Before she moved to fine art photography, she worked in New York and Paris as a fashion photographer for women's magazines such as *Glamour* and *Cosmopolitan*.

Cox has explored issues of power and injustice in her work since the beginning of her career. In 1998, for her first one-woman show in New York, Cox created an alter-ego superhero named Raje, whose mission was to fight racism, challenge stereotypes, and teach African American history to children. Some of the same justice-related themes can be seen in her early piece 'The Liberation of Lady J and UB', in which Raje frees racist commercial icons Aunt Jemima (the pancake lady) and Uncle Ben (the rice caricature) from their respective boxes.

Cox's photo 'The Yo Mama' heralded the introduction of another alter-ego persona: Yo Mama, a larger-than-life super-heroine-esque

figure who appeared in several other works. In 'The Yo Mama', Cox stands tall, naked, and proud in black stilettos, holding her son in front of her waist, almost like a shield.

Not everyone appreciated Cox's sometimes erotic, always visceral images. Her most controversial work, 'Yo Mama's Last Supper', was a massive re-imagining of Leonardo da Vinci's famous painting 'The Last Supper'. In her piece, Cox stands naked in Jesus Christ's place at the table, surrounded by black apostles (save for Judas, who's white). Displayed in the Brooklyn Museum in 2001, the work triggered a massive freak-out on the part of former New York City mayor Rudy Giuliani, who deemed it 'outrageous', 'anti-Catholic', and 'disgusting', telling the *New York Daily News* that he did 'not believe that it is right for public money to be used to desecrate religion, to attack people's ethnicity'. Having grown up Catholic, the ever-intrepid Cox didn't let the drama faze her and said in response, 'We are all created in the likeness of God... The hoopla and the fury are because I'm a black female.'

Cox has also been forthright about her frustration with the way our society views women over the age of forty – namely, the attitude that there's an expiration date on female beauty or relevance. Reflecting on her own aging process, she wrote that when she turned forty, the 'Catherine Deneuve syndrome set in'. Her series *American Family* was born from that, and she called it 'a rebellion against all of the pre-ordained roles I am supposed to maintain: dutiful daughter, diminutive wife, and doting mother'.

Cox continues to create provocative, evocative feminist works that confront, challenge and intrigue viewers – grabbing them by the collars, relentlessly pushing their buttons, and refusing to let go.

HER COOL CREDENTIALS

★ In 1995 Cox and two colleagues founded the Negro Art Collective to fight stereotypes about African Americans. The organisation launched a poster campaign – which it called 'interrogating whiteness' – to challenge people's preconceived ideas about race, poverty, and criminal activity. The project was prompted by Cox's five-year-old son who had asked her, 'Why are all black people bad?' The poster bore a quote from scholar Charles Murray: 'In raw numbers, European American whites are the ethnic group with the most people in poverty, most illegitimate children, most people on welfare, most unemployed men, and most arrests for serious crimes.'

★ Cox's work was shown in the prestigious Venice Biennale in 1999. Somewhat in keeping with her Catholic roots and her open disdain for organised religion, she held the show in the Oratorio di S. Ludivico, a seventeenth-century Catholic church.

★ Cox's Queen Nanny of the Maroons exhibition at the Jamaican Biennial won the Aaron Matalon Award in 2006 for the most outstanding contribution to the Biennial.

QUOTABLES

'Christianity is big in the African American community, but there are no presentations of us. I took it upon myself to include people of colour in these classic scenarios.'

'I use myself as a conduit for my photographs because I think that working with the self is the most honest representation of being.'

'I have a right to interpret The Last Supper just as Leonardo da Vinci created The Last Supper with people who look like him.'

'I guess, unlike other girls, I never felt like I couldn't do what I wanted to do. I never felt that I had restrictions in front of me.'

41.
CAROLINE LUCAS
(1960–)

'We have enormous power if only we would recognise it.'

Claim to Fame	Country of Origin
Politician, writer	England

HER LEGACY

As the co-leader of the Green Party of England and Wales, Caroline Lucas is revamping what the face of modern British politics looks like. She may not 'fit in with the grey suits of Westminster', as she puts it, but she has strong stances on issues that matter – not just to her or to locals in her home town, but to countless women across the UK.

A passionate progressive activist who jumped headfirst into politics because she was frustrated by the lack of change within the traditional three-party system, she is proud to call herself a feminist, and is a tried-and-true champion for women's rights, environmental welfare, animal rights, and more. Known for her gentle, soft-spoken manner, Lucas fights hard battles while turning the stereotype of the angry protester on its head. An expert on climate change, nuclear disarmament, and international trade, she isn't shy about acknowledging the connection between social and environmental justice.

Lucas made history in 2010 when she was voted in as the UK's first Green Party MP. Since then she's held a number of parliamentary positions, but remains steadfast in her determination to do what's right, regardless of whether it makes her look 'likeable' or where it falls on party lines.

HER LIFE STORY

Lucas was born into a Conservative middle-class family in Malvern in 1960. She attended an independent girls' boarding school, and eventually went off to college at the University of Exeter. She also earned her PhD at Exeter with a women-centred thesis called 'Writing for Women: A Study of Woman as Reader in Elizabethan Romance'. It was in college that she began dabbling in activism, becoming involved with the Campaign for Nuclear Disarmament. After finishing her PhD, she worked for Oxfam as a press officer for a few years.

When she first read Jonathon Porritt's book *Seeing Green*, Lucas recalled feeling 'utterly inspired' to dedicate her life to the Green Party and its ideals of sustainability, justice, and equality. She wanted to help shake up the staid, traditional three-party system from within – and she was well aware that people might not appreciate or embrace her right out of the gate.

After joining the party in 1986, she held an assortment of positions (starting out as a press officer). When the party split into three distinct divisions in 1990 for the UK's various constituent parts, she ended up in the Green Party of England and Wales.

In 2008, Lucas became the first leader of the party, winning 92 per cent of the vote. She later spoke out about how she wanted to become a recognisable face of the party, because people correlate faces with the issues that matter to them: 'People don't really relate to abstract ideas, they relate more to the people who embody them.'

In the 2010 general election, Lucas became the Green Party's first MP for Brighton Pavilion, and in 2012 she stood down as party leader. She returned to leadership in 2016, and now serves as co-leader of the Green Party with Jonathan Bartley.

Staunchly devoted to nuclear disarmament and fighting climate change, Lucas acknowledges that her ethos can be hard for some people to grasp. Why? Because these massive, big-picture issues seem so overwhelming. Her aims are to break down the issues into smaller, more digestible chunks. For instance, to help fight climate change and Big Carbon, she tries to strengthen local communities and economies, and encourages people to buy locally and work close to home if possible. As she told *The Guardian* in 2009, 'So many of the changes we need to make for climate change are changes which... are usually pretty positive in themselves, and more likely to mean that we're fulfilled as human beings.'

A frequent contributor to *The Guardian*, *The Independent*, *The Telegraph*, and other publications, Lucas is not shy about vocalising her opposition to Brexit, her distaste for Donald Trump, why the UK must embrace Syrian refugees, and much more. She's also authored various books, and has been deeply, sometimes humorously, critical of the long-running 'boys' club' power hierarchies at play in the UK government. Proudly unwilling to set aside any of her beliefs in order to increase her electability, she once said Westminster was 'like Hogwarts on steroids' and noted its alarming lack of transparency. Fortunately, it looks like Lucas will remain a breath of fresh air for some time to come.

HER COOL CREDENTIALS

★ Lucas has won loads of awards and honours. For instance, she was recently voted 'environmental hero' over many other greats, such as the venerable David Attenborough; she was also dubbed a top 'eco-hero' by *The Guardian* in 2008. She won MP of the Year in 2014 for her work with underserved communities. In 2007, *The Observer* voted her Politician of the Year in their annual Ethical Awards.

★ She's an advisory board member of the think-tanks Protect the Local, Globally and Centre for a Social Europe.

★ Lucas is the vice president of the animal welfare, health and consumer and globalisation cross-party intergroups. She's also co-president of the Peace Initiatives Intergroup.

★ She once kicked off a debate in Parliament about the media's objectification of women. Lucas stirred up a mini furore when she wore a 'No More Page 3' T-shirt in Parliament during a debate about sexism. Page three has been a long-fought feminist battle, and dress code in Parliament is a big thing, so this was a small, but highly impressive act.

★ She's a vegetarian. (She tried being vegan once, but it didn't stick.)

QUOTABLES

'If you want action on climate change and not spin and rhetoric only the Greens can deliver.'

'I am scared. But I am driven by an enormous sense of urgency.'

'One of the most dangerous things is how people have begun to believe in their own lack of power. People do change and things do change.'

42.
KATHLEEN HANNA

(1968–)

'As a woman I was taught to always be hungry. Women are well acquainted with thirst. Yeah, we could eat just about anything. We'd even eat your hate up like love.'

Claim to Fame	Country of Origin
Singer, activist	USA

HER LEGACY

Kathleen Hanna is a punk-rock icon of the highest order. As the frontwoman of the all-girl punk band Bikini Kill, Hanna was one of the founders of riot grrrl, a small but massively influential 1990s feminist movement started in Olympia, Washington, and Washington, DC. Riot grrrl encouraged young women to pick up instruments; start bands; spill their darkest dreams, secrets, and fears in mini hand-produced magazines called fanzines; and stand up against violence, rape, and misogyny. Bikini Kill and other bands like Bratmobile, Excuse 17, and Heavens to Betsy urged young women to start a 'revolution girl-style now', and... they did. The influence of riot grrrl and Hanna herself is still felt today. As one indication, in 2015 the city of Boston named 9 April Riot Grrrl Day in honour of Hanna!

Hanna was born in Portland, Oregon, and her family moved around a lot when she was growing up. She was molested at age seven, her parents divorced, she was raped at fifteen, and she recalled her father being 'sexually inappropriate' and 'creepy' with her. Her feminist consciousness started to awaken around the time her mum began devouring books like Betty Friedan's *The Feminine Mystique* and volunteering at a domestic violence shelter, which Hanna later also did herself. Her mum also took Hanna when she was nine years old to a DC rally where Gloria Steinem spoke.

Hanna described herself as a teenage 'lush/burn-out' in high school, but she went on to study photography at Evergreen State College, where her activism began to take root. She supported herself by stripping and working in a photo lab, and on the side she played in a number of girl bands, performed spoken word poetry, opened an art gallery with a group of girlfriends, and joined forces with other local women to start zines such as *Revolution Girl Style Now* and *Bikini Kill*.

In 1990 she formed Bikini Kill (the band) with guitarist Billy Karren, bassist Kathi Wilcox, and drummer Tobi Vail. In both her zines and her songs, Hanna wrote candidly and evocatively about subjects usually considered way too taboo for women and girls to address publicly, like abortion, rape, domestic violence, and sexual harassment. She also encouraged women to band together, support one another, and take back punk rock from the enduring sexism of the gross guys in the scene. Her writing had a major effect on people, specifically women, and riot grrrl soon sprouted into a countrywide, face-to-face movement of girls meeting up to talk feminism – similar to the consciousness-raising groups of feminism's second wave – as well as to form bands, zines, and more.

Young women flocked to Hanna's shows, and she always encouraged them to stand right in front of the stage so they'd be 'protected' from any violent, grope-y, or obnoxious dudes. Still, Hanna recalled being insulted and worse by men who came to the band's live shows: 'It was super schizo to play shows where guys threw stuff at us, called us cunts and yelled "take it off" during our set, and then the next night perform for throngs of amazing girls singing along to every lyric and cheering after every song.'

Hanna began scrawling things like whore across her stomach as a way to fight back against some of the objectification she feared was happening as the band took off. As she explained once, 'I felt that if I wrote slut or whore or incest victim on my stomach, then I wouldn't just be silent… a lot of guys might be thinking this anyway when they look at my picture, so this would be like holding up a mirror to what they were thinking.'

In her writing, singing, and speaking, Hanna's words were raw but empowering, especially when she tackled the subject of how women are routinely denied pleasure, respect, and self-care.

After the riot grrrl scene fell apart following a painful blitz of sensationalistic, sexist media attention, Hanna went on to release a solo album under the name Julie Ruin. Later she fronted the popular electro-punk group Le Tigre. As a trailblazer in the feminist punk movement, Hanna is awesome because she embodies the multitudes women can possess: beautiful and aggressive, raw, vulnerable, and fearless, painfully honest but also self-protective.

HER COOL CREDENTIALS

★ Riot grrrl had a seriously lasting legacy on pop culture. Both the riot grrrl movement in general and Bikini Kill on its own influenced dozens of bands, artists, and writers, from Sleater-Kinney to Tavi Gevinson to Miranda July to the Gossip and Pussy Riot.

★ Hanna is passionate about pro-choice activism. She has spoken at rallies for Planned Parenthood, and in an interview with me for Salon.com, she was open about having an abortion at age fifteen: 'I worked at McDonald's, raised the money and did it. I'm really, really passionate about pro-choice, because I wouldn't be here talking to you right now if I'd had a kid at fifteen.'

★ She famously inspired Nirvana's crazy-huge-mega-popular 1991 hit 'Smells Like Teen Spirit' – a song that propelled the band into massive worldwide superstardom. Hanna spray-painted the words on Cobain's wall in reference to his girlfriend (and Hanna's bandmate) Tobi Vail's choice in deodorant at the time.

QUOTABLES

'I remember being nervous as a teen, numbed out and self-hating, but it was also such a great time for experimentation and figuring out what my aesthetic was, what kind of music I REALLY liked versus what was cool.'

'I felt like me and my friends were always running. From abusive dads, men on the streets, or even from mean things people would say to us that got stuck in our heads. But running meant we thought we were worth saving.'

'When I first started, I said things like, "It's really great to be beautiful and powerful and sexy," and I take a little bit of that back now. What I was saying was that you don't have to look a certain way or have a certain hairstyle to be a feminist; that just because a

girl wears lipstick that doesn't mean she's not a feminist. But now I realise that I wasn't really challenging the standard of beauty.'

[On speaking about regrets:] 'I wish all my zines didn't have, like, massive amounts of pictures of only white women in them... Let riot grrrl go; let's join groups that are more diverse. Instead of talking about diversity, let's seek out productive dialogue about race and about class.'

43
MARGARET CHO
NÉE MARGARET MORAN CHO (1968–)

'Why am I a feminist? I just am, and I haven't really questioned it.'

Claim to Fame	Country of Origin
Comedian	USA

HER LEGACY

Margaret Cho is a balls-to-the-wall feminist comedian known for her progressive causes as well as her nutty sense of humour. She has transcended all kinds of personal and professional hardships in her life, and her female fans idolise her for how she has used her painful experiences to speak out for others.

In addition to having a super-successful career in stand-up, Cho has acted, sung, directed, and written two popular books: one about her own life, *I'm the One That I Want*, and one about political and social issues, *I Have Chosen to Stay and Fight*. Her shows regularly sell out all over the world, and she's widely applauded for her candour when discussing deeply personal and sometimes traumatic issues like eating disorders, sexism, substance abuse, sexuality, and race. She's a passionate LGBT advocate, and on her website dubs herself a 'patron saint for outsiders', in part because, as she said, 'Some people were raised by wolves – I was raised by… drag queens!'

HER LIFE STORY

Born in San Francisco to Korean parents – who are often the subject of her barbs in many of her routines – Cho was raised by outsiders for the first seven years of her life after her mum followed her dad to Korea when he was deported shortly after Cho's birth. Cho got kicked out of a high school for poor grades, though she did later attend the San Francisco School of the Arts, a public high school, to pursue her interest in the performing arts. She started writing jokes when she was just fourteen and performing at the ripe old age (not!) of sixteen.

In the early 1990s, she moved to the acting and comedy mecca of Los Angeles, where she began gaining notoriety as a feisty (and sometimes crude) comedian. She performed three hundred shows in her first two years in LA. Her first big break was on a night-time talk show, *The Arsenio Hall Show*. She also appeared on a Bob Hope special, which was a massive professional boost especially since Hope was a huge comedy legend in his own right.

In 1994 Cho landed her own show on ABC called *All-American Girl*. But what should have felt like a victory instead turned into something of a nightmare. After producers bashed Cho's appearance – namely for her weight and the fullness of her face – Cho starved herself for weeks in anticipation of filming the show's first episode. This led to kidney failure. Cho recalled later: 'I was told by network executives that I had to lose weight. I was forced to. I went on a very rigid diet and became very sick because I wasn't eating at all.'

Even though she served as the show's executive producer, Cho felt powerless in the face of such intense Hollywood scrutiny, and she watched helplessly as the project she loved was compromised to the point of no return. 'For fear of being too "ethnic", the show got so watered down for television that by the end, it was completely lacking in the essence of what I am and what I do,' she said. Her health got worse when the show was cancelled in 1995 – Cho suffered from anorexia, depression, alcoholism, and drug abuse.

She made it through all those personal demons and has credited getting sober to helping pull her out of her depression: 'You get to the point in addiction where you come to a fork in the road. You have to stay with it and die or get better.' In addition to a new-found commitment to sobriety, she took up healthy practices like yoga, meditation, and service to others, and instead of relying on outsiders to tell her what to do in her work life, she became her own boss. After her one-woman show *I'm the One That I Want* blew up and got crazy successful, Cho launched her own production company with her agent Karen Taussig, Cho Taussig Productions.

Since then she has continued to be a one-woman force of nature, expanding her career into singing and directing. She has received many awards for both her comedy and her activist work in LGBT, feminist, and civil rights issues.

HER COOL CREDENTIALS

★ Cho has long been a passionate LGBT activist, but she has done a ton of other activist and philanthropic work. On Valentine's Day of 2004, Cho spoke at the Marriage Equality Rally at the California

State Capitol. Her speech can be heard in the documentary *Freedom to Marry*. She has been very vocal about her hatred of former president George W. Bush and has worked to campaign against racism and bullying. She also works with homeless people in San Francisco as a tribute to the late Robin Williams.

★ Her concert film, *I'm the One That I Want*, broke records for the most money grossed per print in movie history.

★ Though short-lived, *All-American Girl* did help bring Asian Americans into visibility in the US. It was the first prime-time network sitcom to feature an Asian American family.

QUOTABLES

'Before, [weight and body image] was an obsession; I was so terrified of my appetite and I lived in fear of it, so to not fear it anymore and to actually embrace it was really profound.'

'When we care for ourselves, these are acts of love. Do romantic things for yourself.'

'I don't want young girls to fear the word feminism, because they will desperately need it out in the world, and to fear what will help you, make you stronger, better, happier – it makes no sense.'

'I was scared to turn guys down because I didn't have the self-esteem when I was younger. I never said, "Maybe I should say no to this," because it felt like there may have been consequences. Now I know the only consequence is that I don't have to sleep with them.'

'I talk a lot about abortion and people get really freaked out. I'm not even making a political statement. I'm just talking about what happened! I have had them and I want to talk about them. I don't care what your views are toward abortion, I just think women should be talking about it.'

44.
QUEEN LATIFAH
NÉE DANA ELAINE OWENS (1970–)

'And I decided to love myself.'

Claim to Fame	Country of Origin
Rapper	USA

HER LEGACY

Queen Latifah – a.k.a. the First Lady of Hip Hop – certainly wasn't the first female rapper, but by age nineteen she became one of the few solo women rappers with a deal from a major record label. And she's far from being just a musician. Latifah has done it all and been successful at nearly all of it. She rose to fame as a teenager in the late eighties for her stellar rap game and her commitment to writing for and about strong black women. Since then, Latifah (who still calls herself 'Dana' in everyday life) has proven that her talents extend way beyond the mic. She has mastered the worlds of acting (film and TV); hosting her own talk show; running a record label; managing other musicians; modelling; writing; and more.

Latifah – dubbed 'Princess of the Posse' by her friends as a young woman – made her name on being the embodiment of a smart, powerful, and utterly self-possessed woman who called out misogyny when she saw it, even in her own community. One of the reasons her music is so powerful and relatable to women is its focus on self-esteem and overcoming issues like domestic violence and sexual harassment. For example, in her song 'U.N.I.T.Y.', she describes punching out a man who harasses her on the street, asking him, 'Who you calling a bitch?'

Though she has generally shied away from calling herself a feminist, Latifah has also said, 'I agree with a lot of those same principles. I want women to… set their goals and accomplish them… I want us to have self-confidence. I want us to have equal pay for equal work. I want us to have, most importantly, a voice.'

HER LIFE STORY

Queen Latifah credits her parents with instilling an indomitable foundation of self-confidence and self-love in her. Dana Owens came from humble beginnings in Newark, New Jersey. When she was eight, a Muslim cousin gave her the nickname Latifah, which means 'delicate' in Arabic. She was deemed academically gifted when she was in the second grade, and was a performer almost since day one: as a kid, she sang in the choir at the Baptist church she attended with her family. During her freshman year of high school, she took her passion for music to a new level, casually singing and rapping in women's restrooms and locker rooms. By junior year, Latifah formed a rap group called Ladies Fresh (later known as Flavor Unit) with two friends, Landy D and Tangy B, and the girls began playing shows in their area. The group's demo found its way into the hands of Fab 5 Freddy of the popular TV show *Yo! MTV Raps*. Soon, Latifah had a record deal with Tommy Boy; her feminist-tinged 1989 debut album, *All Hail the Queen*, was released when she was just nineteen.

As her career took off, she realised she had a knack not only for making her own music but also for helping others make theirs. She started producing other artists and took a shine to investing in businesses like a video store and a deli on the ground floor of her apartment building. In 1991 Latifah became CEO of her own Flavor Unit Records and Management Company in Jersey City. By late 1993, the company had signed seventeen rap acts, like Naughty by Nature.

Also in the nineties, Latifah moved over into the world of acting, making her silver-screen debut in Spike Lee's famous *Jungle Fever*. One of her best-known roles was on the TV show *Living Single*, with Kim Coles, Kim Fields, and Erika Alexander. The show focused on a group of six young African American friends living in a Brooklyn brownstone.

Since then Latifah has continued to expand her empire, launching her own talk show and becoming a spokesmodel for Covergirl Cosmetics. Though she's obviously super-successful now, she had to transcend some dark days. She was sexually abused as a child and has spoken openly about struggling with drugs after a particularly dark period in her life: her brother had died in a motorcycle accident, and she had almost lost a friend in a carjacking. 'Drinking a bunch of alcohol, numbing myself. Every day I would be faded, like a painting that's just not vibrant, whose edges are dull, I wasn't living my full life,' she recalled.

And though she is now a big-time champion of body acceptance, she is human – she has had to deal with insecurities, just like most women out there. Self-confidence is something she learned, she said – at least partly by following that famous adage, 'Fake it till you make it.' 'When I was around eighteen, I looked in the mirror and said, "You're either going to love yourself or hate yourself." And I decided to love myself. That changed a lot of things.'

HER COOL CREDENTIALS

★ Latifah's debut album, *All Hail the Queen*, sold more than one million copies. The single 'U.N.I.T.Y.' from her 1993 album, *Black Reign*, helped Latifah snag her first Grammy Award for Best Solo Rap Performance. She's a bona fide superstar in the acting world. Her performance in the musical film *Chicago* earned her an Oscar nomination for best supporting actor.

★ Iconic poet Maya Angelou asked Latifah to recite a poem at Michael Jackson's memorial service in July 2009.

QUOTABLES

*'I realised long ago that something
I did not want to be measured
by was my waistline.'*

'I don't find confidence to be something that if you find your confidence once, there it is forever. It has to be maintained. It's about being true to yourself. Being able to sleep at night and forgive yourself.'

'Nobody can wage a better assault on us than ourselves. It's about treating ourselves as if we were our own best friend.'

45.
ANI DIFRANCO

NÉE ANGELA MARIA DIFRANCO (1970–)

'I am a poster girl with no poster,
I am thirty-two flavours and then some.'

Claim to Fame	Country of Origin
Singer-songwriter	USA

HER LEGACY

To her legions of fans, Ani DiFranco is a self-made feminist superhero. She's known for her guitar-clangy protest music that focuses heavily on politics – think gun control, racism, and gentrification – and also on the broader female experience of sexism, racism, difficult relationships, self-esteem, and messed-up beauty standards. Her lyrics are a good encapsulation of the old feminist adage, 'The personal is political.' Full of biting wit and sharp commentary about, um, nearly everything, DiFranco also conveys a hopeful message of independence and self-reliance that her fans find inspiring. DiFranco may be contradictory in some ways, but she celebrates those contradictions.

HER LIFE STORY

DiFranco grew up in Buffalo, New York. Her parents weren't musical, but they were liberal and politically active, which intensely influenced DiFranco's activism (her Righteous Babe Foundation supports lots of causes like LGBT and abortion rights). She has been into music since she was little, and at age nine DiFranco started busking – playing for handouts in public spaces. Later her mum moved to Connecticut, but fifteen-year-old DiFranco had no desire to go along, so she stayed in Buffalo on her own, legally emancipating herself from her mum, and soon moved to New York City. She went on to launch her own record label, Righteous Babe Records, and throughout the nineties her star continued to rise, largely via word of mouth. She's an anti-corporate indie artist through and through, who dislikes doing interviews for fear of being misconstrued.

As DiFranco began to get more famous – her album *Dilate* debuted in 1996 at number eighty-seven on the Billboard chart, and *Living in Clip*, released in 1997, made it to number fifty-nine – most of her fans stuck by her, but some felt that she changed. She was always an outspoken bisexual, but some folks felt betrayed when she fell in love with a man, got married, and later had kids. DiFranco also began drawing more national attention from mainstream news outlets. This was good for her bottom line, and she began selling more units than many of the cheesy pop groups of the time – all while staying true to her commitment to remaining totally independent.

Though she's long been an icon for women, DiFranco is adamant about including men, too. When a fan yelled out, 'Men are pigs!' at one of her shows, she grew a little irritated, responding, 'It's really nice to be, like, in the groove of a girl vibe… but I so want there to be a feeling of inclusion. There's a lot of sad shit that goes down in my songs… but I never think of it as an us-vs-them situation.'

DiFranco's political activism has been a constant throughout her career. In 2009 she won the Woody Guthrie Award in honour of her work on social issues. She's supportive of anti-war movements and has performed and marched with protesters at the 2004 March for Women's Rights in Washington, DC. She also promotes causes she cares about at her concerts. As a resident of New Orleans, she raised funds for the city's revitalisation after Hurricane Katrina devastated the area in 2005.

She's not immune to controversy or the occasional misguided decision though. In 2013 DiFranco was called out for blatant racism when she announced she'd be hosting an artist retreat at a former slave plantation in Louisiana. Her fans, the press, and the social-media masses were appalled – and even more so when she posted an explanation that read as a flaky non-apology. She later apologised in what most perceived as a more genuine effort. It was a grave blunder on DiFranco's part, but it just shows how far every white woman needs to go when confronting her own racism. No one's feminism is perfect.

Despite all this, DiFranco keeps doing what she does best: writing soul-stirring, often educational songs and delivering them in a way all her own.

HER COOL CREDENTIALS

★ DiFranco has been ranked as one of the top twenty-five most influential musicians of the last twenty-five years.

★ In 2006, the National Organization for Women honoured DiFranco with a Woman of Courage award.

★ Despite being entirely independent in the music world, DiFranco has been nominated for multiple Grammy Awards, which usually tend to recognise big-name mainstream artists on corporate labels.

QUOTABLES

'My idea of feminism is self-determination, and it's very open-ended: every woman has the right to become herself, and do whatever she needs to do.'

'You'd think that the natural progression of feminism would be that, at this point, men and women would all identify as feminist, in our type of society, at least. And yet there was this big break in the chain.'

'Patriarchy is like the elephant in the room that we don't talk about, but how could it not affect the planet radically when it's the superstructure of human society?'

46.
ROXANE GAY

(1974–)

'If I am, indeed, a feminist, I am a rather bad one. I am a mess of contradictions.'

Claim to Fame	Country of Origin
Writer	USA

Roxane Gay is one of the most celebrated feminist writers to hit it big in the past few years – nay, make that the most celebrated feminist writer to hit it big in the past few years. She has been hailed as 'feminism's new rockstar', and her much-anticipated book of non-fiction essays, *Bad Feminist*, debuted on *The New York Times*' bestseller list at number thirteen. The book earned overwhelmingly positive reviews from, well, pretty much everyone and her mother, and as of this writing, it's the number one bestseller in Amazon's Feminist Theory section.

Though some folks assumed Gay was an overnight sensation, she had been writing and publishing for years before gaining widespread notice (she started writing on napkins when she was four!). It's pretty cool to see a woman in her late thirties suddenly earn such big-time accolades – especially a black, queer-identified woman from a mid-western town rather than a big literary hub like New York or Los Angeles.

One of the things that makes Gay so special to her legions of fans and followers is her unabashed commitment to the idea that feminists need not be 'perfect'. As a black woman, she didn't view herself as a feminist for a long time, because she didn't see many women like herself reflected in the movement, and she resisted categorisation. So she created a feminism that fitted her: one that embraces causes like anti-racism and equal pay, but that also allows her to dance shamelessly around to Robin Thicke's infamously skeevy hit 'Blurred Lines'. As she explains in *Bad Feminist*, 'If I am, indeed, a feminist, I am a rather bad one. I am a mess of contradictions.'

She's unapologetic about what she wants and doesn't give a whit if what she wants might detract from her 'feminist cred'. For instance, she wrote, 'I worry about dying alone, unmarried and childless because I spent so much time pursuing my career and accumulating degrees. This kind of keeps me up at night, but I pretend it doesn't because I am supposed to be evolved.' Gay's willingness to embrace all her contradictions has helped make it okay for other women to do the same. After all, what woman doesn't secretly chant along to the occasional derogatory rap lyric. Feminism and a love of low-brow pop culture, or wanting to have a baby, or enjoying sex with men aren't mutually exclusive, and Gay hammers this home.

HER LIFE STORY

Born to Haitian parents in Nebraska, Gay remembered having a pretty great childhood – until she was twelve, when she was gang-raped by a group of her boyfriend's friends from school. The attack had a profound impact on her, but she didn't tell her friends or family for years. She eventually wrote about the experience for the Rumpus, saying the rape made her a 'completely different person'. After the incident, Gay began gaining weight as a way to create a 'fortress' between what had happened to her and who she truly was inside; her body felt like one of the only forces she could control.

Gay's sexual assault haunted her for years, and she tackled it in her writing. She said, 'I don't think I would have a fraction of the fierceness in my writing if I hadn't had to endure that, and the aftermath.' When she was a teenager, her work drew notice from a teacher at her boarding school, who encouraged her to seek counselling to process the rape. Gay later said that teacher saved her life.

After undergraduate college (fun fact: she once dreamed of becoming a doctor!), Gay got a master's degree in creative writing and a PhD in rhetoric. But when she started sending out her work for publication, she got rejection after rejection. She even started a blog called I Have Become Accustomed to Rejection. Gay said she 'wasn't a great writer' back then, so she started to focus on improving her craft and began getting more publishing credits.

Gay has tackled nearly every kind of medium, from short stories to novels to deeply personal essays and pop culture criticism. Some of the common themes running throughout her work are gender issues, body image, privilege, sexual assault, and immigration politics. Many think she's at her best when combining the personal and the political, which she does masterfully and often. In addition to writing multiple books, Gay has contributed to *Best American Mystery Stories 2014*, *Best American Short Stories 2012*, *Tin House*, *The New York Times Book Review*, *The Los Angeles Times*, and *Salon*.

Though she's clearly an outspoken crusader for women's rights, Gay doesn't take herself too seriously, which is totally refreshing. She said her main goal in life is to 'not leave the world a worse place than I found it'.

HER COOL CREDENTIALS

★ Gay has worked tirelessly to help support and boost the profiles of other writers of colour. In 2012 she examined all the books reviewed by major publications the previous year and discovered that 90 per cent of those reviewed by *The New York Times* were written by white authors.

★ She regularly speaks out about the importance of educating young people about media literacy.

★ A Twitter powerhouse with nearly 100,000 followers as of this writing, Gay's tweets effervescently interweave all the divergent streams of awesomeness that make her... HER. For instance, she posts book recommendations alongside freak-outs about Channing Tatum's hotness, paired with sharp takedowns of racist mass media and internal debates about whether sending tipsy emails is a yay or a nay.

QUOTABLES

'I believe feminism is grounded in supporting the choices of women even if we wouldn't make certain choices for ourselves.'

'What goes unsaid is that women might be more ambitious and focused because we've never had a choice. We've had to fight to vote, to work outside the home, to work in environments free of sexual harassment, to attend the universities of our choice, and we've also had to prove ourselves over and over to receive any modicum of consideration.'

'Abandon the cultural myth that all female friendships must be bitchy, toxic, or competitive. This myth is like heels and purses – pretty but designed to SLOW women down.'

'Why do we have to roll out the red carpet and jump through hoops and do cartwheels to get men on board with feminism? It's ridiculous. I want men to grow up and learn they need to get over themselves.'

47.
CHIMAMANDA NGOZI ADICHIE

(1977–)

'Whoever says they're feminist is bloody feminist.'

Claim to Fame	Country of Origin
Author	Nigeria

HER LEGACY

Chimamanda Ngozi Adichie is a Nigerian author who rocketed to worldwide fame after delivering the super-inspiring TED talk 'We Should All Be Feminists' (later published as a bestselling essay). Adichie wasn't an overnight sensation, though – she had been writing acclaimed novels and winning prestigious awards for years. But after her speech went viral, it grabbed the attention of Beyoncé, who sampled it in her song 'Flawless'. After that, Adichie proceeded to blow up even more, becoming a legit household name in the feminist world.

The author's connection with her home country of Nigeria runs deep, and her work, much of which is set in Africa, explores themes of race, love, identity, war, politics, and African postcolonial life. Though Adichie has lived in America off and on for years, she's said she feels most like herself in Nigeria. She's a loud and proud feminist, to be sure, but her feminism is not primarily rooted in the concerns of Western women (who, ironically, have embraced many of her empowering words as catchphrases of their own).

One of the coolest things about Adichie is that she doesn't just critique the way patriarchal society harms women; she also discusses how it affects boys, calling masculinity a 'small, hard cage'. She's been instrumental in broadening the face of mainstream feminism to a wider swath of people and introducing an often-neglected international element to mainstream feminism.

HER LIFE STORY

Adichie was born the fifth of six children to an Igbo family in Enugu, Nigeria, in 1977. The Igbo are an indigenous people in south-eastern Nigeria with a rich history of unique customs. Many Igbo are farmers, and Igbo women are often active in politics and trade. It's still a largely patriarchal society, however, where men are expected to run the show while women remain subservient and docile.

Adichie's parents both worked at the University of Nigeria (Adichie's mum, Grace Ifeoma, was actually the university's first female registrar). As a child, Adichie could be rebellious in her own way. She recalled a kindergarten teacher writing in a report that the five-year-old Adichie was 'brilliant, but she refuses to do any work when she's annoyed'. She was inspired, however, by watching her parents break gender roles in their own ways. For example, she was super-proud of her mum's dedication to her career, and her father's gentle, kind demeanour.

Adichie studied medicine in Nigeria with the intention of eventually becoming a psychiatrist. Though her passion was writing (she started out writing poetry), she didn't think she could support herself with that, and she envisioned incorporating her psychiatric clients' experiences into her stories. But Adichie shifted gears after moving to America at age nineteen and attending Philadelphia's Drexel University on scholarship. Leaving her country to study in the States heavily shaped her views on identity and race, which has influenced her work in turn. She's said she didn't necessarily think of herself as black until she left Nigeria, and that she 'became fascinated by the many permutations of race, especially of blackness' after relocating to America.

At college in the States, she began studying communications, graduating summa cum laude (or with the highest honour) with a communication and political science degree from Eastern Connecticut State University. It was during Adichie's senior year at Eastern that she began writing her award-winning first novel, *Purple Hibiscus*, published in 2003. Next up: a master's degree in creative writing at Baltimore's Johns Hopkins University before publishing more books, which were also met with well-deserved praise.

The same year (2008) she earned an MA in African studies from Yale University, Adichie won a prestigious MacArthur Genius Grant. After Beyoncé sampled Adichie's speech 'We Should All Be Feminists' in 'Flawless', the writer became more popular than ever and a revered face of modern feminism. These days, she splits her time between Maryland and Nigeria. She's still actively writing and speaking out against injustice, and occasionally ruffling feathers (in 2017 she attracted backlash when she implied, in a TV news interview, that there is a difference between transgender women and, well, women who aren't transgender).

HER COOL CREDENTIALS

★ Adichie's TED speech 'We Should All Be Feminists' has been viewed on YouTube more than four million times since it was posted in 2013.

★ Adichie isn't afraid to rock the boat. In 2016, she called out Beyoncé's brand of feminism for not being like her own, saying B's feminism was 'the kind that… gives quite a lot of space to the necessity of men… I don't think that women should relate everything they do to men.'

★ Her work has been translated into thirty languages, and she's won numerous prizes and awards for her writing.

QUOTABLES

'Feminism is, of course, part of human rights in general – but to choose to use the vague expression human rights is to deny the specific and particular problem of gender.'

'This idea of feminism as a party to which only a select few people get to come: this is why so many women, particularly women of colour, feel alienated from mainstream Western academic feminism.'

'I think we need to stop giving men cookies for doing what they should do.'

48.
BEYONCÉ

NÉE BEYONCÉ GISELLE KNOWLES (1981–)

'My goal was independence.'

Claim to Fame	Country of Origin
Singer	USA

HER LEGACY

When Beyoncé orders her fans to 'bow down, bitches', they'd better listen. And they do. Even back in her early days with the all-girl, sixty-million-record-selling super-group Destiny's Child, Queen Bey was all about promoting female empowerment. The group's 1999 hit song 'Independent Women, Pt. 1' was an anthem devoted to women stepping up and doing life for themselves, with crazy-catchy lyrics.

Though she started dabbling in feminist ideas back in her early days, from 2013 onward Beyoncé promoted women's equality, using her massive platform to urge women both younger and older to do, say, and accomplish whatever the hell they want. She is one of a handful of mainstream musical superstars that have boldly proclaimed themselves modern-day feminists. In fact, the stage during her 2014 performance at the MTV Video Music Awards bore a massive neon sign that simply read FEMINIST in towering block letters.

Beyoncé's brand of feminism has been picked apart by pundits who've critiqued her for her sexy image, her supposed hyper-commercialisation, and the tour she did called Mrs. Carter (apparently it's not okay for women to take their husbands' names anymore, even in a cheeky fashion). All the criticism is expected, but not exactly fair.

Do white mega-stars who call themselves feminists get the same level of examination with a fine-tooth comb? In any case, there's no question that having a bona fide 'pop princess' using her massive scope to promote feminist ideals to young girls is something to be applauded.

HER LIFE STORY

Beyoncé grew up in Houston, Texas, and was bitten with the performance bug early. As a little girl she began singing in – and winning – talent shows. When she was eleven, she and her childhood friend LaTavia Roberson joined forces with Kelly Rowland and LeToya Luckett to form the girl group that would eventually call itself Destiny's Child (Bey's dad was their manager). After signing with Columbia Records in 1997, the group became enormously popular, landing number one hits like 'Bills Bills Bills' and 'Say My Name'. While still technically with DC, Beyoncé released her hugely successful first solo album in 2003, *Dangerously in Love* (which won five Grammys!), and Destiny's Child officially disbanded two years later.

Since then Beyoncé has only amassed more popularity and love from the world. She performed at President Barack Obama's inaugural ball in 2009 and at his second inauguration in 2013. She began dating rapper Jay-Z around 2000, but the duo kept their romance on the down low, eventually marrying in 2008. In 2011 she made *Forbes*' top ten list of entertainment's highest-earning women, and by 2013 she had won seventeen Grammys.

In 2013 the thirty-two-year-old superwoman penned a powerful essay, 'Gender Equality Is a Myth' for Maria Shriver's website. In the piece, the singer noted that we must encourage both men and women to embrace women's rights. 'We have to teach our boys the rules of equality and respect, so that as they grow up, gender equality becomes a natural way of life. And we have to teach our girls that they can reach as high as humanly possible.'

And she should know. Beyoncé is a formidable power player on the world stage. Aside from winning twenty Grammys and selling more than seventy-five million records as a solo performer, Beyoncé is one of the top-selling musical artists of all time. She was featured in *Time* magazine's list of the most influential people in both 2013 and 2014. And lest you think she's struggling for money (uh, not that you would), her net worth is reported to be more than $250 million.

HER COOL CREDENTIALS

★ In 2006 Beyoncé was nominated for a Golden Globe Award for her performance in the hit film *Dreamgirls*.

★ In 2011 the singer created an awesome remix of her ultra-catchy song 'Move Your Body' – as well as a music video – for First Lady Michelle Obama's Let's Move! campaign to help fight childhood obesity.

★ In her 2013 hit song 'Flawless', Beyoncé made a powerful statement by sampling lines from a TEDxEuston talk by feminist Nigerian author Chimamanda Ngozi Adichie.

★ After Hurricane Katrina levelled New Orleans in 2005, Beyoncé and her buddy/former bandmate Kelly Rowland founded the Survivor Foundation. The organisation provided transitional housing for victims in the Houston area, and Beyoncé reportedly contributed an initial $250,000. She raised more than $1 million for husband Jay-Z's Shawn Carter Foundation, which helps send low-income kids to college. Beyoncé has also worked in partnership with Feeding America to help give meals to food banks across the US.

QUOTABLES

*'I do believe in equality. Why do you have to
choose what type of woman you are?'*

*'Your self-worth is determined by you. You don't have
to depend on someone telling you who you are.'*

*'The reality is: sometimes you lose. And you're never too good to lose.
You're never too big to lose. You're never too smart to lose. It happens.'*

'Power's not given to you. You have to take it.'

*'It is so liberating to really know what I want, what truly
makes me happy, what I will not tolerate. I have learned
that it is no one else's job to take care of me but me.'*

*'I truly believe that women should be financially independent
from their men. And let's face it, money gives men the power to
run the show. It gives men the power to define value. They define
what's sexy. And men define what's feminine. It's ridiculous.'*

49.
TAVI GEVINSON

(1996–)

'I want [feminism] to not have this stigma around it. For it to be more inclusive… For someone to send out a newsletter to all straight adolescent boys that porn isn't accurate.'

Claim to Fame	Country of Origin
Writer, editor	USA

HER LEGACY

Tavi G. got her start in 2008 as a normal – albeit preternaturally cool and savvy – pre-teen fashion blogger posting about her outfits from her bedroom in suburban Illinois. Just six years later, she was a magazine founder, a Broadway star, an acclaimed writer, and an editor-in-chief. What makes Gevinson so great is that she doesn't see a division between fashion and feminism, and she resents the idea that fashion is 'stupid' while feminism is 'smart'. The intuitive way she managed to blend the two interests sparked her biggest achievement to date: being a hero to teenage girls everywhere. It's a role she has held down since she was in high school, if not earlier.

HER LIFE STORY

Gevinson started a fashion blog, Style Rookie, when she was all of eleven years old. The blog started out small with a few followers, but eventually it blew up, and she started getting invited to major fashion shows all over the world. Though the tween was lavished with admiration from the fashion industry for her impeccably funky style and exhaustive knowledge of haute couture, not everyone took her seriously because of her age.

Citing safety concerns, adults pooh-poohed the idea of young bloggers like Gevinson chronicling their lives and posting photos of themselves on the Internet. They also shamed Gevinson's parents for allowing her to leave school to attend fashion shows. Perhaps most upsettingly, critics started questioning whether she was the age she said she was. Anne Slowey of *Elle* expressed doubts, saying, 'She's either a tween savant or she's got a Tavi team.' *New York* magazine's blog The Cut agreed, questioning her ability to write and maintain her blog on her own: 'We're not sure if a twelve-year-old is actually doing all this or if she's getting some help from a mum or older sister… We're also not sure if we think she's the best thing since the Olsen twins.' And *The Economist* wondered whether she was just 'a little monster'. Naturally the criticism got to her – her dad recalls her waking up in the middle of the night crying. But Gevinson learned to brush off the negative attention, saying, 'A lot of people on the Internet have a problem with a young person doing well. I felt like, there were people… [at fashion week] because of their name, their money or their family, and I didn't have any of those things.' She certainly showed all the naysayers, as her career just kept getting bigger and better.

When Gevinson was fifteen, she decided to retire from fashion-exclusive content and launched *Rookie*, a web magazine covering a range of subjects for teenage girls. The site was intended as a sort of anti-*Seventeen*: smart, sharp, confessional, and direct, all about self-expression and individuality. Gevinson wanted to – and did – address adolescent girls as mature humans instead of as clueless little girl-children. The site features some style spreads, but Gevinson's mission is broader in scope. As she told *Bitch* magazine, 'I want there to be a place where women can… care about fashion, and even be super girly, and it doesn't necessarily mean that you're not also smart or confident or strong.' She also wanted to democratise fashion and let girls know that there's no one way to be or look cool: 'It's mostly about just letting the audience know that they are already smart enough, cool enough.'

Written mostly by teens, *Rookie* immediately stood out from every other teen-targeted magazine out there. It's most similar to *Sassy*, a beloved cult magazine published by media icon Jane Pratt from 1988 through to 1994. *Rookie* was launched as a partnership with Pratt, but Gevinson later took back full ownership of the site. With new content posted five times a week, three times per day, Rookie experienced phenomenal success by covering everything from pop culture to deeply personal essays. Celebrities like Lena Dunham, Jon Hamm, and David Sedaris contribute from time to time.

Today Gevinson lives in New York City and is expanding her work to include Broadway shows, movie acting, and singing. Though her current style is more about 'feeling comfortable' than high-fashion edginess, she's still a feminist style icon for young women. She has shown, all on her own, that smart girls with something to say can take over the media – perhaps even the world.

HER COOL CREDENTIALS

★ Gevinson made *Forbes'* 30 Under 30 in Media list in 2011 and 2012. *Time* magazine dubbed her one of the twenty-five most influential teens of 2014.

★ She was *Harper's Bazaar's* youngest contributor ever when she began writing a column for the magazine at age thirteen. Some people in the fashion industry questioned the hire. *Elle's* Anne Slowey said this choice 'felt a bit gimmicky'.

★ Ira Glass of *This American Life* is one of her mentors. He's the husband of *Rookie's* editorial director Anaheed Alani.

★ Lady Gaga once dubbed Gevinson 'the future of journalism'.

QUOTABLES

'I've heard readers say, "I feel like I'm not cool enough for Rookie*", and I'm like, "Really?" I just hate that, [being exclusionary is] not what I'm trying to do.'*

'I was finally just like, "Once I accept that I'll never be happy with how I look – whether I actually look good or not – then [I could] be free, and focus on the parts of life that are more fulfilling."'

'Look, I'm just trying to put something good out into the world, it's not going to solve patriarchy forever and ever.'

'I wanted to start a website for teenage girls that was not kind of this one-dimensional strong character empowerment thing... girls then think that to be feminists, they have to live up to being perfectly consistent in their beliefs, never being insecure, never having doubts, having all the answers. And this is not true.'

50.
MALALA YOUSAFZAI
(1997–)

'They only shot a body but they cannot shoot my dreams.'

Claim to Fame	Country of Origin
Activist	Pakistan

HER LEGACY

Malala Yousafzai started her activist work in 2009 as an eleven-year-old Pakistani blogger for BBC Urdu. She wrote anonymously about the importance of girls getting an education. If she was ever outed, she would have suffered intense punishment by the Taliban, the powerful Islamic organisation widely known for terrorist attacks, targeted killings, and violent, repressive treatment of women. Danger be damned, Yousafzai chose to risk her life by continuing to speak out about the shoddy conditions for girls in her country – at times the Taliban outright banned girls from going to school at all.

In 2012 Yousafzai rocketed to international stardom, but unfortunately not because of the important stuff she brought to light in her blog. Nope, her sudden fame was triggered by a life-shattering event that happened after she was outed as the BBC blogger in December 2009, which brought her to the Taliban's attention. In October 2012, Yousafzai was on a school bus in her hometown of Swat Valley when some men stopped the bus. A gunman boarded and asked for Yousafzai by name before firing three shots into her head and neck. 'I spoke for education and it means that I'm speaking against the Taliban,' she later said about the motive for the assassination attempt.

Yousafzai was in critical condition after the shooting, but eventually – and amazingly – she recovered with an even more profound passion for human rights and the importance of education for girls. In January 2013 she was released from the British hospital where she was taken for treatment following the attack. She has been a resident of Birmingham ever since.

HER LIFE STORY

Growing up, Yousafzai was educated largely by her father, Ziauddin Yousafzai, a Pakistani diplomat and education activist who ran a number of schools in their area. He was a great role model and a source of inspiration for his daughter, and he has spoken at length about his

immense pride in her work. Like his daughter, he was an anti-Taliban activist and was also an assassination target.

Yousafzai herself had drawn the Taliban's attention long before the group carried out its plans to shoot her on the school bus. The Taliban had been sending her death threats for some time. It even stalked her on Facebook. Unfortunately, she's still a target today, though she no longer lives in Pakistan.

In addition to winning the Nobel Peace Prize in October 2014, Yousafzai has been honoured with a number of awards for her humanitarian work, including the Sakharov Prize for Freedom of Thought from the European Parliament, the National Youth Peace Prize, the Anne Frank Award for Moral Courage, and the Mother Teresa Award for Social Justice. She has donated much of her money to rebuild schools and help provide access to education for children all around the world.

Pakistani Prime Minister Nawaz Sharif has described her as the 'pride of Pakistan, she has made her countrymen proud. Her achievement is unparalleled and unequalled. Girls and boys of the world should take lead from her struggle and commitment.' Girls and women everywhere look up to Yousafzai as a symbol of perseverance and fighting for what she believes in.

HER COOL CREDENTIALS

★ At seventeen, Yousafzai was the youngest person ever – as well as the first Pakistani – to receive the Nobel Peace Prize. She was chosen, along with children's rights activist Kailash Satyarthi, because of their 'struggle against the oppression of children and young people, and for the right of all children to education,' the Norwegian Nobel Committee said.

★ The United Nations officially made 12 July Malala Day, in honour of Yousafzai's bravery.

★ In 2012 she was named *Time* magazine's Person of the Year.

★ In a particularly persuasive speech in 2013, Yousafzai convinced the UN to commit to Millennium Development Goal 2, which says that 'by 2015, children everywhere, boys and girls alike, will be able to complete a full course of primary schooling'. According to the Millennium Development Goals Report, primary school net enrolment in developing regions has reached 91 per cent in 2015 compared to the 83 per cent in 2000.

★ In 2013 she published a bestselling autobiography, *I Am Malala: The Girl Who Stood Up for Education and Was Shot by the Taliban*, authored with British writer Christina Lamb.

QUOTABLES

'When the whole world is silent, even one voice becomes powerful.'

'I don't even hate the Talib who shot me. Even if there is a gun in my hand and he stands in front of me, I would not shoot him.'

'I have the right of education. I have the right to play. I have the right to sing. I have the right to talk. I have the right to go to market. I have the right to speak up.'

'Why shall I wait for someone else? Why shall I be looking to the government, to the army, that they would help us… for them to help me? Why don't I raise my voice? Why don't we speak up for our rights?'

BIBLIOGRAPHY

Mary Wollstonecraft

Falco, Maria J. *Feminist Interpretations of Mary Wollstonecraft*. State College, Pennsylvania: Penn State Press, 2010.

James, Henry Rosher. *Mary Wollstonecraft: A Sketch*. (1932). London: Oxford University, 2008.

Jump, Harriet Devine. *Mary Wollstonecraft and the Critics, 1788–2001*. Volume 1. London/New York: Routledge, 2003.

Laird, Susan. *Mary Wollstonecraft*. London: Bloomsbury, 2014.

Lewis, Jone Johnson. 'Mary Wollstonecraft Legacy'. March 25, 2017. <http://womenshistory.about.com/od/wollstonecraft/a/wollstonecraft-legacy.htm>.

'Mary Wollstonecraft'. <https://humanism.org.uk/humanism/the-humanist-tradition/enlightenment/mary-wollstonecraft/>.

Nehring, Cristina. '"Romantic Outlaws," About the Lives of Mary Wollstonecraft and Mary Shelley'. May 8, 2015. <http://www.nytimes.com/2015/05/10/books/review/romantic-outlaws-about-the-lives-of-mary-wollstonecraft-and-mary-shelley.html>.

Shukla, Bhaskar A. *Feminism: From Mary Wollstonecraft To Betty Friedan*. New Delhi: Sarup and Sons, 2007.

Simkin, John. 'Mary Wollstonecraft'. September, 1997. <http://spartacus-educational.com/Wwollstonecraft.htm>.

Todd, Janet. 'Mary Wollstonecraft: A "Speculative and Dissenting Spirit."' February 17, 2011. <http://www.bbc.co.uk/history/british/empire_seapower/wollstonecraft_01.shtml>.

Tomalin, Claire. *The Life and Death of Mary Wollstonecraft*. London: Penguin, 2004.

Tomaselli, Sylvana. 'Mary Wollstonecraft'. August 19, 2016. <http://plato.stanford.edu/entries/wollstonecraft/>.

Waters, Mary A. '"The First of a New Genus:" Mary Wollstonecraft as a Literary Critic and Mentor to Mary Hays'. Spring 2004. <http://www.jstor.org/stable/25098067>.

Wollstonecraft, Mary. *A Vindication of the Rights of Men: in a Letter to the Right Honourable Edmund Burke*. London: J. Johnson, 1790. <http://oll.libertyfund.org/titles/991>.

Wollstonecraft, Mary. *A Vindication of the Rights of Women: with Strictures on Political and Moral Subjects*. Boston: Thomas and Andrews, 1792. <http://www.bartleby.com/144/>.

'Writer Mary Wollstonecraft Marries William Godwin'. 2009. <http://www.history.com/this-day-in-history/writer-mary-wollstonecraft-marries-william-godwin>.

Sojourner Truth

Horn, Geoffrey M. *Sojourner Truth: Speaking Up for Freedom*. Hove/New York: Crabtree Publishing Company, 2009.

Lewis, Jone Johnson. 'Sojourner Truth'. December 26, 2016. <http://womenshistory.about.com/od/sojournertruth/a/sojourner_truth_bio.htm>.

'Recruiting African American soldiers for the Union Army'. <http://www.frederick-douglass-heritage.org/african-american-civil-war/>.

Reese, Lyn. 'Women's Rights From Past To Present Primary Source Lessons'. <http://www.womeninworldhistory.com/sample-191.html>.

Richardson, Elaine B., and Ronald L. Jackson II. *African American Rhetoric(s): Interdisciplinary Perspectives*. Illinois: Southern Illinois University Press, 2007.

'Sojourner's Words and Music'. <http://sojournertruthmemorial.org/her-words/>.

'Sojourner Truth (1797-1883)'. <https://www.nwhm.org/education-resources/biography/biographies/sojourner-truth/>.

'Sojourner Truth'. <http://www.pbs.org/thisfarbyfaith/people/sojourner_truth.html>.

'Sojourner Truth: Ain't I a Woman?'. 2009. <http://www.history.com/topics/black-history/sojourner-truth>.

'Soujourner Truth's "Ain't I a Woman?"'. <http://www.nolo.com/legal-encyclopedia/content/truth-woman-speech.html>.

'Sojourner Truth: Biography'. <http://www.biography.com/people/sojourner-truth-9511284>.

'Sojourner Truth Biography'. <http://www.notablebiographies.com/St-Tr/Truth-Sojourner.html>.

Stowe, Harriet Beecher. 'Sojourner Truth, the Libyan Sibyl'. April 1863. <http://www.theatlantic.com/magazine/archive/1863/04/sojourner-truth-the-libyan-sibyl/308775/>.

'Who Was Sojourner Truth?'. <http://www.sojournertruthacademy.org/our- mission>.

'Women Suffrage Timeline (1840-1920)'. <https://www.nwhm.org/education-resources/history/woman-suffrage-timeline>.

Emmeline Pankhurst

Gerber, William. *The Deepest Questions You Can Ask about God*. Atlanta: Rodopi, 1995. <http://bit.ly/2nNailj>.

'Emmeline Pankhurst'. <http://www.biography.com/people/emmeline-pankhurst-9432764>.

'Emmeline Pankhurst memorial'. <https://www.royalparks.org.uk/parks/victoria-tower-gardens/things-to-see-and-do/emmeline-pankhurst-memorial>.

'From the archives: Suffragettes on hunger strike'. May 3, 2013. <https://www.theguardian.com/theguardian/from-the-archive-blog/2013/may/03/suffragette-force-feeding-1913>.

'Great speeches of the 20th century: Emmeline Pankhurst's freedom or death'. April 27, 2007. <https://www.theguardian.com/theguardian/2007/apr/27/greatspeeches>.

Pankhurst, Emmeline. *Suffragette: My Own Story*. London: Hesperus Press Ltd. 2016. <http://www.bbc.co.uk/history/historic_figures/pankhurst_emmeline.shtml>.

'The real suffragettes: Emmeline Pankhurst, Emily Davison and Edith New'. October 2, 2015. <http://www.theweek.co.uk/65535/the-real-suffragettes-emmeline-pankhurst-emily-davison-and-edith-new>.

Marie Curie

Cooper-White, Macrina. 'Marie Curie Mixed Science and Sex, and 9 Other Surprising Facts About Famous Chemist'. November 7, 2013. <http://www.huffingtonpost.com/2013/11/07/10-marie-curie-facts_n_4018373.html>.

Curie, Marie. *Pierre Curie*. New York: Macmillan, 1923.

'Einstein's Letter to Marie Curie: Ignore the Haters'. December 8, 2014. <http://www.biography.com/news/albert-einstein-letter-to-marie-curie>.

E., Sarah, and Nyssa Spector. 'Discovery of Radioactivity'. February 12, 2015. <http://chemwiki.ucdavis.edu/Physical_Chemistry/Nuclear_Chemistry/Radioactivity/Discovery_of_Radioactivity>.

Long, Tony. 'Jan. 23, 1911: Science Academy Tells Marie Curie, "Non"'. January 23, 2014. <http://www.wired.com/2012/01/jan-23-1911-marie-curie>.

'Marie Curie – Biographical'. <http://www.nobelprize.org/nobel_prizes/physics/laureates/1903/marie-curie-bio.html>.

'Marie Curie Enshrined in Pantheon'. April 21, 1995. <http://www.nytimes.com/1995/04/21/world/marie-curie-enshrined-in-pantheon.html>.

'Marie Curie: Her Story in Brief'. <http://history.aip.org/history/exhibits/curie/brief/index.html >.

'Marie Curie – Nobel Lecture: Radium and the New Concepts in Chemistry'. <http://www.nobelprize.org/nobel_prizes/chemistry/laureates/1911/marie-curie-lecture.html>.

'Marie Curie – Photo Gallery'. <http://www.nobelprize.org/nobel_prizes/physics/laureates/1903/marie-curie-photo.html>.

'Marie Curie'. September 8, 2014. <http://www.famousscientists.org/marie-curie>.

'Marie Curie's Struggle against Sexism and Xenophobia'. May 1, 2011. <http://fresnoalliance.com/wordpress/?p=2910>.

'Marie Curie: Biography'. <http://www.biography.com/people/marie-curie-9263538>.

'Marie Sklodowska Curie'. <http://www.lchr.org/a/40/b4/sp_marie_curie.htm>.

Mould, R. F. 'Pierre Curie, 1859-1906'. April 14, 2007. <http://www.ncbi.nlm.nih.gov/pmc/articles/PMC1891197/>.

Pycior, Stanley W. 'Marie Skłodowska Curie and Albert Einstein: A Professional And Personal Relationship'. <http://www.jstor.org/stable/25779116>.

'Science Quotes by Marie Curie'. <http://todayinsci.com/C/Curie_Marie/CurieMarie-Quotations.htm>.

Steinke, Ann E. *Marie Curie and the Discovery of Radium*. New York: Barron's Educational Series, 1987.

Quinn, Susan. 'A Test of Courage: Marie Curie and the 1911 Nobel Prize'. 2011. <http://www.clinchem.org/content/57/4/653.full.pdf>.

Valiunas, Algis. 'The Marvelous Marie Curie'. Fall 2012. <http://www.thenewatlantis.com/publications/the-marvelous-marie-curie>.

Williams, Wendy M., and Ceci, Stephen J. 'When Scientists Choose Motherhood'. March-April 2012. <http://www.americanscientist.org/issues/pub/when-scientists-choose-motherhood>.

Virginia Woolf

Crum, Maddie. 'Why Virginia Woolf Should Be Your Feminist Role Model'. <http://www.huffingtonpost.com/2015/01/25/virginia-woolf-feminist_n_6534258.html>.

Epstein, Julia. 'Virginia Woolf and her family's secret life'. May 14, 1989. <https://www.washingtonpost.com/archive/entertainment/books/1989/05/14/virginia-woolf-and-her-familys-secret-life/be2932af-3db9-4274-bf4a-7ad0f20e9b59/?utm_term=.bf7be9c1285d>

Frizzelle, Christopher. 'The day Virginia Woolf brought her mom back to life'. May 6, 2015. <http://lithub.com/the-day-virginia-woolf-brought-her-mom-back-to-life/>.

Fromm, Harold. 'Virginia Woolf: Art and Sexuality'. Summer 1979. <http://www.vqronline.org/essay/virginia-woolf-art-and-sexuality>.

Hiebert, Paul. '59 Things You Didn't Know About Virginia Woolf'. January 25, 2011. <http://flavorwire.com/143610/59-things-you-didnt-know-about-virginia-woolf/4>.

'Hogarth'. <http://crownpublishing.com/archives/imprint/hogarth>.

'Julia Jackson'. <http://www.metmuseum.org/art/collection/search/267426>.

'Leslie Stephen'. <http://www.iep.utm.edu/stephen/>.

Mancini, Mark. '20 Virginia Woolf Quotes to Celebrate Her Birthday'. January 25, 2017. <http://mentalfloss.com/article/74231/20-virginia-woolf-quotes-celebrate-her-birthday>.

Pryor, William (edited by). *Virginia Woolf & the Raverats: A Different Sort of Friendship*. Clear Books. 2003. <http://bit.ly/2omTCVr >.

Scott, Carrie. 'Virginia Woolf's Literary Legacy'. Jan 24, 2014. <https://blog.bookstellyouwhy.com/virginia-woolf-literary-legacy>.

Sellers, Susan (edited by). *The Cambridge Companion to Virginia Woolf*. Cambridge: Cambridge University Press. 2010. <http://bit.ly/2opp9Yu>.

'Virginia Woolf'. <https://www.britannica.com/biography/Virginia-Woolf>

Woolf, Virginia. *A Room of One's Own*. <http://gutenberg.net.au/ebooks02/0200791.txt>

'Virginia Woolf Biography'. < http://www.biographyonline.net/writers/virginia-woolf.html>.

'Virginia Woolf: childhood'. <http://www.shmoop.com/virginia-woolf/childhood.html >.
'Woolf in the World: A Pen and a Press of Her Own'. <http://www.smith.edu/libraries/libs/rarebook/exhibitions/penandpress/case14b.htm>.

Amy Jacques Garvey
'Amy Jacques Garvey'. August 21, 2015. <http://www.blackhistorypages.net/pages/agarvey.php>.
'Amy Jacques Garvey'. <http://sta.uwi.edu/igds/20thanniversary/amyjacquesgarvey.asp>.
Espiritu, Allison. 'Garvey, Amy Jacques (1896-1973)'. <http://www.blackpast.org/aah/garvey-amy-jacques-1896-1973>.
Garvey, Amy Euphemia Jacques. 'Women As Leaders'. October 25, 1925. <http://www.historyisaweapon.com/defcon1/garveywomenasleaders.html>.
Hill, Robert A. *The Marcus Garvey and Universal Negro Improvement Association Papers*. Volume II: August 1919-August 1920. Los Angeles: University of California Press, 1983.
Johnson, Joan. 'In Her Own Right: Amy Jacques Garvey'. August 2003. < https://www.h-net.org/reviews/showpdf.php?id=8053>.
Kuryla, Peter. 'Pan-Africanism'. <http://www.britannica.com/topic/Pan-Africanism>.
'People & Events: Amy Jacques, 1896-1973'. <http:// www.pbs.org/wgbh//amex/garvey/peopleevents/p_jacques.html>.
Taylor, Ula Y. *The Veiled Garvey: The Life and times of Amy Jacques Garvey*. Chapel Hill: University of North Carolina Press, 2002.
Van Leeuwen, David. 'Marcus Garvey and the Universal Negro Improvement Association'. National Humanities Centre. 2000. <http://nationalhumanitiescenter.org/tserve/twenty/tkeyinfo/garvey.htm>.

Frida Kahlo
Alcántara, Isabel, and Sandra Egnolff. *Frida Kahlo and Diego Rivera*. Munich: Prestel, 1999.
Armstrong, Kate. 'Three days with Frida Kahlo and Diego Rivera in Mexico City'. January 21, 2014. <http://www.bbc.com/travel/story/20131230-three-days-with-frida-kahlo-and-diego-rivera-in-mexico-city>.
'Artist Frida Kahlo born'. <http://jwa.org/thisweek/jul/06/1907/frida-kahlo>.
Berne, Emma Carlson. *Frida Kahlo: Mexican Artist*. Edina: ABDO Publishing Company, 2010.
'Chronology'. <http://www.fridakahlofans.com/chronologyenglish.html>.
Collins, Amy Fine. 'Diary Of A Mad Artist'. September 3, 2013. <http://www.vanityfair.com/culture/1995/09/frida-kahlo-diego-rivera-art-diary>.
'Frida and Diego'. <http://www.nytimes.com/fodors/top/features/travel/destinations/mexico/mexicocity/fdrs_feat_101_9.html?n=Top/Features/Travel/Destinations/Mexico/ Mexico%20City>.
'Frida Kahlo and Solidarity of the Strange'. <http://bigthink.com/words-of-wisdom/frida-kahlo-and-solidarity-of-the-strange>.
'Frida Kahlo'. April 28, 2017. <http://www.biography.com/people/ frida-kahlo-9359496>.
'Frida Kahlo Biography'. <http://www.fridakahlo.org/frida-kahlo-biography.jsp>.
'Frida Kahlo Quotes'. <http://www.fridakahlo.org/frida-kahlo-quotes.jsp>.
Johnston, Lissa Jones, and Frida Kahlo. *Frida Kahlo: Painter of Strength*. Mankato: Capstone, 2007.
Julio. 'The Revolutionary Artist: Frida Kahlo'. <http://courses.washington.edu/femart/final_project/wordpress/frida-kahlo/>.

Kahlo, Frida. *The Diary of Frida Kahlo*. London: Bloomsbury, 1995.

Latimer, Joanna. 'Paper 112: Unsettling Bodies: Frida Khalo's portraids and in/dividuality'. < http://orca.cf.ac.uk/25553/1/wp112.pdf >.

McMahan, Elysia. 'Frida Kahlo Quotes'. <http://knoworthy.com/quoteworthy-frida-kahlo/>.

Mencimer, Stephanie. 'The Trouble With Frida Kahlo'. June 2002. <http://www.dalestory.org/LATINAMERICA/Mexico/KahloAndRivera/Kahlo,FridaTheTroubleWithFridaKahlobyStephanie%20Mencimer.pdf >.

Rami, Trupti. 'Return to Sender'. December 1, 2013. <http://nymag.com/news/intelligencer/us-stamp-controversy-2013-12/>.

'Stamps in the News: USPS honours Mexican artist Frida Kahlo'. June 3, 2001. <http://savannahnow.com/stories/060301/LOCstampsap.shtml#.VhhOJPlVhBd>.

Treacy, Christopher. 'A Bisexual Luminary: Frida Kahlo'. April 23, 2015. <http://www.pridesource.com/article.html?article=71111>.

Walter, Natasha. 'Feel my pain'. May 21, 2005. <http://www.theguardian.com/artanddesign/2005/may/21/art>.

Wolfe, Bertram David. *The Fabulous Life of Diego Rivera*. New York: Stein and Day, 1963.

Simone de Beauvoir

Appignanesi, Lisa. 'The heart of Simone de Beauvoir'. January 8, 2008. <https://www.opendemocracy.net/arts-Literature/feminist_2670.jsp>.

Bair, Deirdre. *Simone de Beauvoir: A Biography*. New York: Simon and Schuster, 1991.

De Beauvoir, Simone. *Force of Circumstance: The Autobiography of Simone de Beauvoir*. New York: Paragon House, 1992.

De Beauvoir, Simone. *The Second Sex*. New York: Vintage Books, 2011.

Gillette, Allison. 'Simone de Beauvoir'. <http://www.womeninworldhistory.com/imow-deBeauvoir.pdf>.

Hazareesingh, Sudhir. 'The 10 most celebrated French thinkers'. June 13, 2015. <http://www.theguardian.com/books/2015/jun/13/10-most-celebrated-french-thinkers-philosophy>.

Jones, Josh. 'Simone de Beauvoir Explains "Why I'm a Feminist" in a Rare TV Interview (1975)'. May 23, 2013. <http://www.openculture.com/2013/05/simone_de_beauvoir_explains_why_im_a_feminist_in_a_rare_tv_interview_1975.html>.

Mcclintock, Anne. 'Simone (Lucie Ernestine Marie Bertrand) de Beauvoir'. <http://www.english.wisc.edu/amcclintock/beauvoir.htm>.

Meisler, Stanley. 'De Beauvoir, Writer and Feminist, Dies'. April 15, 1986. <http://articles.latimes.com/1986-04-15/news/mn-4814_1_feminist-movement>.

Mussett, Shannon. 'Simone de Beauvoir (1908–1986)'. <http://www.iep.utm.edu/beauvoir/>.

'Simone Beauvoir – Biography'. <http://www.egs.edu/library/simone-de-beauvoir/biography>.

Smith, Bonnie G. *The Oxford Encyclopedia of Women in World History*. Oxford: Oxford University Press, 2008.

Thurman, Judith. 'Introduction to Simone de Beauvoir's "The Second Sex"'. May 27, 2010. <http://www.nytimes.com/2010/05/30/books/excerpt-introduction-second-sex.html>.

Thurman, Judith. 'Todd Akin and the Second Sex'. August 27, 2012. <http://www.newyorker.com/news/news-desk/todd-akin-and-the-second-sex>.

Wolters, Eugene. 'Incredible Candid Photos of Jean-Paul Sartre and Simone de Beauvoir in Cuba'. June 20, 2014. <http://www.critical-theory.com/incredible-candid-photos-of-jean-paul-sartre-and-simone-de-beauvoir-in-cuba>.

Pauli Murray

'Biography'. <http://paulimurrayproject.org/pauli-murray/biography/>.

Blagg, Deborah. 'Pauli Murray: A One-Woman Civil Rights Movement'. 2013. <https://www.radcliffe.harvard.edu/news/schlesinger-newsletter/pauli-murray-one-woman-civil-rights-movement>.

Cooper, Brittney. 'Black, queer, feminist, erased from history: Meet the most important legal scholar you've likely never heard of'. February 18, 2015. <http://www.salon.com/2015/02/18/black_queer_feminist_erased_from_history_meet_the_most_important_legal_scholar_youve_likely_never_heard_of/>.

Downs, Kenya. 'The "Black, Queer, Feminist" Legal Trailblazer You've Never Heard Of'. February 19, 2015. <http://www.npr.org/sections/codeswitch/2015/02/19/387200033/the-black-queer-feminist-legal-trailblazer-youve-never-heard-of>.

Gebreyes, Rahel. 'How "Respectability Politics" Muted The Legacy of Black LGBT Activist Pauli Murray'. February 10, 2015. <http://www.huffingtonpost.com/2015/02/10/lgbt-activist- pauli-murray_n_6647252.html>.

Guy-Sheftall, Beverly. *Words of Fire: An Anthology of African-American Feminist Thought.* New York: The New Press, 2013.

Hartmann, Susan M. 'Pauli Murray and the "Juncture of Women's Liberation and Black Liberation"'. Summer 2002. <https://muse.jhu.edu/login?auth=0&type=summary&url=/journals/journal_of_womens_history/v014/14.2hartmann.pdf>.

Meyerowitz, Joanne J. *How Sex Changed: A History of Transsexuality in the United States.* Cambridge: Harvard University Press, 2009.

Murray, Pauli. 'An American Credo'. Winter 1945. <http://www.unz.org/Pub/CommonGround-1945q4-00022>.

Murray, Pauli. *Dark Testament and Other Poems.* Norwalk: Silvermine, 1970.

Murray, Pauli. *States' Laws on Race and Color.* Athens: University of Georgia, 1997.

Nahmias, Leah. 'Women Battling Jim Crow and Jane Crow'. April 26, 2010. <http://nowandthen.ashp.cuny.edu/2010/04/when-women-battled-jim-crow-and-jane-crow/>.

'Pauli Murray: Biography'. <http://www.biography.com/people/pauli-murray-214111>.

'Pauli Murray: Early Years and Education'. <https://ncwomenofcivilrights.wordpress.com/pauli-murray/early-years-and-education/>.

'Pauli Murray'. <http://lgbthistorymonth.com/pauli-murray?tab=biography>.

'Pauli Murray'. <https://ncwomenofcivilrights.wordpress.com/pauli-murray/>.

Pinn, Anthony B. *The African American Religious Experience in America.* Westport: Greenwood, 2006.

Rosenberg, Rosalind. 'The Conjunction of Race and Gender'. Winter 2002. <https://muse.jhu.edu/article/17463>.

Simkin, John. 'Anna (Pauli) Murray'. August 2014. <http://spartacus-educational.com/USAmurrayA.htm>.

'The Reverent Pauli Murray, 1910–1985'. <http://www.episcopalarchives.org/Afro-Anglican_history/exhibit/leadership/murray.php>.

'Timeline'. <http://paulimurrayproject.org/pauli-murray/timeline>.

Vintages, Karen. *The Thinking of Simone de Beauvoir.* Bloomington: Indiana University Press, 1996.

Rosa Parks

Boggs, Grace Lee, and Alice B. Jennings. 'Rosa Parks, Champion for Human Rights'. February 4, 2013. <http://www.yesmagazine.org/peace-justice/rosa-parks-champion-for-human-rights>.

Curtis, Mary C. 'Rosa Parks' Other (Radical) Side'. September 21, 2010. <http://www.theroot.com/rosa-parks-other-radical-side-1790880958>.

Fastenberg, Dan. 'Rosa Parks (1913-2005)'. November 18, 2010. <http://content.time.com/time/specials/packages/article/0,28804,2029774_2029776_2031835,00.html>.

Franklin, Morgan. 'More Than Just Sitting Down: The Unyielding Activism of Rosa Parks'. August 26, 2013. <http://cooperproject.org/more-than-just-sitting-down-the-unyielding-activism-of-rosa-parks/>.

Griffin, Rachel. 'Black Herstory: Rosa Parks Did Much More than Sit on a Bus'. February 3, 2012. <http://msmagazine.com/blog/2012/02/03/rosa-parks-did-way-more-than-sit-on- a-bus/>.

McGuire, Danielle. 'Opinion: It's time to free Rosa Parks from the bus'. December 1, 2012. <http://inamerica.blogs.cnn.com/2012/12/01/opinion-its-time-to-free-rosa-parks-from-the-bus/comment-page-2/>.

'Quote of the Week: Rosa Parks'. February 4, 2015. August 27, 2015. <http://www.biography.com/news/rosa-parks-famous-quotes>.

Rathod, Nicholas. 'Honoring Rosa Parks: Moving from Symbolism to Action'. December 1, 2005. <https://www.americanprogress.org/issues/civil-liberties/news/2005/12/01/1743/honoring-rosa-parks-moving-from-symbolism-to-action/>.

Reeves, Joshua. Spiritual Narrative. Lulu.com, 2015. 'Rosa Parks'. 2009. <http://www.history.com/topics/black-history/rosa-parks>.

'Rosa Parks'. <http://www.u-s-history.com/pages/h1697.html>.

'Rosa Parks Biography'. April 28, 2017. <http://www.biography.com/people/rosa-parks-9433715>.

'Rosa Parks Biography'. <http://www.achievement.org/achiever/rosa-parks/>.

'Rosa Parks, "The First Lady of Civil Rights".' <http://billofrightsinstitute.org/rosaparks/>.

Sigerman, Harriet. The Columbia Documentary History of American Women since 1941. New York: Columbia University Press, 2003.

'The Book'. <http://atthedarkendofthestreet.com/the-book/>.

Florynce Kennedy

Africa Woman. Issues 19–24. Africa Journal Limited, 2009.

Burstein, Patricia. 'Lawyer Flo Kennedy Enjoys Her Reputation as Radicalism's Rudest Mouth'. April 14, 1975. <http://www.people.com/people/archive/article/0,,20065145,00.html>.

Finkelman, Paul. Encyclopedia of African American History, 1896 to the Present. New York: Oxford University Press, 2009.

'Florynce Kennedy Biography'. <http://www.notablebiographies.com/supp/Supplement-Ka-M/Kennedy-Florynce.html>.

French, Ellen, and Christine Minderovic. 'Kennedy, Florynce 1916–2000'. <http://www.encyclopedia.com/topic/Florynce_Kennedy.aspx>.

Kennedy, Florynce. Color Me Flo: My Hard Life and Good Times. Englewood: Prentice-Hall, 1976.

Kennedy, Florynce. 'Papers of Florynce Kennedy, 1915-2004 (inclusive), 1947-1993 (bulk)'. April 2009. <http://oasis.lib.harvard.edu/oasis/deliver/~sch01221>.

Love, Barbara, and Cott, Nancy. Feminists Who Changed America, 1963-1975. Chicago: University of Illinois Press, 2015.

Martin, Douglas. 'Flo Kennedy, Feminist, Civil Rights Advocate and Flamboyant Gadfly, Is Dead at 84'. December 23, 2000. <http://www.nytimes.com/2000/12/23/us/flo-kennedy-feminist-civil-rights-advocate-and-flamboyant-gadfly-is-dead-at-84.html>.

Randolph, Sherie M. 'The Lasting Legacy of Florynce Kennedy, Black Feminist Fighter'. May-June 2011. <https://www.solidarity-us.org/node/3272>.

Scanlon, Jennifer. *Significant Contemporary American Feminists: A Biographical Sourcebook*. Westport: Greenwood Press, 1999.

Steinem, Gloria. 'The Verbal Karate of Florynce R. Kennedy, Esq'. Summer 2011. <http://www.msmagazine.com/summer2011/verbalkarate.asp>.

Theoharis, Jeanne, and Woodard, Komozi. *Want to Start a Revolution?* New York: NYU Press, 2009.

Woo, Elaine. 'Florynce Kennedy; Irreverent Activist for Equal Rights'. December 28, 2000. <http://articles.latimes.com/2000/dec/28/local/me-5531>.

Maya Angelou

Angelou, Maya. *And Still I Rise*. New York: Random House, 1978.

Angelou, Maya. *I Know Why the Caged Bird Sings*. New York: Random House, 1970.

'Biography'. <http://www.mayaangelou.com/biography>.

Kelly, Cara. 'Before Maya Angelou, there was Miss Calypso'. May 28, 2014. <https://www.washingtonpost.com/news/style-blog/wp/2014/05/28/before-maya-angelou-there-was-miss-calypso/>.

'Maya Angelou'. <http://www.poetryfoundation.org/bio/maya-angelou>.

'Maya Angelou Biography'. April 28, 2017. <http://www.biography.com/people/maya-angelou-9185388>.

'Maya Angelou Biography'. < http://www.achievement.org/achiever/maya-angelou/>.

'Maya Angelou – the most banned author in the US'. August 5, 2014. <http://newafricanmagazine.com/maya-angelou-banned-author-us/>.

Nichols, John. 'Maya Angelou's Civil Rights Legacy'. May 28, 2014. <http://www.thenation.com/article/maya-angelous-civil-rights-legacy/>.

'Remembering Dr. Maya Angelou: Maya Angelou Teacher'. <http://mayaangelou.wfu.edu/story/>.

Salters, J.N. '35 Maya Angelou Quotes That Changed My Life'. July 30, 2014. <http://www.huffingtonpost.com/jn-salters/35-maya-angelou-quotes-th_b_5412166.html>.

Serwer, Adam. 'Maya Angelou, radical activist'. May 29, 2015. <http://www.msnbc.com/msnbc/maya-angelou-radical-activist>.

Sorel, Nancy Caldwell. 'When Maya Angelou met Billie Holiday'. July 21, 1995. <http://www.independent.co.uk/arts-entertainment/when-maya-angelou-met-billie-holiday-1592757.html>.

Stephens, Rodeena. 'Dr. Maya Angelou: Phenomenal Woman'. February 4, 2014. <http://www.nywici.org/blog/aloud/dr-maya-angelou-phenomenal-woman>.

Stringer, Mary. 'Nine of the most amazing women of 2014'. January 2, 2015. <http://metro.co.uk/2015/01/02/nine-of-the-most-amazing-women-in-2014-5003919/>.

Vilkomerson, Sara. 'Maya Angelou: Saying goodbye to a literary giant'. May 28, 2014. <http://www.ew.com/article/2014/05/28/maya-angelou-obituary>.

Wills, Amanda. '15 Other Jobs Maya Angelou Once Held'. May 28, 2014. <http://mashable.com/2014/05/28/maya-angelou-jobs/#T4wdWbzuqqkV>.

Winfrey, Oprah, and Janet Lowe. *Oprah Winfrey Speaks: Insight from the World's Most Influential Voice*. New York: Wiley, 1998.

Yayoi Kusama

Adams, Tim. 'Yayoi Kusama – review'. February 12, 2012. <http://www.theguardian.com/artanddesign/2012/feb/12/yayoi-kusama-tate-modern-review>.

Corbett, Rachel. 'Yayoi Kusama: The Last Word'. <http://www.artnet.com/magazineus/books/corbett/yayoi-kusama-autobiography-2-15-12.asp>.

Darling, Gala. 'Yayoi Kusama'. September 29, 2009. <http://galadarling.com/article/yayoi-kusama>.

Foster, Gwendolyn Audrey. 'Self-Stylization and Performativity in the Work of Yoko Ono, Yayoi Kusama and Mariko Mori'. June 28, 2010. <http://www.tandfonline.com/doi/abs/10.1080/10509200802350307?journalCode=gqrf20>.

Frank, Priscilla. 'Polka Dot Queen: Yayoi Kusama On Her Whitney Retrospective and Vuitton Collaboration (PHOTOS, INTERVIEW)'. August 23, 2012. <http://www.huffingtonpost.com/2012/08/07/yayoi-kusama-interview_n_1749378.html>.

Gómez, Edward M. 'Kusama, In Her Own Words'. April 2, 2012. <http://www.brooklynrail.org/2012/04/art_books/kusama-in-her-own-words>.

Itoi, Kay. 'Kusama Speaks'. August 22, 1997. <http://www.artnet.com/ Magazine/features/itoi/itoi8-22-97.asp>.

'Love Forever: Yayoi Kusama, 1958-1968'. December 13, 1998–March 7, 1999. <http://www.walkerart.org/archive/8/A973D5586AA1C2926161.htm>.

Morris, Frances. 'The fantastical world of Yayoi Kusama'. February 3, 2012. <http://www.phaidon.com/agenda/art/picture-galleries/2012/february/02/the-fantastical-world-of-yayoi-kusama/?idx=1>.

Osborne, Catherine. 'Yayoi Kusama's Obliteration Room'. January 10, 2012. <http://www.azuremagazine.com/article/yayoi-kusamas-obliteration-room/>.

Patel, Nilesh. 'Yayoi Kusama: The Self-Obliteration Of Japan's Troubled Artist'. <http://theculturetrip.com/asia/japan/articles/the-self-obliteration-of-yayoi-kusama/>.

Suhr, Trine. 'Yayoi Kusama'. <http://courses.washington.edu/femart/final_project/wordpress/yayoi-kusama/>.

Turner, Grady T. 'Yayoi Kusama'. Winter 1999. <http://bombmagazine.org/article/2192/yayoi-kusama>.

'Yayoi Kusama'. <http://www.gagosian.com/artists/yayoi-kusama>.

'Yayoi Kusama'. <http://www.victoria-miro.com/artists/31-yayoi-kusama/overview/>.

'Yayoi Kusama'. <http://www.yayoi-kusama.jp/e/biography/index.html>.

Zwirner, David. 'Yayoi Kusama'. <http://www.davidzwirner.com/artists/yayoi-kusama/biography/>.

Faith Ringgold

Biggs, Mary. *Women's Words: The Columbia Book of Quotations by Women*. New York: Columbia University Press, 1996.

'Faith Ringgold'. <https://www.brooklynmuseum.org/eascfa/feminist_art_base/faith-ringgold>.

'Faith Ringgold'. <http://www.craftinamerica.org/artists/faith-ringgold/>.

'Faith Ringgold'. <http://www.makers.com/faith-ringgold>.

'Faith Ringgold'. <http://www.pbs.org/americaquilts/century/stories/faith_ringgold.html>.

'Faith Ringgold Biography'. May 10, 2016. <http://www.biography.com/people/faith-ringgold-9459066>.

'Faith Ringgold Chronology'. <http://www.faithringgold.com/ringgold/chron_rev.pdf>.

'Faith Ringgold: No 'Knock Down, Drag Out Black Woman Story'. August 19, 2013. <http://www.npr.org/templates/story/story.php?storyId=213500929>.

'Faith Ringgold: Story Quilts'. <http://www.danforthart.org/faith_ringgold_quilt.html>.

'Faith Ringgold: Street Story Quilt (1990.237a-c)'. <http://www.metmuseum.org/toah/works-of-art/1990.237a-c>.

Koolish, Lynda. *African American Writers: Portraits and Visions*. Jackson: University Press of Mississippi, 2001.

Ringgold, Faith. 'Biography'. <http://www.faithringgold.com/ringgold/bio.htm>.

Ringgold, Faith. 'Faith Ringgold Biography'. <http://www.scholastic.com/teachers/contributor/faith-ringgold>.

Ringgold, Faith. 'Frequently Asked Questions'. <http://www.faithringgold.com/ringgold/faq.htm>.

Ringgold, Faith. *Talking to Faith Ringgold.* New York: Knopf, 1996.

Ringgold, Faith. *We Flew Over the Bridge: The Memoirs of Faith Ringgold.* Durham: Duke University Press, 2005.

Zimmer, William. 'ART; Politics With Subtlety, On Quilts and in Books'. April 14, 2002. <http://www.nytimes.com/2002/04/14/nyregion/art-politics-with-subtlety-on-quilts-and-in-books.html>.

Yoko Ono

Adler, Margot. 'After 40 Years, The Bed-In Reawakens'. August 25, 2009. <http://www.npr.org/ templates/story/story.php?storyId=112082796>.

Barnett, Emma. 'Yoko Ono to judge Twitter haiku competition'. May 18, 2009. <http://www.telegraph.co.uk/technology/twitter/5343746/Yoko-Ono-to-judge-Twitter-haiku-competition.html>.

Blaney, John. *John Lennon: Listen to This Book.* John Blaney, 2005.

Carmen. 'Artist Attack! Yoko Ono is My Hero and I'm Not Sorry'. February 20, 2012. <http://www.autostraddle.com/artist-attack-yoko-ono-is-my-hero-and-im-not-sorry-127603/>.

Cott, Jonathan. 'Yoko Ono and Her Sixteen-Track Voice'. March 18, 1971. <http://www.rollingstone.com/music/news/yoko-ono-and-her-sixteen-track-voice-19710318>.

Douglass, Lynn. 'Yoko Ono Honored For Feminist Art, Says Not Saying Anything With Art "A Waste".' November 19, 2012. <http://www.forbes.com/sites/lynndouglass/2012/11/19/yoko-ono-honored-for-feminist-art-says-not-saying-anything-with-art-a-waste/>.

Frank, Peter. 'Yoko Ono As An Artist'. <http://www.artcommotion.com/Issue2/VisualArts/>.

Halliday, Ayun. 'Yoko Ono Lets Audience Cut Up Her Clothes in Conceptual Art Performance (Carnegie Hall, 1965)'. May 19, 2015. <http://www.openculture.com/2015/05/yoko-ono-lets-audience-cut-up-her-clothes.html>.

Kumeh, Titania. '15 Minutes With Yoko Ono'. February 22, 2010. <http://www.motherjones.com/riff/2010/02/music-monday-yoko-ono-john-lennon-noise-pop-deerhoof>.

Lifton, Dave. '46 Years Ago: John Lennon and Yoko Ono Begin 'Bed-in for Peace'.' March 25, 2016. <http://ultimateclassicrock.com/john-lennon-yoko-ono-bed-in/>.

Mahoney, J.W. 'From the Archives: Transmodern Yoko'. February 1, 2012. <http://www.artinamericamagazine.com/news-features/magazine/from-the-archives-transmodern-yoko/>.

Meecham, Pam, and Sheldon, Julie. *Modern Art: A Critical Introduction.* New York: Routledge, 2013.

'Ono launches peace prize'. October 10, 2002. <http://news.bbc.co.uk/2/hi/entertainment/2315665.stm>.

Rutkowski, Stephanie. 'Dec. 8: John Lennon Shot, Killed 1980'. December 8, 2011. <http://abcnews.go.com/blogs/extras/2011/12/08/dec-8-john-lennon-shot-killed-1980/>.

Silverman, Stephen M. 'Dixie Chick Marries, Emmys Tone Down'. September 26, 2001. <http://www.people.com/people/article/0,,622259,00.html>.

Sturges, Fiona. '"I was doing this before you were born": Yoko Ono on John Lennon, infidelity and making music into her eighties'. August 31, 2013. <http://www.independent.co.uk/news/people/profiles/i-was-doing-this-before-you-were-born-yoko-ono-on-john-lennon-infidelity-and-making-music-into-her-8788694.html>

Valdimarsson, Omar, and Niklas Pollard. 'Yoko Ono awards Lady Gaga peace prize in Iceland'. October 10, 2012. <http://www.reuters.com/article/entertainment-us-ladygaga-prize-idUSBRE8981G820121010 >.

'What is fracking and why is it controversial?'. December 16, 2015. <http://www.bbc.com/news/uk-14432401>.

'Yoko Ono and Artists Against Fracking Find Out What Fracking Has Done to Pennsylvania'. <http://artistsagainstfracking.com/about/>.

'Yoko Ono Biography'. April 28, 2017. <http://www.biography.com/people/ yoko-ono-9542162>.

Yoshimoto, Midori. *Into Performance: Japanese Women Artists in New York*. New Brunswick/London: Rutgers University Press, 2005.

Audre Lorde

'Audre Lorde'. <http://www.britannica.com/biography/Audre-Lorde>.

'Audre Lorde'. <http://www.poetryfoundation.org/bio/audre-lorde>.

'Audre Lorde'. <https://www.poets.org/poetsorg/poet/audre-lorde>.

Demakis, Joseph M. *The Ultimate Book of Quotations*. Createspace, 2012.

Gerund, Katharina. *Transatlantic Cultural Exchange: African American Women's Art and Activism in West Germany*. Bielefeld: Transcript-Verlag, 2013.

Kulii, Beverly Threatt, Ann E. Reuman, and Ann Trapasso. 'Audre Lorde's Life and Career'. <http://www.english.illinois.edu/maps/poets/g_l/lorde/life.htm>.

Lorde, Audre. *A Burst of Light: Essays*. Ithaca: Firebrand, 1988.

Lorde, Audre. *Cables to Rage*. London: Paul Breman, 1970.

Lorde, Audre. *I Am Your Sister: Collected and Unpublished Writings of Audre Lorde*. New York: Oxford University Press. 2011.

Lorde, Audre. *Sister Outsider: Essays and Speeches*. Berkeley: Crossing, 2007.

Lorde, Audre. *The Cancer Journals*. Argyle: Spinsters, Ink, 1980.

Lorde, Audre. *Zami, a New Spelling of My Name*. Trumansburg: Crossing, 1982.

Lorde, Audre, and (edited by) Hall, Joan Wylie. *Conversations with Audre Lorde*. Jackson: University of Mississippi, 2004.

Ulysse, Gina Athena. 'How Audre Lorde Made Queer History'. October 31, 2011. <http://msmagazine.com/blog/2011/10/31/how-audre-lorde-made-queer-history/>.

Jane Goodall

Bagley, Mary. 'Jane Goodall Biography'. March 29, 2014. <http://www.livescience.com/44469-jane-goodall.html>.

Bardhan-Quallen, Sudipta. *Up Close: Jane Goodall: A Twentieth-century Life*. New York: Penguin Group/Viking, 2008.

Hollow, Michele C. and Rives, William P. *The Everything Guide to Working with Animals: From dog groomer to wildlife rescuer—tons of great jobs for animal lovers*. Massachusetts: Adams Media, 2009.

'Jane Goodall'. <http://www.nationalgeographic.com/explorers/bios/jane-goodall>.

'Jane Goodall Biography'. April 28, 2017. <http://www.biography.com/people/jane-goodall-9542363>.

'Jane Goodall Biography'. < http://www.achievement.org/achiever/jane-goodall/>.

Lewis, Jone Johnson. 'Jane Goodall Quotes'. May 1, 2017. <http://womenshistory.about.com/od/quotes/a/jane_goodall.htm>.

Loriggio, Paola. '"Little things" change world: Jane Goodall'. November 14, 2008. <http://www.thestar.com/news/gta/2008/11/14/little_things_change_world_jane_goodall.html>.

Peterson, Dale. *Jane Goodall: The Woman Who Redefined Man*. Boston: Houghton Mifflin Harcourt, 2006.

Schnall, Marianne. 'Exclusive Interview with Dr. Jane Goodall'. June 1, 2010. <http://www.huffingtonpost.com/marianne-schnall/exclusive-interview-with_b_479894.html>.

'Study Corner – Biography'. <http://www.janegoodall.org/study-corner-biography>.

Judy Blume

Blume, Judy. *Forever...* New York: Simon and Schuster, 2012.

Blume, Judy. 'How I Became an Author'. <http://www.judyblume.com/about/author/author.php>

Blume, Judy. 'Judy Blume Talks About Censorship'. <http://www.judyblume.com/censorship.php>.

Blume, Judy. 'Judy's Official Bio'. <http://www.judyblume.com/about.php>.

Blue, Judy. 'National Book Awards Acceptance Speeches: Judy Blume, Winner of the 2004 Distinguished Contribution to American Letters Award'. November 17, 2004. <http://www.nationalbook.org/nbaacceptspeech_jblume04.html#.Vh6FJflVhBd>.

Blume, Judy. *Tiger Eyes*. New York: Simon and Schuster, 2014.

Dunham, Lena. 'Lena Dunham meets Judy Blume'. June 1, 2014. <http://www.telegraph.co.uk/culture/hay-festival/10848610/Lena-Dunham-meets-Judy-Blume.html>.

Gottlieb, Amy. 'Judy Blume'. March 1, 2009. <http://jwa.org/encyclopedia/article/blume-judy>.

Green, Michelle. 'After Two Divorces, Judy Blume Blossoms as An Unmarried Woman—and Hits the Best-Seller List Again'. March 19, 1984. <http://www.people.com/people/archive/article/0,,20087381,00.html>.

'Judy Blume'. <http://www.scholastic.com/teachers/article/judy-blume>.

'Judy Blume Biography'. November 3, 2016. <http://www.biography.com/people/judy-blume-9216512>.

'Judy Blume – Living Legends'. <http://www.loc.gov/about/awards-and-honors/living-legends/judy-blume>.

'Judy Blume: Often Banned, But Widely Beloved'. November 28, 2011. <http://www.npr.org/2011/11/28/142859819/judy-blume-banned-often-but-widely-beloved>.

'Most frequently challenged authors of the 21st century'. <http://www.ala.org/bbooks/frequentlychallengedbooks/challengedauthors>.

Nemy, Enid. 'It's Judy Blume, New Yorker'. October 3, 1982. <http://www.nytimes.com/1982/10/03/style/it-s-judy-blume-new-yorker.html>.

Prichep, Deena. 'This Blumesday Celebrates Judy, Not Joyce'. June 17, 2013. <http://www.npr.org/2013/06/17/191651560/this-blumesday-celebrates-judy-not-joyce>.

Tracy, Kathleen. *Judy Blume: A Biography*. Westport: Greenwood, 2008.

West, Mark I. 'Judy Blume: A Leader in the Anticensorship Movement'. January/February 2000. <http://www.judyblume.com/censorship/leader.php>.

Whitelocks, Sadie. 'Author Judy Blume reveals she is suffering from breast cancer and has had a mastectomy'. September 5, 2012. <http://www.dailymail.co.uk/femail/article-2198830/Judy-Blume-reveals-suffering-breast-cancer-mastectomy.html>.

Judy Chicago

Beckman, Rachel. 'Her Table Is Ready'. April 22, 2007. <http://www.washingtonpost.com/wp-dyn/content/article/2007/04/20/AR2007042000419.html>.

Bennetts, Leslie. 'Judy Chicago: Women's Lives and Art'. April 8, 1985. <http://www.nytimes.com/1985/04/08/style/judy-chicago-women-s-lives-and-art.html>.

'Biography'. <http://www.judychicago.com/about/biography/ >.

Bloch, Avital H., and Lauri Umanski. *Impossible to Hold*. New York: NYU Press, 2005.

'Chicago in L.A.: Judy Chicago's Early Work, 1963–74'. <https://www.brooklynmuseum.
 org/exhibitions/judy_chicago_los_angeles/>.
Chicago, Judy. 'Judy Chicago: What I Learned From Male Chauvinists'. September
 22, 2011. <http://www.laweekly.com/arts/judy-chicago-what-i-learned-from-male-
 chauvinists-2172063>.
Chicago, Judy. *Through the Flower: My Struggle as a Woman Artist.* Lincoln: iUniverse, 2006.
Cooke, Rachel. 'The art of Judy Chicago'. November 4, 2012. <http://www.theguardian.
 com/artanddesign/2012/nov/04/judy-chicago-art-feminism-britain>.
Dixler, Elsa. 'A Place at the Table'. March 4, 2007. <http://www.nytimes.com/2007/03/04/
 books/review/Dixler.t.html?_r=0>.
Gerhard, Jane F. *The Dinner Party: Judy Chicago and the Power of Popular Feminism,
 1970–2007.* Athens: University of Georgia Press, 2013.
'Judy Chicago'. <http://www.theartstory.org/artist-chicago-judy.htm>.
'Judy Chicago Biography'. April 2, 2014. <http://www.biography.com/people/judy-
 chicago-9246631>.
'Judy Chicago: Through the Archives'. <https://www.radcliffe.harvard.edu/schlesinger-
 library/exhibition/judy-chicago-through-the-archives>.
'The Dinner Party: Place Settings: Sojourner Truth'. <https://www.brooklynmuseum.
 org/eascfa/dinner_party/place_settings/sojourner_truth>.
'The Dinner Party: Place Settings: Susan B. Anthony'. <https://www.brooklynmuseum.
 org/eascfa/dinner_party/place_settings/susan_b_anthony>.
'The Dinner Party: Place Settings: Virginia Woolf'. <https://www.brooklynmuseum.org/
 eascfa/dinner_party/place_settings/virginia_woolf>.
Wacks, Debra. 'Judy Chicago'. March 1, 2009. <http://jwa.org/encyclopedia/article/
 chicago-judy>.
Yood, James W. 'Judy Chicago'. <http://www.britannica.com/biography/Judy-Chicago>.

Frances M. Beal

'Black Women's Manifesto'. <http://library.duke.edu/digitalcollections/wlmpc_wlmms01009/>.
Breines, Winifred. *The Trouble Between Us: An Uneasy History of White and Black
 Women in the Feminist Movement.* New York: Oxford University Press, 2006.
Carson, Clayborne, and Heidi Hess. 'Student Nonviolent Coordinating Committee'.
 <http://web.stanford.edu/~ccarson/articles/black_women_3.htm>.
Crow, Barbara A. *Radical Feminism.* New York/London: NYU Press, 2000.
Hartmann, Maureen. 'Frances Beal: A Voice for Peace, Racial Justice and the Rights
 of Women'. May 6, 2015. <http://www.thestreetspirit.org/frances-beal-a-voice-for-
 peace-racial-justice-and-the-rights-of-women/>.
Keetley, Dawn, and Pettegrew, John. *Public Women, Public Words.* Volume 2. Lanham:
 Rowman & Littlefield, 2005.
Kinser, Amber E. *Motherhood and Feminism.* Berkeley: Seal Press, 2010.
Love, Barbara J. and F. Cott, Nancy. *Feminists Who Changed America, 1963–1975.*
 Urbana: University of Illinois Press, 2015.
Ross, Loretta J. 'Voices of Feminism Oral History Project'. March 18, 2005. <https://
 www.coursehero.com/file/11726918/Beal/>.
Springer, Kimberly. *Living for the Revolution: Black Feminist Organizations, 1968–
 1980.* Durham: Duke University Press, 2005.
'The Death of Emmett Till'. 2010. <http://www.history.com/this-day-in-history/the-
 death-of-emmett-till>.
Vidal, Ava. '"Intersectional feminism". What the hell is it? (And why you should care.)'.
 January 15, 2014. <http://www.telegraph.co.uk/women/womens-life/10572435/
 Intersectional-feminism.-What-the-hell-is-it-And-why-you-should-care.html>.

Wangari Maathai

Gettleman, Jeffrey. 'Wangari Maathai, Nobel Peace Prize Laureate, Dies at 71'. September 26, 2011. <http://www.nytimes.com/2011/09/27/world/africa/wangari-maathai-nobel-peace-prize-laureate-dies-at-71.html?_r=0>.

Gilbert, Natasha. 'Nobel peace prize laureate and environmental campaigner dies'. September 26, 2011. <http://blogs.nature.com/news/2011/09/nobel_peace_prize_laureate_and.html>.

Hoagland, Jim. 'Seeds of Hope in Africa'. May 12, 2005. <http://www.washingtonpost.com/wp-dyn/content/article/2005/05/11/AR2005051101765.html>.

Lechter, Sharon. *Think and Grow Rich for Women: Using Your Power to Create Success and Significance.* New York: Penguin, 2014.

Lewis, Jone Johnson. 'Wangari Maathai'. March 11, 2017. <http://womenshistory.about.com/od/wangarimaathai/p/wangari_maathai.htm>.

Maathai, Wangari. *Unbowed: A Memoir.* New York: Knopf, 2006.

MacDonald, Mia. 'The Green Belt Movement: The Story of Wangari Maathai'. March 25, 2005. <http://www.yesmagazine.org/issues/media-that-set-us-free/the-green-belt-movement-the-story-of-wangari-maathai>.

MacNair, Rachel M. *ProLife Feminism: Yesterday and Today.* New York: Xlibris Corporation, 2006.

North, Anna. 'Peace Prize-Winner Wangari Maathai Dies At 71'. September 26, 2011. <http://jezebel.com/5843853/peace-prize-winner-wangari-maathai-dies-at-71>.

O'Connor, Karen. *Gender and Women's Leadership.* Thousand Oaks: SAGE Publications, 2010.

O'Neill, Patrick. 'Pro-life, eco-feminists work for consist ethic of life'. January 22, 2009. <http://ncronline.org/news/pro-life-eco-feminists-work-consist-ethic-life>.

Schnall, Marianne. 'Conversation with Wangari Maathai'. September 19, 2015. <http://www.feminist.com/resources/artspeech/interviews/wangarimaathai.html>.

Seay, Bob. 'A Pioneering African Environmentalist's Legacy Lives On'. October 14, 2011. <http://www.wgbh.org/articles/A-Pioneering-African-Environmentalists-Legacy-Lives-On-4509>.

Taylor, Alice. *The Gift of a Garden.* Dublin: O'Brien Press, 2013.

'Wangari Maathai'. <http://www.britannica.com/biography/Wangari-Maathai>.

'Wangari Maathai – Biographical'. <http://www.nobelprize.org/nobel_prizes/peace/laureates/2004/maathai-bio.html>.

'Wangari Maathai Biography'. April 2, 2014. <http://www.biography.com/people/wangari-maathai-13704918>.

'Wangari Maathai: Biography'. <http://www.greenbeltmovement.org/wangari-maathai/biography>.

'Wangari Maathai Biography'. <http://www.notablebiographies.com/newsmakers2/2005-La-Pr/Maathai-Wangari.html>.

'Wangari Maathai – Facts'. <http://www.nobelprize.org/nobel_prizes/peace/laureates/2004/maathai-facts.html>.

'Who We Are'. <http://www.greenbeltmovement.org/who-we-are>.

Wilma Rudolph

Biggs, Mary. *Women's Words: The Columbia Book of Quotations by Women.* New York: Columbia University Press, 1996.

Engel, KeriLynn. 'Wilma Rudolph, Olympic gold medalist & civil rights pioneer'. August 14, 2012. <http://www.amazingwomeninhistory.com/wilma-rudolph-olympic-gold-medalist-civil-right-pioneer/>.

Litsky, Frank. 'Wilma Rudolph, Star of the 1960 Olympics, Dies at 54'. November 13, 1994. <http://www.nytimes.com/1994/11/13/obituaries/wilma-rudolph-star-of-the-1960-olympics-dies-at-54.html>.

Porter, David L. *African-American Sports Greats: A Biographical Dictionary.* Westport: ABC-CLIO, 1995.

Roberts, M.B. 'Rudolph ran and the world went wild'. <https://espn.go.com/sportscentury/features/00016444.html>.

Stiller, Joachim K. *Success By Quotes.* Lulu Press, 2015.

'Wilma Rudolph'. <http://www.knowsouthernhistory.net/Biographies/Wilma_Rudolph/>.

'Wilma Rudolph'. <http://www.tnhistoryforkids.org/history/people/people/wilma-rudolph.2448237 >.

'Wilma Rudolph Biography'. June 17, 2016. <http://www.biography.com/people/wilma-rudolph-9466552>.

'Women Subjects on United States Postage Stamps'. <https://about.usps.com/who-we-are/postal-history/women-stamp-subjects.pdf>.

Angela Davis

'Angela Davis Biography'. May 27, 2016. <http://www.biography.com/people/angela-davis-9267589>.

Applewhite, Ashton, Tripp Evans, and Andrew Frothingham. *And I Quote: The Definitive Collection of Quotes, Sayings, and Jokes for the Contemporary Speechmaker.* Revised ed. New York: Macmillan, 2003.

Caldwell, Earl. 'Angela Davis Acquitted on All Charges'. June 5, 1972. <https://www.nytimes.com/books/98/03/08/home/davis-acquit.html>.

'Civil Rights Activist Angela Davis Speaks at PSC March 17'. <http://www.pensacolastate.edu/civil-rights-activist-angela-davis-speaks-at-psc-march-17/>.

Davis, Angela Y. *Are Prisons Obsolete?* New York: Seven Stories Press, 2003.

'Davis, Angela Yvonne'. <http://www.encyclopedia.com/topic/Angela_Yvonne_Davis.aspx>.

Davis, Angela Y. *Women, Culture & Politics.* New York: Knopf Doubleday, 2011.

Davis, Angela Y. *Women, Race & Class.* New York: Vintage Books, 2011.

Goodman, Amy. 'Angela Davis on the Prison Abolishment Movement, Frederick Douglass, the 40th Anniversary of Her Arrest and President Obama's First Two Years'. October 19, 2010. <http://www.democracynow.org/2010/10/19/angela_davis_on_the_prison_abolishment>.

Greene, Helen Taylor and Gabbidon, Shaun L. *Encyclopedia of Race and Crime.* Thouosand Oaks: SAGE Publications, 2009.

'Is Prison Obsolete? Conference 2014'. <http://www.sistersinside.com.au/conference2014.htm>.

Jones, Ann. 'Black Women: On Their Own'. January 10, 1982. <https://www.nytimes.com/books/98/03/08/home/davis-raceclass.html>.

Marable, Manning and Mullings, Leith. *Let Nobody Turn Us Around: An African American Anthology.* Lanham: Rowman & Littlefield, 2009.

McDuffie, Erik S. *Sojourning for Freedom.* Durham: Duke University Press, 2011.

Mitchell, Charlene. *The Fight to Free Angela Davis.* New York: Outlook, 1972.

O'Brien, Matt. 'Angela Davis commemorates 50th anniversary of Alabama church bombing'. September 12, 2013. <http://www.mercurynews.com/breaking-news/ci_24078761/angela- davis-commemorates-50th-anniversary-alabama-church-bombing>.

Parker, Suzi. 'Activist Angela Davis: Education Is Critical for Prison Reform'. October 26, 2012. <http://www.takepart.com/article/2012/10/26/political-activist-angela-davis-says-education-critical-prison-reform>.

Radosh, Ronald. 'Jury isn't out on Angela Davis'. March 11, 2012. <http://www.washingtontimes.com/news/2012/mar/11/jury-isnt-out-on-angela-davis/?page=all>.

Rockefeller, Terry and Massiah, Louis. 'Interview with Angela Davis'. May 24, 1989. <http://digital.wustl.edu/e/eii/eiiweb/dav5427.0115.036marc_record_interviewer_process.html>.

Warner, Carolyn. *The Words of Extraordinary Women*. New York: Newmarket Press, 2010.

'Women on FBI's most wanted list: Angela Yvonne Davis'. <http://www.cbsnews.com/pictures/women-on-fbis-most-wanted-list/3/>.

Alice Walker

'Alice Walker. Author. Pulitzer Prize Winner. Publisher. Voter Registration Activist'. <http://www.black-ladies.org/alice-walker-literature>.

'Alice Walker Biography. April 28, 2017. <http://www.biography.com/people/alice-walker-9521939>.

'Alice Walker Biography'. <http://www.notablebiographies.com/Tu-We/Walker-Alice.html>.

Bloom, Harold. *Alice Walker*. New York: Infobase, 2009.

Chang, Larry, and Roderick Terry. *Wisdom for the Soul of Black Folk*. Washington: Gnosophia, 2007.

Clark, Alex. 'Alice Walker: "I feel dedicated to the whole of humanity".' March 9, 2013. <http://www.theguardian.com/books/2013/mar/09/alice-walker-beauty-in-truth-interview>.

Collins, Patricia Hill. *Black Feminist Thought: Knowledge, Consciousness, and the Politics of Empowerment*. New York: Routledge, 2002.

Donnelly, Mary. *Alice Walker: The Color Purple and Other Works*. New York: Marshall Cavendish, 2009.

Gumbs, Alexis Pauline, China Martens, and Mai'a Williams. 'Alice Walker: Official Biography'. < http://alicewalkersgarden.com/about/>.

G., Waddie. '18 Most Profound & Inspiring Quotes by Alice Walker'. <http://www.glistsociety.com/2014/08/18-most-profound-inspiring-quotes-by-alice-walker/>.

Hoover, Julie, and (edited by) Jack Canfield, Mark Victor Hansen, Kimberly Kirberger, and Mitch Claspy. 'More than Just Sisters'. *Chicken Soup for the Teenage Soul IV*. New York: Chicken Soup for the Soul, 2012. <http://www.chickensoup.com/book-story/50469/more-than-just-sisters>.

Hospital, Janette Turner. 'What They Did to Tashi'. June 28, 1992. <https://www.nytimes.com/books/98/10/04/specials/walker-secret.html>.

Kreitner, Richard and The Almanac. 'April 18, 1983: Alice Walker Becomes the First Woman of Color to Win the Pulitzer Prize for Fiction'. April 18, 2015. <http://www.thenation.com/article/april-18-1983-alice-walker-becomes-first-woman-color-win-pulitzer-prize-fiction/>.

Labrise, Megan. 'Alice Walker: Writing What's Right'. October 1, 2012. <https://www.guernicamag.com/daily/alice-walker-writing-whats-right/>.

Maslin, Janet. 'The Color Purple (1985): Film: 'The Color Purple,' from Steven Spielberg'. December 18, 1985. <http://www.nytimes.com/movie/review?res=9F06E5DC153BF93BA25751C1A963948260>.

Napikoski, Linda. 'Womanist'. August 31, 2016. <http://womenshistory.about.com/od/feminism/a/womanist.htm>.

'Pratibha Parmar'. <http://www.wmm.com/filmcatalog/makers/fm48.shtml>.

'Quote Page: Alice Walker'. February 1, 2012. <http://www.yesmagazine.org/issues/9-strategies-to-end-corporate-rule/quote-page-alice-walker>.

Schacht, Steven. *Feminism and Men: Reconstructing Gender Relations*. New York: NYU Press, 1998.

'The Darlings of Broadway: 2006 Tony Award Winners'. May 16, 2006. <http://www.nytimes.com/2006/06/11/theater/16tony.list.html>.

Walker, Alice. 'After 20 Years, Meditation Still Conquers Inner Space'. October 23, 2000. <http://www.nytimes.com/2000/10/23/arts/23WALK.html>.

Walker, Alice. *In Search of Our Mothers' Gardens: Prose.* New York: Open Road Media, 2011.

Walker, Alice. *The World Has Changed: Conversations with Alice Walker.* New York: New Press, 2013.

White, Evelyn C. *Alice Walker: A Life.* New York: W.W. Norton & Company, 2004.

White, Evelyn C. 'An interview with Alice Walker: Alice Walker: On Finding Your Bliss'. September/ October 1999. <https://www.bookbrowse.com/author_interviews/full/index.cfm/author_number/314/alice-walker#interview>.

Whitted, Quiana. 'Alice Walker (b. 1944)'. August 12, 2014. <http://www.georgiaencyclopedia.org/articles/arts-culture/alice-walker-b-1944>.

Wilma Mankiller

Berns, Roberta. *Child, Family, School, Community: Socialization and Support.* Stamford: Cengage Learning, 2015.

Colich, Abby. *Wilma Mankiller.* North Mankato: Capstone, 2014.

Geffcken, Glenn. *Shift: Indigenous Principles for Corporate Change.* Bloomington: iUniverse, 2014.

Gould, Suzanne. 'Wilma Mankiller, the Inspiring First Woman Cherokee Chief'. November 20, 2013. <http://www.aauw.org/2013/11/20/wilma-mankiller/>.

'Judgement Day: The Trail of Tears'. <http://www.pbs.org/wgbh/aia/part4/4h1567.html>.

Keetley, Dawn, and John Pettegrew. *Public Women, Public Words: A Documentary History of American Feminism.* Volume 2. New York: Rowman & Littlefield, 2005.

Krull, Kathleen. *Lives of Extraordinary Women: Rulers, Rebels (and What the Neighbors Thought).* Boston: Houghton Mifflin Harcourt, 2000.

Mankiller, Wilma. *Every Day is a Good Day: Reflections by Contemporary Indigenous Women.* Golden: Fulcrum, 2004.

Mankiller, Wilma, and Michael Wallis. *Mankiller: A Chief and Her People.* New York: Macmillan, 2000.

'Statement by the President on the Passing of Wilma Mankiller'. April 6, 2010. <https://obamawhitehouse.archives.gov/the-press-office/statement-president-passing-wilma-mankiller>.

Strange, Mary Zeiss, Carol K. Oyster, and Jane E. Sloan. *Encyclopedia of Women in Today's World.* Volume 1. Los Angeles: SAGE Publications, 2011.

Stubben, Jerry D. *Native Americans and Political Participation: A Reference Handbook.* Santa Barbara: ABC-CLIO, 2006.

U.S. News & World Report. Vol 100. U.S. News Publishing Corporation, 1986.

Verhovek, Sam Howe. 'Wilma Mankiller, Cherokee Chief and First Woman to Lead Major Tribe, Is Dead at 64'. April 6, 2010. <http://www.nytimes.com/2010/04/07/us/07mankiller.html>.

Shirin Ebadi

Adarlan, Davar, and Rasool Nafisi. 'My Name is Iran'. <http://americanradioworks.publicradio.org/features/iran/htmlversion/cast.html>.

Afary, Janet, and Kevin B. Anderson. *Foucault and the Iranian Revolution: Gender and the Seductions of Islamism.* Chicago: University of Chicago Press, 2010.

Ebadi, Shirin and Azadeh Moaveni. *Iran Awakening. From Prison to Peace Prize: One Woman's Struggle at the Crossroads of History.* Toronto: Knopf Canada, 2011.

'Ebadi Wins Round with U.S. over Memoirs'. December 19, 2004. <http://www.npr.org/templates/story/story.php?storyId=4235765>.

Goodman, Amy. 'Iranian Nobel Peace Prize Laureate Shirin Ebadi on Nuclear Deal, Islamic State, Women's Rights'. April 28, 2015. <http://www.democracynow.org/2015/4/28/iranian_nobel_peace_prize_laureate_shirin>.

LoLordo, Ann. 'Girl's murder shames Iran Torture: She was as much a victim of Iran's child custody laws as of relatives who killed her'. January 28, 1998. <http://articles.baltimoresun.com/1998-01- 8/news/1998028066_1_ebadi-iran-arian>.

Mattin, David. 'Iranian author Shirin Ebadi talks about writing a personal history'. August 15, 2011. <http://www.thenational.ae/arts-culture/books/iranian-author-shirin-ebadi-talks-about-writing-a-personal-history>.

Monshipouri, Mahmood. 'The Road to globalization runs through women's struggle: Iran and the impact of the Nobel Peace Prize'. 2004. <http://www.iranchamber.com/society/articles/globalization_women_struggle_iran1.php>.

Penketh, Anne. 'The new suffragettes: Shirin Ebadi – the campaigner who has become an international figurehead for women's rights'. May 30, 2013. <http://www.independent.co.uk/news/people/profiles/the-new-suffragettes-shirin-ebadi-the-campaigner-who-has-become-an-international- figurehead-for-8638504.html>.

'Shirin Ebadi'. <http://www.doonething.org/heroes/pages-e/ebadi-quotes.htm>.

'Shirin Ebadi – Biographical'. <http://www.nobelprize.org/nobel_prizes/peace/laureates/2003/ebadi-bio.html>.

'Shirin Ebadi Fast Facts'. June 7, 2016. <http://www.cnn.com/2013/01/01/world/meast/shirin-ebadi---fast-facts/>.

'Shirin Ebadi – Iran, 2003'<http://nobelwomensinitiative.org/meet-the-laureates/shirin-ebadi/>.

Wallbridge, Wendy. *Spiraling Upward: The 5 Co-Creative Powers for Women on the Rise.* Brookline: Bibliomotion, 2015.

Hillary Clinton

Barcella, Laura. 'Hillary Isn't Even Running For President Yet, & She's Already Winning'. February 9, 2015. <http://www.refinery29.com/2015/02/82028/hillary-clinton-winning-president-2016-polls>.

Black, Allida. 'Hillary Rodham Clinton'. <https://www.whitehouse.gov/1600/first-ladies/hillaryclinton>.

Bombardieri, Marcella. 'From conservative roots sprang a call for change'. October 21, 2007. <http://www.boston.com/news/nation/articles/2007/10/21/from_conservative_roots_sprang_a_call_for_change/?page=full>.

Chozick, Amy. 'Hillary Clinton Draws Scrappy Determination From a Tough, Combative Father'. July 19, 2015. <http://www.nytimes.com/2015/07/20/us/politics/hillary-clinton-draws-scrappy-determination-from-a-tough-combative-father.html?_r=0>.

Clinton, Hillary Rodham, and Bill Frist. 'Save the Children's Insurance'. February 12, 2015. <http://www.nytimes.com/2015/02/13/opinion/hillary-clinton-and-bill-frist-on-health-care-for-americas-kids.html>.

Clinton, Hillary Rodham. *Hard Choices.* New York: Simon & Schuster, 2014.

Clinton, Hillary Rodham. 'Helping Women Isn't Just a "Nice" Thing to Do'. April 5, 2013. <http://www.thedailybeast.com/witw/articles/2013/04/05/hillary-clinton-helping-women-isn-t-just-a-nice-thing-to-do.html>.

Clinton, Hillary Rodham. *Living History.* New York: Simon & Schuster, 2014.

Clinton, Hillary Rodham. 'Remarks for the United Nations Fourth World Conference on Women'. September 5, 1995. <http://www.un.org/esa/gopher-data/conf/fwcw/conf/gov/950905175653.txt>.

Collins, Laura. 'EXCLUSIVE: Hillary Clinton's camp fears a new "bimbo eruption" will put the kibosh on candidacy – especially from Gennifer Flowers who claimed Bill liked to be blindfolded and tied up with silk scarves and called his wife "Hilla the Hun".' July 31, 2015. <http://www.dailymail.co.uk/news/ article-3180398/ Hillary-Clinton-s-camp-fears-new-bimbo-eruption-kibosh-candidacy-especially-Gennifer-Flowers-claimed-Bill-liked-blindfolded-tied-silk-scarves-called-wife-Hilla-Hun.html>.

Garber, Megan. 'Hillary Clinton Traveled 956,733 Miles During Her Time as Secretary of State'. January 29, 2013. <http://www.theatlantic.com/politics/archive/2013/01/ hillary-clinton-traveled-956-733-miles-during-her-time-as-secretary-of-state/272656/>.

Goodman, Amy. 'Iranian Nobel Peace Prize Laureate Shirin Ebadi on Nuclear Deal, Islamic State, Women's Rights'. April 28, 2015. <http://www.democracynow. org/2015/4/28/iranian_nobel_peace_prize_laureate_shirin>.

'Hillary Clinton: On the Issues'. <http://www.ontheissues.org/Hillary_Clinton.htm>.

Kahn, Mattie. '7 Best Lines From Hillary Clinton's Impossibly Gracious Concession Speech'. November 9, 2016. <http://www.elle.com/culture/career-politics/news/ a40596/hillary-clinton-concession-speech-best-quotes-lines/>.

Kanyoro, Musimbi. 'Hillary's Legacy: Women and Girls Take A Front Seat'. February 1, 2013. <http://www.trust.org/item/20130201133000-9ni2s/>.

Klein, Edward. *Blood Feud: The Clintons vs. The Obamas.* New York: Kensington, 2015.

Klein, Rick. 'What Went Wrong? How Hillary Lost'. June 3, 2008. <http://abcnews. go.com/Politics/Vote2008/story?id=4978839>.

'Most Admired Man and Woman'. <http://www.gallup.com/poll/1678/most-admired-man-woman.aspx>.

Penketh, Anne. 'The new suffragettes: Shirin Ebadi – the campaigner who has become an international figurehead for women's rights'. May 30, 2013. <http://www. independent.co.uk/news/people/profiles/the-new-suffragettes-shirin-ebadi-the-campaigner-who-has-become-an-international- figurehead-for-8638504.html>.

Rogak, Lisa. *Hillary Clinton in Her Own Words.* Berkeley: Seal Press, 2014.

Sugarman, Eli. '5 Top Highlights in Hillary Clinton's Secretary of State Tenure'. January 2, 2013. <http://mic.com/articles/21829/5-top-highlights-in-hillary-clinton-s-secretary-of-state-tenure>.

Waldman, Ayelet. 'Is This Really Goodbye?' October 18, 2012. <http://www.marieclaire. com/politics/news/a7354/hillary-clinton-farewell/>.

Kate Bornstein

'An interview with Kate Bornstein on Gender Outlaws'. April 26, 2012. <http:// fivebooks.com/interviews/kate-bornstein-on-gender>.

'Book Reviews: Gender Outlaw'. April 15, 1994. <https://www.kirkusreviews.com/ book-reviews/kate-bornstein/gender-outlaw/>.

Bornstein, Kate. 'About'. <http://katebornstein.typepad.com/about.html>.

Bornstein, Kate. *A Queer and Pleasant Danger.* Boston: Beacon Press, 2012.

Bornstein, Kate. 'Don't Be Mean? Really?' October 6, 2010. <http://katebornstein. typepad.com/kate_bornsteins_blog/2010/10/dont-be-mean-really.html>.

Bornstein, Kate. *Hello, Cruel World.* New York: Seven Stories Press, 2006.

Bornstein, Kate. 'Lambda Literary Pioneer Award Talks, 2014'. June 05, 2014. <http:// katebornstein.typepad.com/kate_bornsteins_blog/2014/06/lambda-literary-pioneer-award-talks-2014.html>.

Bornstein, Kate. *My Gender Workbook.* New York: Routledge, 1997.

'Kate Bornstein Biography'. <http://www.speakoutnow.org/speaker/bornstein-kate>.

Ortega, Tony. 'Kate Bornstein's Amazing Voyage'. May 2, 2012. <http://www.villagevoice.com/news/kate-bornsteins-amazing-voyage-6434753>.

Pasulka, Nicole. '"A Queer and Pleasant Danger": Kate Bornstein, Trans Scientology Survivor'. May 5, 2012. <http://www.motherjones.com/media/2012/04/kate-bornstein-gender-outlaw-queer-and-pleasant-danger-interview>.

Signorile, Michelangelo. 'Kate Bornstein, Transgender Writer and Activist, Discusses Life In And Exit From The Church Of Scientology'. May 5, 2012. <http://www.huffingtonpost.com/2012/05/05/kate-bornstein-transgender-scientology_n_1483590.html>.

'The Thetan'. <http://www.scientology.org/what-is-scientology/basic-principles-of-scientology/the-thetan.html>.

Pam Grier

Adolphus, Emell Derra. 'Pam Grier on "Foxy Brown" and Black Feminism'. Feburary 2014. <http://www.blacdetroit.com/BLAC-Detroit/February-2014/Pam-Grier-on-Foxy-Brown-and-Black-Feminism/>.

Bailey, Jason. 'The Enduring Appeal (and Unfortunate Novelty) of Pam Grier, Our Favorite Movie Badass'. June 9, 2015. <http://flavorwire.com/522058/the-enduring-appeal-and-unfortunate-novelty-of-pam-grier-our-favorite-movie-badass>.

Canby, Vincent. 'Screen: 'Beyond the Valley of the Dolls':Film Seems to Parody His Earlier Efforts'. June 27, 1970. <http://www.nytimes.com/movie/review?res=9E07E7D7123FE336A05754C2A9609C946190D6CF?>.

Faraci, Devin. 'The Badass Interview: Pam Grier On JACKIE BROWN And Trading Recipes With Fellini'. October 14, 2011. <http://birthmoviesdeath.com/2011/10/14/the-badass-interview-pam-grier-on-jackie-brown-and-trading-recipes-with-fel>.

Grier, Pam. *Foxy: My Life in Three Acts*. New York: Grand Central Publishing, 2010.

Lambert, Craig. 'The Blaxploitation Era'. January-February 2003. <http://harvardmagazine.com/2003/01/the-blaxploitation-era>.

Lee, Felicia R. 'Pam Grier's Connection of Lessons Learned'. May 4, 2010. <http://www.nytimes.com/2010/05/05/books/05grier.html>.

Mask, Mia. 'Pam Grier: Part Foxy, Part Feminist, All Sexy'. March 2, 2010. <http://www.npr.org/ templates/story/story.php?storyId=124009543>.

Morris, Wesley. 'Sweet Vengeance'. March 15, 2013. <http://grantland.com/features/the-career-legacy-pam-grier/>.

'Pam Grier Biography'. April 2, 2014. <http://www.biography.com/people/pam-grier-17181346>.

Petkovic, John. 'Pam Grier, queen of 1970s Blaxploitation films, speaks in Cleveland on her book tour'. September 18, 2010. <http://www.cleveland.com/goingout/index.ssf/2010/09/pam_grier_queen_of_1970s_blaxp.html>.

Tisdale, Stacey. 'Gloria Steinem on Black Women: "They Invented the Feminist Movement".' March 19, 2015. <http://www.blackenterprise.com/lifestyle/arts-culture/be-womens-history-month-feminist-icon-gloria-steinem-talks-black-women-feminism/>.

Leslie Feinberg

'Biography'. <http://transgenderwarrior.org/biography/fullbio.htm>.

Currah, Paisley. 'Leslie Feinberg's Gender Revolution'. <http://brooklynquarterly.org/leslie-feinbergs-gender-revolution-paisley-currah/>.

Enszer, Julie R. 'Leslie Feinberg, Transgender Warrior'. December 2, 2014. <http://the-toast.net/2014/12/02/leslie-feinberg-transgender-warrior/>.

Feinberg, Leslie. *Transgender Warriors: Making History from Joan of Arc to Dennis Rodman*. Boston: Beacon Press, 1996.

Feinberg, Leslie. *Trans Liberation: Beyond Pink Or Blue*. Boston: Beacon Press, 1999.

'Leslie Feinberg'. <http://jwa.org/people/feinberg-leslie>.

Miller, Shauna. 'The Importance of Leslie Feinberg'. November 17, 2014. <http://www.theatlantic.com/entertainment/archive/2014/11/the-importance-of-leslie-feinberg/382852/>.

Pratt, Minnie Bruce. 'Transgender Pioneer and Stone Butch Blues Author Leslie Feinberg Has Died'. November 17, 2014. <http://www.advocate.com/arts-entertainment/books/2014/11/17/transgender-pioneer-leslie-feinberg-stone-butch-blues-has-died>.

Pratt, Minnie Bruce. 'Transgender warrior Leslie Feinberg united all struggles for liberation'. March 31, 2015. <http://www.workers.org/articles/2015/03/31/transgender-warrior-leslie-feinberg-united-all-struggles-for-liberation/>.

Schaub, Michael. 'Author and transgender activist Leslie Feinberg is dead at 65'. November 18, 2014. <http://www.latimes.com/books/jacketcopy/la-et-jc-author-and-transgender-activist-leslie-feinberg-is-dead-at-65-20141117-story.html >.

Stryker, Susan, and Stephen Whittle. *The Transgender Studies Reader*. New York: Routledge, 2013.

Weber, Bruce. 'Leslie Feinberg, Writer and Transgender Activist, Dies at 65'. November 24, 2015. <http://www.nytimes.com/2014/11/25/nyregion/leslie-feinberg-writer-and-transgender-activist-dies-at-65.html?_r=0>.

Williams, Cristan. '1993: The Life and Times of a Gender Outlaw: An Interview with Leslie Feinberg'. <http://transadvocate.com/1993-the-life-and-times-of-a-gender-outlaw-an-interview-with-leslie-feinberg_n_8350.htm>

Sally Ride

'Astronaut Sally Ride: In Her Own Words'. July 24, 2012. <http://www.space.com/16732-sally-ride-quotes-women-science.html>.

Bilger, Audrey. 'The Private Life and Natural Feminism of Sally Ride'. November 4, 2014. <http://msmagazine.com/blog/2014/11/04/the-private-life-and-natural-feminism-of-sally-ride/>.

Burby, Liza N. *Mae Jemison: The First African American Woman Astronaut*. New York: Rosen Publishing, 1997.

'Dr. Sally Ride'. <https://www.sallyridescience.com/about/sallyride/about-sallyride/>.

'Dr. Sally Ride Former astronaut, first American woman in space CEO of Sally Ride Science and Professor Emerita University of California, San Diego'. <http://www.nasa.gov/offices/hsf/members/ride-bio.html>.

Grady, Denise. 'American Woman Who Shattered Space Ceiling'. July 23, 2012. <http://www.nytimes.com/2012/07/24/science/space/sally-ride-trailblazing-astronaut-dies-at-61.html?_r=0>.

'Kalpana Chawla (Ph.D.)'. May 2004. <http://www.jsc.nasa.gov/Bios/htmlbios/chawla.html>.

Kramer, Melody. 'New Female Astronauts Show Evolution of Women in Space'. June 19, 2013. <http://news.nationalgeographic.com/news/2013/06/130618-space-female-astronauts-sally-ride-nasa-science/>.

May, Sandra, and Flint Wild. 'Who Was Sally Ride?' June 18, 2014. <http://www.nasa.gov/audience/forstudents/k-4/stories/nasa-knows/who-was-sally-ride-k4.html>.

Redd, Nola Taylor. 'Kalpana Chawla: Biography & Columbia Disaster'. August 10, 2012. <http://www.space.com/17056-kalpana-chawla-biography.html>.

Ruskai, Mary Beth. 'Why Women Are Discouraged From Becoming Scientists'. March 5, 1990. <http://www.the-scientist.com/?articles.view/articleNo/10951/title/Why-Women-Are-Discouraged-From-Becoming-Scientists/>.

'Sally Ride'. September 2012. <https://hbr.org/2012/09/sally-ride/ar/1>.

'Sally Ride Interview'. June 2, 2006. <http://www.achievement.org/achiever/sally-ride-ph-d/#interview>.

Severn, Stacey. 'The Top 6 Female Astronauts Every Scientista Should Know About'. July 29, 2013. <http://www.scientistafoundation.com/scientista-spotlights/the-top-6-female-astronauts-every-scientista-should-know-about>.

The 'How to' of performance management. (E-book). Management Training Australia, 2015.

'The World's Top 6 Female Astronauts – Inspiring Girls & Young Women To "Reach For The Stars"'. October 20, 2013. <http://www.spaceflightinsider.com/space-flight-news/the-worlds-top-6-female-astronauts-inspiring-girls-young-women-to-reach-for-the-stars/>.

Trex, Ethan. '5 Things You Didn't Know About Sally Ride'. July 23, 2012. <http://mentalfloss.com/article/31275/5-things-you-didnt-know-about-sally-ride>.

'Valentina Tereshkova'. <http://starchild.gsfc.nasa.gov/docs/StarChild/whos_who_level2/tereshkova.html>.

bell hooks

Adams, Maggie, and Soojung Chang. 'Famed feminist preaches peace'. January 16, 2003. <https://news.google.com/newspapers?nid=2706&dat=20030116&id=4QNKAAAAIBAJ&sjid=YB4NAAAAIBAJ&pg=3125,434381&hl=en >.

'bell hooks'. <http://conservancy.umn.edu/bitstream/handle/11299/166225/hooks%2c%20bell.pdf?sequence=1&isAllowed=y>.

'bell hooks'. January/February 1995. <http://www.utne.com/arts/bell-hooks-postmodernism-racism-sexism.aspx>.

'Bell Hooks'. February 17, 2000. <http://www.cnn.com/chat/transcripts/2000/2/hooks/index.html>.

'Bell Hooks (1952–) Biography - Personal, Addresses, Career, Honors Awards, Writings, Sidelights'. <http://biography.jrank.org/pages/2287/Hooks-Bell-1952.html>.

'Bell hooks: American Scholar'. <http://www.britannica.com/biography/bell-hooks>.

'bell hooks talks to John Perry Barlow'. September 1, 1995. <http://www.lionsroar.com/bell-hooks-talks-to-john-perry-barlow/>.

Davidson, Maria del Guadalupe, and George Yancy. Critical Perspectives on Bell Hooks. New York: Routledge, 2009.

Hewlett, Jennifer. 'Noted feminists celebrate opening of institute'. September 20, 2010. <http://www.kentucky.com/news/local/education/article44049879.html>.

hooks, bell. Feminism Is for Everybody: Passionate Politics. Cambridge: South End, 2000.

hooks, bell. Feminist Theory: From Margin to Center. New York: Routledge, 2014.

hooks, bell. Outlaw Culture: Resisting Representations. New York: Routledge, 1994. 106.

Jankowski, Lauren. 'bell hooks'. <http://womenshistory.about.com/od/second-wave-feminists/a/Bell-Hooks.htm>.

McLeod, Melvin. 'Angelou'. January 1998. <http://www.hartford-hwp.com/archives/45a/249.html>.

Cindy Sherman

Behrooz, Anahit. '10 Artists Who Changed the Course of 20th Century Art'. January 10, 2017. <http://theculturetrip.com/north-america/usa/articles/10-artists-who-changed-the-course-of-20th-century-art/>.

Berne, Betsy. 'Studio: Cindy Sherman'. June 1, 2003. <http://www.tate.org.uk/context-comment/articles/studio-cindy-sherman>.

Blessing, Jennifer. 'Cindy Sherman: Untitled, #264'. <http://www.guggenheim.org/new-york/collections/collection-online/artwork/10791>.

'Cindy Sherman'. <https://art21.org/artist/cindy-sherman/>.

'Cindy Sherman'. <http://www.britannica.com/biography/Cindy-Sherman>.

'Cindy Sherman'. < https://www.guggenheim.org/artwork/artist/cindy-sherman>.

'Cindy Sherman'. November 29, 2008. <http://www.interviewmagazine.com/art/cindy-sherman>.

'Cindy Sherman'. <http://www.theartstory.org/artist-sherman-cindy.htm>.

'Cindy Sherman Talks to David Frankel. ('80S Then)'. March 2003. <https://www.questia.com/magazine/1G1-98918643/cindy-sherman-talks-to-david-frankel-80s-then>.

Collins, Glenn. 'A Portraitist's Romp Through Art History'. February 1, 1990. <http://www.nytimes.com/1990/02/01/arts/a-portraitist-s-romp-through-art-history.html>.

Hattenstone, Simon. 'Cindy Sherman: Me, myself and I'. January 15, 2011. <http://www.theguardian.com/artanddesign/2011/jan/15/cindy-sherman-interview>.

Heartney, Eleanor. *After the Revolution: Women who Transformed Contemporary Art.* New York: Dorsky Gallery, 2007.

Karlen, Neal. *Babes in Toyland: The Making and Selling of a Rock and Roll Band.* New York: Crown/Archetype, 2013.

Kimmelman, Michael. *Portraits: Talking with Artists at the Met, the Modern, the Louvre, and Elsewhere.* New York: Random House, 1998.

O'Neill, Claire. 'Meet The World's Most Expensive Photo'. May 13, 2011. <http://www.npr.org/sections/pictureshow/2011/05/13/136273419/meet-the-worlds-most-expensive-photo>.

Respini, Eva, Johanna Burton, and John Waters. *Cindy Sherman.* New York: Museum of Modern Art, 2012.

Schmelzer, Paul. '"Completely Punk Rock": Cindy Sherman's (Nearly) Forgotten History with Babes in Toyland'. February 7, 2013. <http://blogs.walkerart.org/visualarts/2013/02/07/cindy-sherman-babes-in-toyland-punk-rock/>.

Schwabsky, Barry. 'ART; A Photographer's Many Faces'. April 18, 1999. <http://www.nytimes.com/1999/04/18/nyregion/art-a-photographer-s-many-faces.html?ref=cindysherman>.

'Sherman, Cindy'. <http://www.mocp.org/detail.php?type=related&kv=12996&t=objects>.

Silver, Alain and James Ursini. *The Horror Film Reader.* Milwaukee: Hal Leonard, 2000.

'The Complete Untitled Film Stills Cindy Sherman'. 1997. <http://www.moma.org/interactives/exhibitions/1997/sherman/>.

Vogel, Carol. 'Cindy Sherman Unmasked'. February 16, 2012. <http://www.nytimes.com/2012/02/19/arts/design/moma-to-showcase-cindy-shermans-new-and-old-characters.html?_r=0>.

Oprah

'Accused Child Predators Caught'. October 19, 2005. <https://www.fbi.gov/news/stories/2005/october/oprah-television-viewers>.

Alderman, Abigail. 'O, The Oprah Magazine Celebrates 15 Years of Publication'. April 22, 2015. <http://www.hearst.com/newsroom/o-the-oprah-magazine-celebrates-15-years-of-publication>.

'All About Oprah: Winfrey Reflects On Her Life History In "MAKERS" Documentary (VIDEO)'. February 28, 2013. <http://www.huffingtonpost.com/2013/02/28/about-oprah-winfrey-life-history-makers_n_2760337.html>.

Cooper, Ilene. *Up Close: Oprah Winfrey.* New York: Puffin, 2008.

Ebert, Roger. 'How I Gave Oprah Her Start'. November 16, 2005. <http://www.rogerebert.com/rogers-journal/how-i-gave-oprah-her-start>.

Jacobson, Murrey. 'The Oprah Effect, by the Numbers'. May 25, 2011. <http://www.pbs.org/newshour/rundown/the-oprah-phenomenon-by-the-numbers/>.

Kelley, Kitty. *Oprah: A Biography.* New York: Crown/Archetype, 2010.

Kniffel, Leonard. 'Reading For Life: Oprah Winfrey'. August 10, 2015. <http://www.ilovelibraries.org/article/reading-life-oprah-winfrey>.

Krohn, Katherine E. *Oprah Winfrey: Global Media Leader.* Minneapolis: Twenty-First Century Books, 2008.

Miller, Matthew. 'The Wealthiest Black Americans'. May 6, 2009. <http://www.forbes.com/2009/05/06/richest-black-americans-busienss-billionaires-richest-black-americans.html>.

Minzesheimer, Bob. 'How the "Oprah Effect" changed publishing'. May 22, 2011. <http://usatoday30.usatoday.com/life/books/news/2011-05-22-Oprah-Winfrey-Book-Club_n.htm>.

Paprocki, Sherry Beck. *Oprah Winfrey: Talk Show Host and Media Magnate.* New York: Infobase Publishing, 2009.

'Oprah: Charity Work, Events and Causes'. <https://www.looktothestars.org/celebrity/oprah>.

'Oprah gets another award: The Presidential Medal of Freedom'. November 20, 2013. <https://www.washingtonpost.com/news/reliable-source/wp/2013/11/20/oprah-gets-another-award-the-presidential-medal-of-freedom/>.

'Oprah goes national'. <http://www.history.com/this-day-in-history/oprah-goes-national>.

'Oprah opens up about drugs, abuse'. November 14, 2005. <http://www.today.com/popculture/oprah-opens-about-drugs-abuse-2D80556369>.

'Oprah Winfrey'. <http://www.fembio.org/english/biography.php/woman/biography/oprah-winfrey/>.

'Oprah Winfrey'. October 9, 2008. <http://www.entrepreneur.com/article/197558>.

'Oprah Winfrey Biography'. <http://www.achievement.org/achiever/oprah-winfrey/>.

'Oprah Winfrey Biography'. April 28, 2017<http://www.biography.com/people/oprah-winfrey-9534419>.

'Oprah Winfrey Interview'. February 25, 1991. <http://www.achievement.org/achiever/oprah-winfrey/#interview>.

'Oprah Winfrey Show, The'. <http://www.emmytvlegends.org/interviews/shows/oprah-winfrey-show-the>.

Pine, Joslyn. *Book of African-American Quotations.* Mineola: Courier Corporation, 2012.

'President Obama Names Medal of Freedom Recipients'. July 30, 2009. <https://obamawhitehouse.archives.gov/the-press-office/president-obama-names-medal-freedom-recipients >.

Schnall, Marianne. 'Conversation with Oprah Winfrey'. <http://www.feminist.com/resources/artspeech/interviews/oprahwinfrey.html>.

Sellers, Patricia. 'The Business Of Being Oprah'. April 1, 2002. <http://archive.fortune.com/magazines/fortune/fortune_archive/2002/04/01/320634/index.htm>.

'So Much for One Person, One Vote'. August 6, 2008. <http://freakonomics.com/2008/08/06/so-much-for-one-person-one-vote/>.

'The Academy'. <https://www.owla.co.za/owlag_academy>.

Western, Robin. *Oprah Winfrey: A Biography of a Billionaire Talk Show Host.* Berkeley Heights: Enslow Publishers, 2013.

Wilmouth, Brad. 'NYT's Maureen Dowd: Clinton's Lying "Endearing," While Bush "Lies" In His Bubble'. January 27, 2006. <http://newsbusters.org/blogs/brad-

wilmouth/2006/01/27/nyts-maureen-dowd-clintons-lying-endearing-while-bush-lies-his-bubble>.
'YMCA of Michiana, Inc'. <http://force4good.org/2012/nominee/ymca-michiana-inc>.

Geena Davis
'About Us'. <http://seejane.org/about-us/>.
Coyne, Kate. 'Geena Davis from Heartbreak to Happiness'. March 31, 2006. <http://www.goodhousekeeping.com/life/inspirational-stories/interviews/a17444/geena-davis-interview-arp06/>.
Davis, Geena. 'Geena Davis' Two Easy Steps To Make Hollywood Less Sexist (Guest Column)'. December 11, 2013. <http://www.hollywoodreporter.com/news/geena-davis-two-easy-steps-664573>.
Hajek, Daniel. 'From Mannequin To Actor: Geena Davis' "Ridiculous, Ridiculous" Break'. October 19, 2014. <http://www.npr.org/2014/10/19/353323280/from-mannequin-to-actor-geena-davis-ridiculous-ridiculous-break>.
'Harry Belafonte, Geena Davis to receive Muhammad Ali awards'. August 18, 2015. <http://www.washingtontimes.com/news/2015/aug/18/belafonte-davis-to-receive-ali-humanitarian-awards/>.
Hitchens, Christopher. 'The Eggheads and I'. September 1996. <http://www.vanityfair.com/news/1996/09/hitchens-199609>.
'Interview With Actress Geena Davis'. March 22, 2006. <http://www.cnn.com/TRANSCRIPTS/0603/22/lol.05.html>.
Jones, Emma. 'Geena Davis: Thelma and Louise star on setting up her own film festival and getting more women on screen'. May 10, 2015. <http://www.independent.co.uk/arts-entertainment/films/features/geena-davis-thelma-and-louise-star-on-setting-up-her-own-film-festival-and-getting-more-women-on-10239457.html>.
Lipsitz, Raina. '"Thelma & Louise": The Last Great Film About Women'. August 31, 2011. <http://www.theatlantic.com/entertainment/archive/2011/08/thelma-louise-the-last-great-film-about-women/244336/>.
Litsky, Frank. 'OLYMPICS; Geena Davis Zeros In With Bow and Arrows'. August 6, 1999. <http://www.nytimes.com/1999/08/06/sports/olympics-geena-davis-zeros-in-with-bow-and-arrows.html>.
'Prominent Mensans'. <https://www.mensa.org/prominent-mensans>.
Rabin, Nathan. 'Geena Davis launches Bentonville Film Festival'. January 6, 2015. <https://thedissolve.com/news/4372-geena-davis-helps-launch-bentonville-film-festival/>.
Richardson, Sarah. 'We Heart: Geena Davis'. August 17, 2011. <http://msmagazine.com/blog/2011/08/17/we-heart-geena-davis>.
Silverstein, Melissa. 'Geena Davis Uses Her Celebrity Power to Help Improve the Gender Disparity in Film and TV for Kids'. June 7, 2010. <http://www.huffingtonpost.com/melissa-silverstein/geena-davis-uses-her-cele_b_528284.html>.
Yates, Carolyn. 'Geena Davis Is My Feminist Hero'. August 20, 2011. <http://www.autostraddle.com/geena-davis-is-my-feminist-hero-106349/>.

Anita Hill
'Anita F. Hill'. <http://www.leighbureau.com/speakers/AHill/>.
Armstrong, Connie G. 'Hill, Anita F'. <http://www.okhistory.org/publications/enc/entry.php?entry=HI005>.
Gibbs, Nancy. 'Hill Vs. Thomas: An Ugly Circus'. October 21, 1991. <http://content.time.com/time/magazine/article/0,9171,974074,00.html>.
Grana, Sheryl J. *Women and Justice.* Lanham: Rowman & Littlefield, 2010.

'Hill, Anita'. <http://www.encyclopedia.com/topic/Anita_Hill.aspx>.

Hill, Anita. 'Opening Statement: Sexual Harassment Hearings Concerning Judge Clarence Thomas'. October 11, 1991. <http://gos.sbc.edu/h/hill.html>.

Kasson, Elisabeth Greenbaum. 'Speaking Truth to Power: "Anita" Tells a Tale of Transformation'. <http://www.documentary.org/feature/speaking-truth-power-anita-tells-tale-transformation>.

Krupa, Charles. 'Anita Hill vs. Clarence Thomas: The Backstory'. October 20, 2010. <http://www.cbsnews.com/news/anita-hill-vs-clarence-thomas-the-backstory/>.

Lithwick, Dahlia. 'All These Issues Are Still With Us'. March 21, 2014. <http://www.slate.com/articles/double_x/doublex/2014/03/talking_to_anita_hill_at_57_the_woman_who_stood_up_to_clarence_thomas_is.html>.

Markovitz, Jonathan. *Legacies of Lynching: Racial Violence and Memory.* Minneapolis: University of Minnesota, 2004.

Palmer, Barbara. 'Ten years later, Anita Hill revisits the Clarence Thomas controversy'. April 3, 2002. <http://news.stanford.edu/news/2002/april3/anitahill-43.html>.

Paludi, Michele A. *The Psychology of Teen Violence and Victimization.* Volume 2. Santa Barbara: ABC-CLIO, 2011.

Smolowe, Jill. 'Sex, Lies and Politics: He Said, She Said'. October 21, 1991. <http://content.time.com/time/magazine/article/0,9171,974096,00.html>.

Williams, Patricia J. 'The Legacy of Anita Hill, Then and Now'. October 5, 2011. <http://www.thenation.com/article/legacy-anita-hill-then-and-now/>.

Poly Styrene

Billet, Alexander. 'Defiance in Day-Glo: Remembering Poly Styrene'. May 6, 2011. <http://www.thenation.com/article/defiance-day-glo-remembering-poly-styrene/>.

Boy George. 'Poly Styrene remembered by Boy George'. December 11, 2011. <http://www.theguardian.com/theobserver/2011/dec/11/poly-styrene-obituary-boy-george>.

jaymusseato. 'X-Ray Spex / Poly Styrene interview '77 punk'. April 6, 2013. <https://www.youtube.com/watch?v=D8hAqdx7g4M>.

Philby, Charlotte. 'My secret life: Poly Styrene, Singer, 51'April 18, 2008. <http://www.independent.co.uk/news/people/profiles/my-secret-life-poly-styrene-singer-51-811129.html>.

Ryzik, Melena. 'Poly Styrene, Punk Singer of X-Ray Spex, Is Dead at 53'. April 26, 2011. <http://www.nytimes.com/2011/04/27/arts/music/poly-styrene-brash-frontwoman-of-x-ray-spex-dies-at-53.html?_r=0>.

Salewicz, Chris. 'Poly Styrene: Singer who blazed a trail for punk’s feminist revolutionaries'. April 26, 2011. <http://www.independent.co.uk/news/obituaries/poly-styrene-singer-who-blazed-a-trail-for-punkrsquos-feminist-revolutionaries-2275032.html>.

Simpson, Dave. 'Poly Styrene: The Spex factor'. March 23, 2011. <http://www.theguardian.com/music/2011/mar/23/poly-styrene-interview>.

Sweeting, Adam. 'Poly Styrene Obituary'. April 26, 2011. <http://www.theguardian.com/music/2011/apr/26/poly-styrene-obituary>.

Sandi Toksvig

Griffiths, Josie. 'GIRLS ARE BEST. Who is Sandi Toksvig? The Great British Bake Off host, QI presenter and writer – all you need to know'. April 14, 2017. <https://www.thesun.co.uk/tvandshowbiz/3112181/sandi-toksvig-great-british-bake-off-qi/>.

Husband, Stuart. 'This much I know: Sandi Toksvig'. December 6, 2009. <https://www.theguardian.com/lifeandstyle/2009/dec/06/sandi-toksvig-this-much-i-know>.

'Sandi Toksvig becomes chancellor of Portsmouth University'. January 23, 2012. <https://www.theguardian.com/education/2012/jan/23/sandi-toksvig-chancellor-portsmouth-university>.

'Sandi Toksvig: Can Social Change Start With Laughter?'. March 24, 2017. <http://www.npr.org/2017/03/24/520942402/sandi-toksvig-can-social-change-start-with-laughter>.

'Sandi Toksvig: quote'. <http://learninglog.tumblr.com/post/486438324/when-i-was-a-student-at-cambridge-i-remember-an>.

TED. 'A political party for women's equality | Sandi Toksvig'. December 14, 2016. <https://www.youtube.com/watch?v=r92jUj7gNRw>.

'TED: Sandi Toksvig'. <https://www.ted.com/speakers/sandi_toksvig>.

Toksvig, Sandi. 'Sandi Toksvig: "Today we can all celebrate whom we choose to love"'. March 28, 2014. <https://www.theguardian.com/lifeandstyle/2014/mar/28/sandi-toksvig-gay-marriage-renewing-vows>.

Madonna

'About Us - Raising Malawi'. <http://www.raisingmalawi.org/about-us/ >.

Barcella, Laura. *Madonna and Me: Women Writers on the Queen of Pop.* Berkeley: Soft Skull Press, 2012.

'Best-selling female recording artist'. 2014. <http://www.guinnessworldrecords.com/world-records/best-selling-female-recording-artist>.

Curry, Tyler. '10 Celebrity Icons of HIV Activism'. April 5, 2015. <http://www.advocate.com/health/hiv-aids/2015/04/05/10-celebrity-icons-hiv-activism>.

Dobnik, Verena. 'Video a "Celebration of Sex"—Madonna'. December 4, 1990. <http://articles.latimes.com/1990-12-04/entertainment/ca-6106_1_video>.

Gandhi, Neha. 'Madonna Is A True Feminist Icon – & You Need To Pay Attention To What She's Saying'. March 9, 2015. <http://www.refinery29.com/2015/03/83104/madonna-rebel-heart-feminism-interview>.

Jerome, Jim. 'Lady Madonna'. March 13, 2000. <http://www.people.com/people/archive/article/0,,20130712,00.html>.

Landrum, Gene N. *Profiles of Female Genius.* Buffalo: Prometheus Books, 1994.

Lynch, Joe. 'Madonna Was Nearly Arrested for Simulating Masturbation 25 Years Ago Today'. May 29, 2015. <http://www.billboard.com/articles/news/6582939/madonna-masturbation-like-a-virgin-controversy-toronto-anniversary>.

Madonna. 'Express Yourself'. Music video. Like a Prayer. Sire Records. May 9, 1989. <https://www.youtube.com/watch?v=GsVcUzP_O_8>.

'Madonna Music Career Statistics'. September 5, 2016. <http://www.statisticbrain.com/madonna-music-career-statistics/>.

Mitchell, John. 'Dick Clark, Thank You For Introducing Madonna to The World'. April 19, 2012. <http://www.mtv.com/news/1683483/dick-clark-madonna/>.

Morton, Andrew. *Madonna.* New York: Macmillan, 2001.

Munier, Paula. *On Being Blonde.* Gloucester: Fair Winds Press, 2004.

Nagourney, Adam. 'Madonna's Charity Fails in Bid to Finance School'. March 24, 2011. <http://www.nytimes.com/2011/03/25/us/25madonna.html?_r=0>.

Paglia, Camille. 'Madonna – Finally, a Real Feminist'. December 14, 1990. <http://www.nytimes.com/1990/12/14/opinion/madonna-finally-a-real-feminist.html>.

Robertson, Pamela. *Guilty Pleasures.* London: I.B. Tauris, 1996.

Sawyer, Forrest. 'Interview with Madonna'. December 3, 1990. <http://allaboutmadonna.com/madonna-tv/videos-1990>

Sexton, Adam. *Desperately Seeking Madonna.* New York: Random House, 2008.

Taranto, Denis. 'Madonna Interview: I Am A Nice Little Ducky'. May 1987. <http://see-aych.com/madonna/madonna_interview.htm>.

Wolf, Naomi. 'Madonna: The Director's Cut'. November 9, 2011. <http://www.
harpersbazaar.com/celebrity/latest/news/a841/madonna-interview-1211/>.

Renée Cox

Colangelo, Lisa and Michael R. Blood. 'Commission Could Face Many Legal Obstacles'.
February 16, 2001. <http://www.nydailynews.com/archives/news/commission-face-
legal-obstacles-article-1.914190>.

Cox, Renee, Fo Wilson, and Tony Cokes. 'Fighting Cultural Misinformation About
African-Americans'. <http://www.brown.edu/Departments/MCM/people/cokes/
NAC.html>.

Croft, Karen. 'Using her body'. February 22, 2001. <http://www.salon.com/2001/02/22/
renee_cox/>.

Paglia, Camille. *Glittering Images*. New York: Pantheon Books, 2012.

Plett, Nicole. 'Renée Cox interviewed by Nicole Plett'. October 21, 2008. <http://
www.libraries.rutgers.edu/sites/default/files/dwas/pdfs/Cox_interview_by_Plett_
Oct_2008.pdf>.

'Renee Cox'. <https://www.brooklynmuseum.org/eascfa/feminist_art_base/renee-
cox>.

'Renee Cox'. <http://www.reneecox.org/#!about/ciaa>.

Williams, Monte. '"Yo Mama" Artist Takes On Catholic Critic'. February 21, 2001.
<http://www.nytimes.com/2001/02/21/nyregion/yo-mama-artist-takes-on-catholic-
critic.html>.

Caroline Lucas

Aitkenhead, Decca. 'Caroline Lucas: "We've got to get better at painting a positive
vision of a post-carbon world. This is not about sitting around a candle in a cave"'.
May 18, 2009. <https://www.theguardian.com/politics/2009/may/18/interview-
caroline-lucas-green-party>.

'Caroline Lucas: articles'. <http://journalisted.com/caroline-lucas?allarticles=yes>.

'Caroline Lucas: books'. <https://www.amazon.co.uk/Books-Caroline-Lucas/s?ie=UTF
8&page=1&rh=i%3Abooks%2Cp_27%3ACaroline%20Lucas>.

Gold, Tanya. 'Caroline Lucas: the Green in beige who could be Nick Clegg's
nemesis'. September 3, 2010. <http://www.telegraph.co.uk/news/politics/green-
party/7981297/Caroline-Lucas-the-Green-in-beige-who-could-be-Nick-Cleggs-
nemesis.html>.

'Green Party: Caroline Lucas'. <https://www.greenparty.org.uk/people/caroline-lucas.
html>.

Lucas, Caroline. 'Caroline wins "MP of the Year" award for work with deprived and
minority communities'. July 16, 2013. <https://www.carolinelucas.com/latest/
caroline-wins-mp-of-the-year-award-for-work-with-deprived-and-minority-
communities>.

Lucas, Caroline. 'Equal rights for women'. <https://www.carolinelucas.com/issues/
equality/women>.

Lucas, Caroline. 'What I stand for and why'. <https://www.carolinelucas.com/caroline>.

Siobhan, Ryan. 'Caroline Lucas named "environmental hero". April 22, 2017. <http://
www.theargus.co.uk/news/15239923.Caroline_Lucas_named____environmental_
hero___/>.

Kathleen Hanna

Aaron, Charles. 'Trend of the Year: Rap-Rock Mooks'. September 2005. <http://www.
spin.com/2014/02/rap-rock-mook-nation-charles-aaron-september-2005/>.

Barcella, Laura. 'Kathleen Hanna Is My Absolute Favorite Fantasy Best Friend'. November 23, 2013. <http://www.xojane.com/entertainment/kathleen-hanna-is-one-of-my-favorite-people>.

Barcella, Laura. 'The A-word'. September 20, 2004. <http://www.salon.com/2004/09/20/t_shirts>.

Breihan, Tom. 'Video: The Mountain Goats and Kathleen Hanna Support Planned Parenthood at New York Rally'. March 2, 2011. <http://pitchfork.com/news/41737-video-the-mountain-goats-and-kathleen-hanna-support-planned-parenthood-at-new-york-rally/>.

Brockes, Emma. 'What happens when a riot grrrl grows up?' May 9, 2014. <http://www.theguardian.com/music/2014/may/09/kathleen-hanna-the-julie-ruin-bikini-kill-interview>.

Darms, Lisa. *The Riot Grrrl Collection.* New York: The Feminist Press at CUNY, 2014.

Hanna, Kathleen. 'Kathleen Hanna: My Herstory'. <http://www.letigreworld.com/sweepstakes/html_site/fact/khfacts.html>.

Hanna, Kathleen. 'Teenager'. July 9, 2011. <http://www.kathleenhanna.com/teenager>.

'Kathleen Hanna Biography'. April 2, 2014. <http://www.biography.com/people/kathleen-hanna-17178854>.

Kreps, Daniel. 'Kathleen Hanna Honored With "Riot Grrrl Day" in Boston'. April 9, 2015. <http://www.rollingstone.com/music/news/kathleen-hanna-honored-with-riot-grrrl-day-in-boston-20150409>.

Monem, Nadine. *Riot Grrrl: Revolution Girl Style Now!* London: Black Dog Publishing, 2007.

'Revolution, Girl Style'. November 22, 1992. <http://www.newsweek.com/revolution-girl-style-196998>.

Richards, Chris. 'Bikini Kill was a girl punk group ahead of its time'. November 18, 2012. <https://www.washingtonpost.com/lifestyle/style/bikini-kill-was-a-girl-punk-group-ahead-of-its-time/2012/11/18/3fdc61bc-31d8-11e2-bfd5-e202b6d7b501_story.html>.

'Riot Grrrl Collection Development Policy'. January 2016. <http://guides.nyu.edu/riot-grrrl/coll-dev>.

'Riot Grrrl Respect: Creative Women Influenced by the Punk Movement of the 90s'. February 5, 2015. <http://www.makers.com/blog/riot-grrrl-respect-creative-women-influenced-punk-movement-90s>.

Stern, Marlow. 'Punk Rock-Feminist Pioneer Kathleen Hanna on Her SXSW Doc and More'. March 13, 2013. <http://www.thedailybeast.com/articles/2013/03/13/punk-rock-feminist-pioneer-kathleen-hanna-on-her-sxsw-doc-more.html>.

Thompson, Stacy. *Punk Productions.* New York: SUNY Press, 2004.

True, Everett. 'Kathleen Hanna: the riot grrrl returns'. January 14, 2014. <http://www.theguardian.com/music/australia-culture-blog/2014/jan/14/kathleen-hanna-julie-ruin-riot-grrrl>.

Wang, Yiyang. 'Riot Grrrl's Lasting Effect on Feminism'. June 26, 2013. <http://www.nwlc.org/our-blog/riot-grrrl%E2%80%99s-lasting-effect-feminism>.

Wickman, Forrest. '"Girls to the Front": How Kathleen Hanna Helped Make Punk Safe for Women'. November 29, 2013. <http://www.slate.com/blogs/browbeat/2013/11/29/the_punk_singer_documentary_clip_kathleen_hanna_explains_the_riot_grrrl.html>.

Margaret Cho

Caswell, Michelle. 'Margaret Cho: She's the One that She Wants'. <http://asiasociety.org/margaret-cho-shes-one-she-wants>.

Cho, Margaret. 'Feminism'. November 13, 2012. <http://margaretcho.com/2012/11/13/feminism/>.

Cho, Margaret. *I'm the One That I Want*. New York: Random House, 2007.

Cho, Margaret. 'You're the fattest ballerina'. July 8, 2008. <http://www.cnn.com/2008/LIVING/personal/07/08/o.fattest.ballerina/index.html?iref=nextin>.

Eisenbach, Helen. 'Cho & Tell'. July 12, 1999. <http://nymag.com/nymetro/arts/features/758/>.

McCombs, Emily. 'The Same 5 Questions We Always Ask: Margaret Cho'. December 5, 2011. <http://www.xojane.com/entertainment/same-5-questions-we-always-ask-margaret-cho>.

Miserandino, Dominick. 'Cho, Margaret'. August 21, 2000. <http://thecelebritycafe.com/2000/08/cho-margaret/>.

'The Woman! The Comic! The Legend!' <http://margaretcho.com/bio/>.

Tiger, Caroline. *Margaret Cho*. New York: Infobase Learning, 2013.

Queen Latifah

'37th Annual GRAMMY Awards'. <http://www.grammy.com/awards/37th-annual-grammy-awards>.

Allen, Amy Ruth. *Queen Latifah: From Jersey Girl to Superstar*. Minneapolis: Twenty-First Century Books, 2012.

DeLuzio, Crista. *Women's Rights: People and Perspectives*. Santa Barbara: ABC-CLIO, 2009.

Johns, Robert L., and (edited by) Jessie Carney Smith. 'Queen Latifah'. *Notable Black American Women*. Book 2. Bonn: VNR AG, 1996.

Keeps, David A. 'Queen Latifah on Surviving Her Darkest Moment – and Finding Joy'. December 10, 2013. <http://www.goodhousekeeping.com/life/inspirational-stories/interviews/a19546/queen-latifah-interview/>.

Koestler-Grack, Rachel A. *Queen Latifah*. New York: Infobase Publishing, 2009.

Latifah, Queen. *Ladies First*. New York: Harper Paperbacks, 2000.

'Queen Latifah'. <https://www.britannica.com/biography/Queen-Latifah>.

'Queen Latifah Biography'. April 28, 2017. <http://www.biography.com/people/queen-latifah-9542419>.

Robertson, Regina R. 'Queen Latifah Reveals Past Sexual Abuse in July 2009 Issue of ESSENCE'. December 16, 2009. <http://www.essence.com/2009/06/10/queen-latifah-reveals-past-sexual-abuse>.

Rudulph, Heather Wood. 'Why Beyoncé, Nicki, & Taylor Owe A Debt To Queen Latifah'. August 5, 2015. <http://www.refinery29.com/2015/08/91904/queen-latifah-unity-feminist-legacy>.

Tracy, Liz. 'Is Queen Latifah A Feminist?' March 21, 2013. <http://www.browardpalmbeach.com/2013-03-21/music/is-queen-latifah-a-feminist/full>.

Vena, Jocelyn. 'Maya Angelou's Poem About Michael Jackson: "We Had Him".' July 7, 2009. <http://www.mtv.com/news/1615416/maya-angelous-poem-about-michael-jackson-we-had-him/>.

Williams, Brennan. 'Queen Latifah: Domestic Violence Is A Problem "Every Part Of Society".' September 19, 2014. <http://www.huffingtonpost.com/2014/09/19/queen-latifah-domestic-violence_n_5850858.html>.

Ani DiFranco

'Ani DiFranco'. <http://www.billboard.com/artist/279330/ani-difranco/biography>.

'Ani DiFranco Biography'. April 2, 2014. <http://www.biography.com/people/ani-difranco-20874409>.

Baine, Wallace. 'With her new album "Which Side Are You On?," Ani DiFranco connects the progressive spirit of yesterday to today's political challenges'. March 22, 2012. <http://www.santacruzsentinel.com/general-news/20120322/with-her-new-album-which-side-are-you-on-ani-difranco-connects-the-progressive-spirit-of-yesterday-to-todays-political-challenges>.

Baker-Whitelaw, Gavia. 'Why feminist icon Ani DiFranco is being accused of "blatant" racism'. December 29, 2013. <http://www.dailydot.com/lifestyle/ani-difranco-nottoway-plantation-facebook/>.

Cochrane, Kira. '"I'm considering a revolution".' October 10, 2007. <http://www.theguardian.com/music/2007/oct/10/folk.gender>.

Dicker, Rory. *A History of U.S. Feminisms.* Berkeley: Seal Press, 2008.

'Help Victims of Hurricane Katrina'. July 6, 2005. <http://www.righteousbabe.com/blogs/news/6242194-help-victims-of-hurricane-katrina>.

Himan, Eric. 'Regarding Ani'. February 14, 2014. <http://www.out.com/entertainment/music/2014/02/14/regarding-ani>.

'March for Women's Lives 2004'. <http://www.righteousbabe.com/products/ani-marches-and-sings-in-washington-d-c>.

'Musician and Activist Ani DiFranco to receive the prestigious Woody Guthrie Award on Thursday October 8th, 2009'. October 8, 2009. <http://www.prweb.com/releases/anidifranco/guthrieaward/prweb3013504.htm>.

'Open Letter From Ani Difranco to Ms. Editors'. January 12, 1998. <http://www.mtv.com/news/2474/open-letter-from-ani-difranco-to-ms-editors>.

Claude J. Summers. *The Queer Encyclopedia of Music, Dance, & Musical Theater.* San Francisco: Cleis Press, 2004.

Revkin, Andrew C. 'Righteous Babe Saves Hometown; A Fiercely Independent Folk Singer's Soaring Career Lifts Buffalo, Too'. February 16, 1998. <http://www.nytimes.com/1998/02/16/nyregion/righteous-babe-saves-hometown-fiercely-independent-folk-singer-s-soaring-career.html>.

Ruehl, Kim. 'Ani DiFranco's Best Songs'. February 10, 2017. <http://folkmusic.about.com/od/anidifranco/tp/AniDiFrancoSongs.htm>.

Sion, Mike. 'Going off-script with Ani DiFranco'. March 17, 2015. <http://www.rgj.com/story/life/arts/2015/03/16/ani-difranco-reno-concert/24866971>.

Van Meter, Jonathan. 'Righteous Babe'. SPIN. Vol 13, No 5. August 1997. SPIN Media, 1997.

Varga, George. 'Ani DiFranco sings and marches on'. March 13, 2015. <http://www.sandiegouniontribune.com/entertainment/music/sdut-ani-di-franco-moves-through-controversy-2015mar13-story.html>.

Warner, Jay. *Notable Moments of Women in Music.* Milwaukee: Hal Leonard, 2008.

Roxane Gay

Cochrane, Kira. 'Roxane Gay: meet the bad feminist'. August 2, 2014. <http://www.theguardian.com/world/2014/aug/02/roxane-gay-bad-feminist-sisterhood-fake-orgasm>.

Essmaker, Tina. 'Roxane Gay'. June 3, 2014. <http://thegreatdiscontent.com/interview/roxane-gay>.

Flood, Alison. 'Books reviewed in New York Times are "predominantly by white authors".' June 12, 2012. <http://www.theguardian.com/books/2012/jun/12/reviews-new-york-times-white-authors>.

Gay, Roxane. *Bad Feminist.* New York: HarperCollins, 2014.

Gay, Roxane. 'Bad Feminist'. September 22, 2012. <http://www.vqronline.org/essay/bad-feminist>.

Gay, Roxane. 'What We Hunger For'. April 12, 2012. <http://therumpus.net/2012/04/what-we-hunger-for/>.

Kocak, Courtney. 'Bad Feminist's Roxane Gay: "I'm loath to use the word 'success'"'. October 9, 2014. <http://www.bustle.com/articles/41797-bad-feminists-roxane-gay-im-loath-to-use-the-word-success>.

Long, Dayna. 'Roxane Gay'. <http://ffrf.org/news/day/dayitems/item/22884-roxane-gay>.

Sullivan, Rebecca. 'Roxane Gay, author of Bad Feminist, on Q & A: "Men need to get over themselves".' March 11, 2015. <http://www.news.com.au/lifestyle/real-life/roxane-gay-author-of-bad-feminist-on-q-a-men-need-to-get-over-themselves/story-fnq2o7dd-1227255978472>.

Zimmerman, Jess. 'How a "Bad Feminist" Inspired Me to Become a Better One'. September 29, 2014. <http://www.damemagazine.com/2014/09/29/how-bad-feminist-inspired-me-become-better-one>.

Chimamanda Ngozi Adichie

Adichie, Chimamanda Ngozi. *We Should All Be Feminists*. New York: Vintage. 2014.

Adicie, Chimamanda Ngozi. 'We Should All be Feminists: Quotes'. <https://www.goodreads.com/work/quotes/42278179-we-should-all-be-feminists>.

'Award-winning author Adichie explores faith, feminism at Georgetown Event'. March 17, 2017. <https://www.georgetown.edu/chimamanda-ngozi-adichie-talks-faith-feminism>.

Brokes, Emma. 'Chimamanda Ngozi Adichie: "Can people please stop telling me feminism is hot?"'. March 4, 2017. <https://www.theguardian.com/books/2017/mar/04/chimamanda-ngozi-adichie-stop-telling-me-feminism-hot>.

'Chimamanda Ngozi Adichie: biography'. <http://www.cerep.ulg.ac.be/adichie/cnabio.html>.

'Chimamanda Ngozi Adichie: interview'. <http://www.percontra.net/archive/2adichie.htm>.

'Chimamanda Ngozi Adichie: profile'. <https://www.macfound.org/fellows/69/>.

Dandridge-Lemco, Ben. 'Chimamanda Ngozi Adichie On Beyoncé: "Her Type Of Feminism Is Not Mine"'. October 7, 2016. <http://www.thefader.com/2016/10/07/chimamanda-ngozi-adichie-beyoncs-feminism-comment>.

Danielle, Britni. 'Chimamanda Ngozi Adichie Defends Beyoncé: "Whoever Says They're Feminist is Bloody Feminist". March, 2014. <http://www.clutchmagonline.com/2014/03/chimamanda-ngozi-adichie-defends-beyonce-asks-shouldnt-women-sexuality/>.

Heimback, Alex. '13 inspiring quotes from Chimamanda Ngozi Adichie'. September 23, 2015. <https://www.bustle.com/articles/112328-13-inspiring-quotes-from-chimamanda-ngozi-adichie>.

'Igbo'. <https://www.britannica.com/topic/Igbo>.

TEDx Talks. 'We should all be feminists | Chimamanda Ngozi Adichie | TEDxEuston'. (April 12, 2013) <https://www.youtube.com/watch?v=hg3umXU_qWc>.

Wilkinson, Carl. 'I left home to find home'. March 6, 2015. <https://www.theguardian.com/travel/2005/mar/06/observerescapesection3>.

Beyoncé

Adichie, Chimamanda Ngozi. 'Excerpt from WE SHOULD ALL BE FEMINISTS'. <http://www.feminist.com/resources/artspeech/genwom/adichie.html>.

Alexis, Nadeska. 'Beyonce's 2014 VMA Performance: Fearless, Feminist, Flawless, Family Time'. August 25, 2014. <http://www.mtv.com/news/1910270/beyonce-2014-vma-perfomance/>.

'Beyoncé & Jay-Z Raise $1 Million for Charity'. October 4, 2011. <http://www.people. com/people/article/0,,20533903,00.html>.

'Beyoncé Helps Combat Hunger with Feeding America'. June 23, 2009. <http:// www.seventeen.com/celebrity/news/a4962/beyonce-helps-combat-hunger-with-feeding-america/>.

Cubarrubia, RJ. 'Beyonce Calls Herself a "Modern-Day Feminist".' April 3, 2013. <http://www.rollingstone.com/music/news/beyonce-calls-herself-a-modern-day-feminist-20130403#ixzz3Mw8CP7QN>.

Frank, Alex. 'Chimamanda Ngozi Adichie on Her "Flawless" Speech, Out Today as an eBook'. July 29, 2014. <http://www.vogue.com/946843/chimamanda-ngozi-adicihie-feminism-beyonce-book/>.

Greenburg, Zack O'Malley. 'Beyonce's Net Worth In 2015: $250 Million'. May 27, 2015. <http://www.forbes.com/sites/zackomalleygreenburg/2015/05/27/beyonce-net-worth-in-2015-250-million/>.

Johnson, Rachael. 'There's one huge difference between Madonna and Beyoncé'. March 31, 2014. <http://qz.com/193390/theres-one-huge-difference-between-beyonce-and-madonna/>.

Kaufman, Gil. 'Destiny's Child Announce Split'. June 12, 2005. <http://www.mtv.com/news/1503975/destinys-child-announce-split/>.

Knowles-Carter, Beyoncé. 'Gender Equality Is a Myth'. January 12, 2014. <http://shriverreport.org/gender-equality-is-a-myth-beyonce/>.

Leopold, Todd. 'Beyonce tops with five Grammys'. February 9, 2004. <http://www.cnn. com/2004/SHOWBIZ/Music/02/08/grammy.night/index.html?iref=newssearch>.

McCall, Erika R. *Go For Yours*. CreateSpace, 2013.

Nastasi, Alison. '15 Things We Learned from "Beyoncé: Life Is But a Dream".' February 17, 2013. <http://flavorwire.com/371704/15-things-we-learned-from-beyonce-life-is-but-a-dream>.

Payne, Chris. 'Beyonce Drops New Hit Boy-Produced Track, "Bow Down/I Been On".' March 17, 2013. <http://www.billboard.com/articles/news/1552441/beyonce-drops-new-hit-boy-produced-track-bow-downi-been-on>.

Rice, Francesca. '20 Of Beyoncé's Best & Most Brilliant Quotes'. September 7, 2015. <http://www.marieclaire.co.uk/blogs/545716/bow-down-bitches-15-beyonce-quotes-that-cemented-her-place-as-one-of-the-most-inspiring-women-ever.html>.

Rife, Katie. 'No, the Beyoncé building isn't shaped like a giant butt'. July 8, 2015. <http://www.avclub.com/article/no-beyonce-building-isnt-shaped-giant-butt-221964>.

Serpick, Evan. 'Beyoncé Biography'. <http://www.rollingstone.com/music/artists/beyonce/biography>.

Silman, Anna. 'A Comprehensive History of Jay Z and Beyoncé's Relationship'. September 19, 2014. <http://www.vulture.com/2014/07/jay-z-beyonce-relationship-history.html>.

Swash, Rosie. 'Why is Beyoncé calling herself Mrs Carter?' February 5, 2013. <http://www.theguardian.com/lifeandstyle/the-womens-blog-with-jane-martinson/2013/feb/05/beyonce-calling-herself-mrs-carter>.

'The Survivor Foundation Established by Knowles and Rowland Families to Provide Transitional Housing for Hurricane Evacuees'. September 16, 2005. <http://www.businesswire.com/news/home/20050916005663/en/Survivor-Foundation-Established-Knowles-Rowland-Families-Provide#.Vgx-baarSRs>.

Ulaby, Neda. 'Beyonce (And Michelle Obama) Get The Kids Moving'. May 3, 2011. <http://www.npr.org/sections/therecord/2011/05/03/135958485/beyonce-and-michelle-obama-get-the-kids-moving>.

Vena, Jocelyn. 'Beyonce Considers Herself A "Modern-Day Feminist".' April 3, 2013. <http://www.mtv.com/news/1704878/beyonce-feminist-vogue-uk/>.

Waxman, Olivia B. 'Beyoncé and Destiny's Child to Release Original Track for First Time in Eight Years'. January 11, 2013. <http://entertainment.time.com/2013/01/11/beyonce-and-destinys-child-to-release-original-track-for-first-time-in-eight-years/>.

Witherspoon, Chris. 'Annie Lennox calls Beyoncé a "token" feminist with "cheap" lyrics'. October 7, 2014. <http://thegrio.com/2014/10/07/annie-lennox-beyonce-feminist/>.

Tavi Gevinson

Adams, Rebecca. 'Tavi Gevinson Talks Her Right To Be At Fashion Week & That Giant Bow Incident (VIDEO)'. February 24, 2013. <http://www.huffingtonpost.com/2013/02/24/tavi-gevinson-fashion-week-bow_n_2753370.html>.

Bateman, Kristen. 'My List: Tavi Gevinson in 24 Hours'. October 30, 2014. <http://www.harpersbazaar.com/culture/features/a4171/tavi-gevinson-rookie-magazine/>.

Bazilian, Emma. '16-Year-Old Media Mogul Tavi Gevinson Is Expanding Her Empire'. April 14, 2013. <http://www.adweek.com/news/advertising-branding/16-year-old-media-mogul-tavi-gevinson-expanding-her-empire-148565>.

Bercovici, Jeff. '30 Under 30: These People Are Building The Media Companies Of Tomorrow'. January 6, 2014. <http://www.forbes.com/sites/jeffbercovici/2014/01/06/30-under-30-these-people-are-building-the-media-companies-of-tomorrow/>.

Bercovici, Jeff. '30 Under 30: The Next Generation of Media Moguls, Machers and Mavens'. December 17, 2012. <http://www.forbes.com/sites/jeffbercovici/2012/12/17/30-under-30-the-next-generation-of-media-moguls-machers-and-mavens/>.

Carlson, Erin. '"Rookie" Blogger Tavi Gevinson Sings Pet Shop Boys' "Heart" (Audio)'. January 16, 2013. <http://www.hollywoodreporter.com/news/rookie-blogger-tavi-gevinson-sings-413048>.

Cutruzzula, Kara. 'Tavi Gevinson writes her future as she lives it'. April 24, 2015. <http://nytlive.nytimes.com/womenintheworld/2015/04/24/tavi-gevinson-writes-her-future-as-she-lives-it/>.

Gevinson, Tavi. 'A teen just trying to figure it out'. May 2012. <http://www.ted.com/talks/tavi_gevinson_a_teen_just_trying_to_figure_it_out/transcript>.

Kwan, Amanda. 'Young fashion bloggers are worrisome trend to parents'. August 13, 2008. <http://usatoday30.usatoday.com/tech/webguide/internetlife/2008-08-12-girl-fashion-blogs_N.htm>.

Larson, Jordan. 'Rookie hits home run for young, fashionable feminists'. October 5, 2012. <http://chicagomaroon.com/2012/10/05/rookie-hits-home-run-for-young-fashionable-feminists/>.

'Meet Tavi, the 12-Year-Old Fashion Blogger'. July 22, 2008. <http://nymag.com/thecut/2008/07/meet_tavi_the_12yearold_fashio.html>.

Miller, Julie. 'Tavi Gevinson on Shifting from Fashion to Feminism, Surviving Blogger Mortification, and Her First Acting Gig'. November 9, 2012. <http://www.vanityfair.com/culture/2012/11/tavi-gevinson-interview-rookie-magazine-road-trip-nicole-holofcener-acting>.

Odell, Amy. 'Editors Like Tavi But Don't Take Her Fashion Advice Seriously'. December 9, 2009. <http://nymag.com/thecut/2009/12/tavi_the_13-year-old_fashion_b.html>.

Osgerby, Bill. *Youth Media*. London/New York: Routledge, 2004.

'Out of the mouths of babes'. May 18, 2010. <http://www.economist.com/node/16155471>.

Sauers, Jenna. 'Elle Editor Leads Backlash Against 13-Year-Old Fashion Blogger'. December 10, 2009. <http://jezebel.com/5423555/elle-editor-leads-backlash-against-13-year-old-fashion-blogger>.

Schulman, Michael. 'The Oracle of Girl World'. July 27, 2012. <http://www.nytimes.com/2012/07/29/fashion/tavi-gevinson-the-oracle-of-girl-world.html?_r=0>.

Stoeffel, Kat. 'Sayonara, SAY Media! Tavi Gevinson Ditches Jane Pratt's Publisher'. August 5, 2011. <http://observer.com/2011/08/sayanora-say-media-tavi-gevinson-ditches-jane-pratts-publisher/>.

Taras, Rebecca. 'Inside A Surprising Chicago Friendship: Tavi &…Ira Glass'. August 24, 2012. <http://www.refinery29.com/2012/08/35836/tavi-gevinson-ira-glass>.

'Tavi Gevinson'. <http://www.makers.com/tavi-gevinson>.

'Tavi Gevinson'. <https://www.ted.com/speakers/tavi_gevinson>.

'Tavi Gevinson: Teenage 'Rookie' still figuring it out'. October 24, 2012. <http://www.metronews.ca/entertainment/2012/10/24/tavi-gevinson-teenage-rookie-still-figuring-it-out.html>.

'The 25 Most Influential Teens of 2014'. October 13, 2014. <http://time.com/3486048/most-influential-teens-2014/>.

Widdicombe, Lizzie. 'Tavi Says'. September 20, 2010. <http://www.newyorker.com/magazine/2010/09/20/tavi-says>.

Wiseman, Eva. 'Girlhood explained online'. April 22, 2012. <http://www.theguardian.com/lifeandstyle/2012/apr/22/girls-internet-rookie-eva-wiseman>.

Zeisler, Andi. 'An Interview With Rookie Editor Tavi Gevinson'. December 9, 2013. <https://bitchmedia.org/post/an-interview-with-rookie-editor-tavi-gevinson>.

Malala Yousafzai

Blumberg, Naomi. 'Malala Yousafzai'. <https://www.britannica.com/biography/Malala-Yousafzai>.

Brenner, Marie. 'The Target'. April 2013. <http://www.vanityfair.com/news/politics/2013/04/malala-yousafzai-pakistan-profile>.

Bryant, Ben. 'Malala Yousafzai recounts moment she was shot in the head by Taliban'. October 13, 2013. <http://www.telegraph.co.uk/news/worldnews/asia/pakistan/10375633/Malala-Yousafzai-recounts-moment-she-was-shot-in-the-head-by-Taliban.html>.

Couric, Katie. '"He Named Me Malala": An inside look at Davis Guggenheim's new film'. October 1, 2015. <https://www.yahoo.com/katiecouric/he-named-me-malala-an-inside-look-at-davis-130276827663.html>.

Dias, Chelsea. '10 Ways Malala Yousafzai Has Changed the World'. July 23, 2013. <http://mic.com/articles/55333/10-ways-malala-yousafzai-has-changed-the-world>.

Fantz, Ashley. 'Malala at U.N.: The Taliban failed to silence us'. July 12, 2013. <http://www.cnn.com/2013/07/12/world/united-nations-malala>.

Husain, Mishal. 'Malala: The girl who was shot for going to school'. October 7, 2013. <http://www.bbc.com/news/magazine-24379018>.

Jordan, Carol. '16-year-old Malala Yousafzai wins Sakharov Prize for Freedom of Thought'. October 10, 2013. <http://www.cnn.com/2013/10/10/world/malala-wins-sakharov-prize/>.

Kallon, Baindu. '12 incredible Malala quotes that will make you want to give her the Nobel Peace Prize all over again'. October 11, 2014. <http://www.salon.com/2014/10/11/12_incredible_malala_quotes_that_will_make_you_want_to_give_her_the_nobel_peace_prize_all_over_again_partner/>.

Kwan, Amanda. 'Young fashion bloggers are worrisome trend to parents'. August 13, 2008. <http://usatoday30.usatoday.com/tech/webguide/internetlife/2008-08-12-girl-fashion-blogs_N.htm>.

MacQuarrie, Brian. 'Malala Yousafzai addresses Harvard audience'. September 28, 2013. <https://www.bostonglobe.com/metro/2013/09/27/malala-yousafzai-pakistani-teen-shot-taliban-tells-harvard-audience-that-education-right-for-all/6cZBan0M4J3cAnmRZLfUmI/story.html>.

'Malala Day 2015'. July 12, 2015. <http://globalwomensinstitute.gwu.edu/malala-day-2015>.

'Malala gets Mother Teresa Memorial Award'. December 10, 2012. <http://nation.com.pk/national/10-Dec-2012/malala-gets-mother-teresa-memorial-award>.

'Malala Yousafzai to receive Anne Frank courage award'. January 29, 2014. <http://www.bbc.com/news/uk-25951120>.

Meikle, James. 'Malala Yousafzai's father appointed to diplomatic job at UK consulate'. January 3, 2013. <http://www.theguardian.com/world/2013/jan/03/malala-yousafzai-father-given-diplomatic-role-uk>.

Mosbergen, Dominique. 'Malala Yousafzai Tells CNN's Christiane Amanpour: "I Want To Be Prime Minister" (VIDEO)'. October 12, 2013. <http://www.huffingtonpost.com/2013/10/12/ christiane-amanpour-malala_n_4089844.html>.

Mullin, Gemma. 'Nobel Peace Prize winner Malala Yousafzai given two 24-hour armed guards after "terror death threats"'. August 22, 2015. <http://www.dailymail.co.uk/news/article-3207225/Nobel-Peace-   Prize-winner-Malala-Yousafzai-two-24-hour-armed-guards-terror-death-threats.html>.

Simpson, David and Ben Brumfield. 'Malala Yousafzai turns the other cheek to the Taliban'. October 9, 2013. <http://www.cnn.com/2013/10/07/world/asia/taliban-malala/>.

Smith-Spark, Laura. 'Malala Yousafzai and Kailash Satyarthi share Nobel Peace Prize'. October 14, 2014. <http://www.cnn.com/2014/10/10/world/europe/nobel-peace-prize/>.

'The Nobel Peace Prize for 2014 – Press Release'. October 10, 2014. <http://www.nobelprize.org/nobel_prizes/peace/laureates/2014/press.html>.

United Nations. 'The Millennium Development Goals Report 2015'. June 2015. <http://www.undp.org/content/undp/en/home/librarypage/mdg/the-millennium-development-goals-report-2015.html>.

Walsh, Declan. 'Girl Shot by Taliban in Critical Condition After Surgery'. October 10, 2012. <http://www.nytimes.com/2012/10/11/world/asia/girl-shot-by-taliban-in-critical-condition-after-surgery.html>.

Yousafzai, Malala. *I Am Malala: The Girl Who Stood Up for Education and Was Shot by the Taliban*. New York: Little, Brown, 2013.

ACKNOWLEDGEMENTS

Thanks to Massiel Torres for her time, dedication, and research help. Thanks to my small but mighty cohort of true-blue friends. Thanks to my mum for being nice to me 99.9 per cent of the time, even when I don't deserve it. Thanks to my late dad for his unwavering pride in everything I ever did, said, or created. Thanks to my late Henny-dog for her gentle companionship and acceptance, and my late Joon-cat for allowing me to be her person for sixteen perfect years.

ABOUT THE AUTHOR

Laura Barcella is a writer, editor, and forever feminist. She's the author of the forthcoming *Know Your Rights: A Modern Kid's Guide to the American Constitution; The End: 50 Apocalyptic Visions From Pop Culture That You Should Know About… Before It's Too Late;* and *Madonna & Me: Women Writers on the Queen of Pop.* She's obsessed with horror movies and gummy candy, and she works part-time in a kitten nursery. Find her online at **laurabarcella.com** and on Twitter **@laurabarcella**.

If you're interested in finding out more
about our books, find us on Facebook at
Summersdale Publishers and follow
us on Twitter at **@Summersdale**.

www.summersdale.com